Remaking Citizenship

Remaking Citizenship

Latina Immigrants and New American Politics

Kathleen M. Coll

Stanford University Press
Stanford, California

Stanford University Press
Stanford, California

Printed in the United States of America on acid-free, archival-quality paper

Library of Congress Cataloging-in-Publication Data

Coll, Kathleen M.
    Remaking citizenship : Latina immigrants and new American politics / Kathleen M. Coll.
        p. cm.
    Includes bibliographical references and index.
    ISBN 978-0-8047-5821-5 (cloth : alk. paper)—ISBN 978-0-8047-5822-2 (pbk. : alk. paper)
    1. Hispanic American women—California—San Francisco—Political activity.
    2. Women immigrants—California—San Francisco—Political activity.   3. Hispanic American women—California—San Francisco—Societies and clubs.   4. Women immigrants—California—San Francisco—Societies and clubs.   5. Citizenship—Social aspects—United States.   6. United States—Emigration and immigration—Social aspects. I. Title.
    F870.S75C65   2010
    323.3'408968073—dc22   2009025677

Typeset by Westchester Book Group in 10/14 Minion

For Cecilia, Daniela, and Charlotte,
y las miembras de Mujeres Unidas y Activas

Contents

Acknowledgments

ALTHOUGH MY GREATEST DEBT FOR THIS PROJECT is clearly to the past and present members and staff of Mujeres Unidas y Activas and their comrades in San Francisco's immigrant rights struggles (especially the Women's Collective of the Day Laborers Program, PODER/POWER, and the Chinese Progressive Association), many other people also contributed to the research that has become this book.

The Stanford Anthropology department, Professors George Collier, Renato Rosaldo, and Sylvia Yanagisako in particular, helped me through years that included the illness and death of my mother, the birth of my second child, and my relocation to Massachusetts. Today I encounter my wonderful former graduate school classmates as oases of peace and good humor in the rough seas of professional meetings. Mónica Dehart, Anu Sharma, Arzoo Osanloo, Bobby Vaughn, Scott Wilson, Mei Zhan, Tom Boellstorff, and Federico Besserer have become supportive colleagues, inspirational teachers, and role models for me.

Rina Benmayor, Alejandro Lugo, Sunaina Maira, David G. Sweet, and anonymous reviewers generously offered constructive comments and critiques, along with solidarity and encouragement. Members of the Gender and Cultural Citizenship Working Group (Kia Lilly Caldwell, Tracy Fisher, Renya Ramirez, Lok Siu) encouraged me not only to see this project through to publication, but to stay in a profession that, despite all its vagaries and problems, could offer me such meaningful collegial relationships.

I thank my friends and my writing group in Cambridge (Cameron MacDonald, Laura Miller, Kimberly McClain Dacosta) for keeping me writing even when the happy distractions of parenting and teaching and less happy anxiety about the future occupied most of my energies. I have Frances Kunreuther to thank for introducing me to Ann Holder, whose scholarship on race, gender, and sexuality in the American South after the Civil War sets the highest standard for precision and historicity in understanding American citizenship. I owe Juliet Schor my gratitude for first asking me to teach in Harvard's undergraduate program in Women, Gender and Sexuality. WGS provided gainful employment with wonderful students and a community of warm and supportive colleagues, especially Kath Weston and Afsaneh Najmabadi. Along with the staff of WGS and the scholars at the David Rockefeller Center for Latin American Studies, I appreciated the many opportunities I had to share my work with the community of scholars at Harvard. Fellowships from the Radcliffe Public Policy Center / Radcliffe Institute and the Social Science Research Council helped me situate this project regionally and nationally by enabling my subsequent research on movements for noncitizen voting rights in U.S. cities. Pat Katayama, Kate Wahl, Jennifer Helé, and Joa Suorez all played crucial roles in this book's publication by Stanford University Press.

Since my return to California, similar thanks is due Stanford's Feminist Studies and Introduction to the Humanities (IHUM) programs for support in the form of lectureships and fellowships. Penny Eckert, Michelle Zamora, Alisa Bierria, Barb Voss, Jim Ferguson, and Heather Hadlock have been wonderful colleagues and also role models in their dedication to excellence in both scholarship and teaching. For the past two years, my thinking and writing about citizenship has developed in the context of an ongoing interdisciplinary and international collaboration with John Clarke, Evelina Dagnino, and Catherine Neveu, supported by the Fondation Maison des Sciences de l'Homme of Paris. This collaboration has energized and challenged me, changing the way I see myself and my work in relationship to the broader field of citizenship studies.

I started this book for myself, developed it further for the members of Mujeres Unidas y Activas, but finished it for my husband and children, Alejandro, Cecilia, and Daniela, who lovingly sent me out of the house and even out of the country for days, weeks, and months at a time—"whatever it takes" to get it done. My father, John Coll, a retired San Francisco librarian, taught me to love books, politics, my heritage, and San Francisco. He read drafts of this book, corrected many errors, and provided countless hours of research and bibliographic support. My mother, Charlotte Gaffney Coll, taught me to appreciate every educational opportunity afforded me. She also taught me to respect the knowledge of everyday people, women in particular, as authorities not only about their own lives, but also about the world around them. Though she had withdrawn from doctoral studies and the tenure track when I was a toddler in favor of adjunct teaching at community and state colleges, she made sure I studied at her bedside during her many months of chemotherapy. Since her death, my aunts, my sister, and my mother's best women friends keep Mom's memory alive for me and my daughters.

For all these people, resources, and opportunities, I am extremely grateful. They all contributed to what is meaningful and worthwhile about this book. For any weaknesses, omissions, and errors that remain in the final text, I bear sole responsibility.

Remaking Citizenship

Introduction

One way to undertake a historically rich inquiry into American citizenship is to investigate what citizenship has meant to those women and men who have been denied all or some of its attributes, and who ardently wanted to be full citizens.

—Shklar, 1991

SANDWICHED BETWEEN THE WORKING-CLASS immigrant neighborhoods of Chinatown and the Tenderloin, and bordering the downtown financial district, San Francisco's Nob Hill is home to some of the city's most elegant condominiums and to spectacular views of San Francisco Bay. The neighborhood that once flaunted the palatial homes of the Big Four California railroad financiers is now filled with exclusive hotels, condominiums, and the Episcopal Cathedral.[1] Crouched among them, near the intersection of the California and Powell Street cable car lines, sits the Masonic Auditorium, its marble steps and massive Corinthian columns signaling monumental status. Both history and locale have linked the white auditorium with the nineteenth-century magnates whose wealth was created by the labor of Chinese, Irish, and Mexican railroad workers.

One summer morning in 1996, Ximena Monreal and I entered the Masonic Auditorium, up the marble stairs and between the massive columns. We were late, and the new citizen naturalization ceremony was about to begin. We strode briskly to the community group's volunteer table, where the coordinator told us that our help was needed to register voters, but first one of us should help hold up the banner announcing what we were doing. Ximena volunteered—a bit nervously—and soon found herself on stage with another woman, each holding the end of a twenty-foot banner reading "Congratulations New Citizens! Register to Vote Today!" As the volunteer coordinator made a brief statement from the stage explaining our purpose, a dozen volunteers and I held stacks of voter registration forms over our heads, walked up and down the aisles, and called out in English, Spanish, Chinese, Tagalog, and Vietnamese, "Register to vote!"

Looking up at Ximena, who appeared confident before the crowd of 1,800, I wondered if the audience would have been surprised to know that this petite mother in her early twenties was herself an undocumented immigrant from Guatemala, unable to understand most of the English being spoken on stage. Ximena was volunteering at the ceremony in part at the suggestion of her immigration attorney, who suggested that her residency application would be stronger if she had some community service activities demonstrating the good moral character that the Immigration and Naturalization Service (INS) demanded of petitioners for legal permanent residence. A few weeks before showing up to help register voters, she had traveled to the office of Mujeres Unidas y Activas (MUA), a local community organization of Latin American immigrant women, to ask for a letter attesting to her good standing in the community. Staff members responded that, of course, they would help her in any way they could, but first she would have to do something for them to bear witness to. They told her about the naturalization ceremonies and voter registration campaign, which she thought would fit well into her work and child care schedules.

After the ceremony, Ximena told me how good it had felt to help register other immigrants to vote and how she looked forward to coming back again. At a women's group meeting shortly thereafter, I listened as she dynamically conveyed to the other women how the ceremony itself was very interesting, and that the actual experience was not as scary as she had imagined it would be. Ximena succeeded in encouraging other women to participate, and we went back to register new citizen voters at these ceremonies every other week for several months.

Earlier in 1996, a presidential election year, Congress had passed legislation limiting public benefits to noncitizen residents. Soon after, the Clinton administration had authorized extra funding to the Immigration and Naturalization Service to address the enormous backlog of applications for naturalization. More than one million new citizens swore their oaths of allegiance that year at ceremonies like the one Ximena and I attended.[2] Each of them received a letter of congratulations on White House letterhead with President Clinton's electronic signature.

The San Francisco INS office allowed the nonprofit Coalition for Immigrant and Refugee Rights and Services, of which Mujeres Unidas y Activas was a part, to register voters inside the auditorium. INS officers incorporated the dispersal and collection of voter registration forms from new voters, as well as their guests, into the program itself. States and localities also began promoting citizenship drives because immigration and welfare eligibility changes threatened the social services they could provide low-income immigrants.

By October 1996, this coalition of immigrant groups, service providers, and state agencies had registered over twenty thousand voters at the San Francisco ceremonies and in door-to-door campaigns in San Francisco, San Mateo, and Sonoma counties, all of which have high numbers of Latino residents. According to the San Francisco county registrar of voters, 78 percent of these new voters cast ballots in the November 1996 elections, compared to the 62 percent voter turnout for San Francisco overall. Newly registered voters living in the city's most heavily Latino neighborhoods turned out in even greater numbers (82 percent in the Excelsior District and 85 percent in the Mission).

In August, I wondered whether conservative legislators were aware of the huge numbers of citizens being naturalized and the increasing number of immigrant citizens who were motivated to register to vote for the first time. By fall, it seemed that they had caught on. The Republican majority in the U.S. Congress passed legislation requiring more extensive FBI background checks on naturalizing immigrants, which drastically slowed the rate of naturalization. Within a year, the INS was again reporting eighteen-month backlogs for eligible permanent residents waiting to take the naturalization oath. New fingerprinting requirements further slowed the visa application process at U.S. consular offices around the world, while increased income requirements for residents sponsoring relatives for immigration further limited migrants' legal entry. The short-lived experiment in reemphasizing the naturalization part of the Immigration and Naturalization Service's charter was over, and California found itself with the highest number of immigrants, but also the lowest rates of naturalization, of any state.[3]

My visit with Ximena to the Masonic Auditorium was memorable because it was our first experience with registering voters at the naturalization ceremonies, and also because of the conflicting emotions it raised for me as both researcher and U.S.-born white citizen. I found the ritual swearing of allegiance to be disconcertingly powerful. New citizens must foreswear all loyalty to their nation of birth, even though it is not illegal for U.S. citizens to hold passports from other nations and neither the State Department nor the INS seeks to enforce that clause of the oath. Speeches alternated between celebrating the history of immigration to the United States and emphasizing that, in the words of the white-haired, black-robed INS judge who presided, "After today, you will never be the same. You will be an American."[4] I was simultaneously moved by the speakers' rhetoric and repelled by my susceptibility to it, knowing as I did how shallow such speeches felt in the context of national efforts to restrict immigrant rights and social welfare benefits for all Americans.

I wondered what the event meant to the Asian elders I could see in the auditorium, several of whom looked to be in their eighties or nineties. Two of these new citizens were hunched over in wheelchairs at the back of the auditorium, with their family members helping them hold up their hands for the oath. I had not noticed them filling out voter registration forms. Perhaps, I thought, they had been moved to naturalize by that summer's immigration reform legislation, which eliminated Social Security benefits, Medicaid, and food stamps for noncitizens, even long-term permanent residents who for years had contributed toward these benefits through their payroll taxes.[5] Lynn Fujiwara has documented immigrant communities' panic, but also their successful political mobilization, in opposition to aspects of the welfare reform legislation called the Personal Responsibility and Work Opportunity Reconciliation Act (PRWORA) of 1996 (Fujiwara, 2005).

Long after staff members wrote a letter in support of her successful application for legal residency, Ximena continued participating in Mujeres Unidas y Activas and encouraged her peers to engage in more public political actions. Ximena had found the women's group for the most self-interested reasons: the state's requirement of good moral character and a recommendation from her immigration attorney. Yet by her own account, her experiences there transformed her sense of her relationship to the United States. Because she was the mother of a U.S.-born child, this transformation had implications for her son as well as for Ximena.

Ximena told me that her main motivation for legalizing her immigration status was to be able to see to the well-being of her eighteen-month-old son, since she and his father—also undocumented—had separated. Even though Ximena hoped to someday return to Guatemala to live and had already made sure to register her son's Guatemalan citizenship at her consulate, she wanted to make sure she could continue living in the United States with him, legally and with the proper work permits. Because his father was Mexican, she also hoped someday to register her son with the Mexican consulate. When she came to the United States to work, she had anticipated neither falling in love nor having a child and ending up a single mother struggling to make ends meet as a low-wage restaurant worker. She was conscious of the power of citizenship to convey rights and saw part of her responsibility as a parent as making sure her child could claim a legal right to study, live, or work in any of these countries if necessary.

Ximena was clear about the importance of citizenship, even if she might never be able to obtain it for herself. Although there are multiple "legal" immigrant statuses, to obtain the right to naturalize, an immigrant must first obtain lawful permanent resident (also known as LPR or green card) status and then wait five years to apply for naturalization. Depending on factors such as nationality, date of immigration, and initial and subsequent visa statuses, an immigrant might wait twenty years to qualify for naturalization.[6] The English-language requirement, naturalization exam, and rising application fees all pose additional burdens, particularly on low-income immigrants with low literacy rates in their native language.

Anthropology and Cultural Citizenship

At the turn of the twenty-first century, with the global realignments after the end of the cold war and the rapid dominance of neoliberal policies in both northern and southern countries, immigrant Latino/as face particular obstacles in claiming their rights and gaining recognition as contributing members of U.S. society. Members of the Inter-University Project on Cultural Studies first used the term *cultural citizenship* to describe the processes through which "a subordinated group of people arrives at a common identity, establishes solidarity, and defines a common sense of interests" (quoted in Benmayor, Torruellas, and Juarbe, 1992, 72). Cultural citizenship as an analytic frame offers an important position from which to highlight the situation of certain groups of citizens who, though formally entitled to full legal political rights, are socially recognized neither as first-class citizens nor as contributors to the vernacular meanings of citizenship as it plays a role in day-to-day life in the United States. "The concept of cultural citizenship allows us to see the notion of rights as it is defined not by the legal code but by the cultural foundations and practices of people themselves, in their own philosophical and political terms" (Benmayor, Torruellas, and Juarbe, 1992, 73).

The idea that anthropology or ethnography might contribute to understanding citizenship is relatively new. Precisely because of the cultural notion that citizenship is a governmental rather than a social domain, citizenship studies have traditionally been the terrain of sociologists, political scientists, historians, and legal scholars. Sociologist T. H. Marshall (1964) elaborated one of the first post–World War II theories of citizenship, linking the development of citizenship ideals to earlier shifts in economic and political structures. Contemporary British and U.S. perspectives on citizenship are often rooted in a critique of Marshall's assumptions about universal and unilineal development of citizenship rights and who belongs in the modern nation-state (Hall and Held, 1989).[7] They suggest that ethnic diversity and globalization represent the central issues around which new citizenship theory will emerge (Turner, 1990, 222).

Marshallian assumptions about individual needs and rights versus collective interests and structures undergird many formulations of citizenship. The individual and collective dichotomy is also reflected in the distinction between private and public social spheres common to Western European and North American cultures. The idea of citizenship as an essentially public, political domain dates back at least as far as Enlightenment notions of the clear division between a rational, male, civic-minded citizenry and the emotive, female domestic world that male citizens both control and receive comfort from. With the elaboration of the modern nation-state, imperial capitalism, and Victorian social ideals, this ideological division became entrenched and eventually invisible through the cultural common sense about citizenship in the United States (Collier, 2000; M. Rosaldo, 1980).

The emergence of ideas about cultural citizenship is part of a broader set of discussions about the inadequacies of traditional citizenship forms and politics that emerged at the end of the twentieth century. The combined effects of economic and political globalization, devolution of industrial welfare states, and the postcolonial, civil rights, human rights, and feminist movements led to proposals for more process- and practice-oriented approaches to understanding citizenship (Brubaker, 1989; Taylor, 1994; Turner, 1990, 1993; Somers, 1993). Some political philosophers, sociologists, and anthropologists sought out new ideas about citizenship based on the experiences of people historically excluded from either formal or substantive first-class status. The subject positions theorized in this literature include women (Barbalet, 1988; Pateman, 1989; Orloff, 1993, 1996; Walby, 1994; Yuval-Davis and Anthias, 1994; Lister, 1997), people of color and diasporic communities (Hall and Held, 1989; Dagnino, 1994; R. Rosaldo, 1994; Ong, 1996; Flores, 2003; Flores and Benmayor, 1997; Rosaldo, Flores, and Silvestrini, 1993; De Genova and Ramos-Zayas, 2003), lesbian/gay/bisexual/transgender (LGBT) people (Herrell, 1996; Berlant, 1997; Bell and

Binnie, 2000), and transnational migrants (Brubaker, 1989; Shklar, 1991; Mouffe, 1992; Soysal, 1994; P. Clarke, 1996; Bhabha, 1998; Yuval-Davis, 1999; Goldring, 2001). In some cases, renewed academic concern with citizenship focused on liberal defenses of inclusion (Kymlicka, 2001), while others promised more radical challenges to global political economic systems of inequality (Lowe, 1996, 33).

Contemporary studies of U.S. citizenship situate cultural norms and practices of citizenship within the relationships of power and inequality that circumscribe American politics and society. Some argue that the internal contradiction in citizenship between the ideology of democracy and actual exclusions of groups from political rights dates back to ancient Athens (Shklar, 1991). Both Aristotelian and modern U.S. republican ideas about citizenship are products of societies in which slaves, women, and male laborers were excluded from the political class. When the economic and political life of the United States was predicated on the enslavement of 20 percent of its population, "black slavery and racial caste served as the floor upon which white, ethnic, and gender struggles could be diffused and diverted," as Cornel West notes (1994, 156). U.S. political culture included an ideology of citizenship that linked the right to vote with the right to labor for wages, while defining good citizenship as public political participation in local and national issues through public meetings and voluntary organizations contributing to the public good (Shklar, 1991, 5). From the beginning, this meant that, at different times and to differing degrees, people of color, the poor, and women have been excluded from the definition of the U.S. citizenry.

Notions of cultural citizenship integrate this history of the exclusivity of citizenship in different ways because they are neither uniform nor unified. However, they do share the impulse to reformulate the concept of citizenship at the turn of the twenty-first century, when people, capital, and productive processes span national boundaries, where national, ethnic, and sexual minorities, women, and postcolonial subjects demand consideration as citizens in their own right. Until recently, the field of citizenship studies focused on formal definitions and expressions of citizenship, rather than on people's everyday lived experiences. The fieldwork for this book took place in the context of growing political opposition to efforts by traditionally excluded citizens and noncitizen immigrants to claim civil and political rights as well as access to public benefits and resources—what Marshall (1964) would call "social rights."

No matter what other differences they espoused, the principal theorists of cultural citizenship in anthropology represented it as processual rather than simply as a static bundle of rights and entitlements. For Aihwa Ong, cultural citizenship is "a process of 'subjectification,' in the Foucauldian sense of self-making and being-made by power relations that produce consent through schemes of surveillance, discipline, control and administration" (1996, 737). For Renato Rosaldo, "[c]ultural citizenship is a process by which rights are claimed and expanded . . . the manner in which groups claim cultural citizenship may very well affect a renegotiation of the basic social contract of America. So-called new citizens—people of color, recent immigrants, women, gays, and lesbians—are not only 'imagining' America; they are creating it anew" (1994, 62). Both Rosaldo and Ong draw on British cultural studies of citizenship, specifically those of Stuart Hall and David Held, who define citizenship in terms of belonging, rights, and entitlement in a given society and assert that "issues around membership—who does and who does not belong—is where the politics of citizenship begins" (1989, 175). The concept of cultural citizenship is ethnographically productive for anthropologists entering the terrain of citizenship studies because it provides a frame of reference to study people's experiences and interpretations of their own political, cultural, and economic position in the United States in the context of relationships of power, the U.S. state, and other groups in society. Rosaldo, Ong, and Hall and Held all emphasize the perspectives of immigrant and diasporic communities as critical for reformulating citizenship, suggesting that the framework of cultural studies of citizenship holds great promise for new approaches to studying immigrant lives and the politics of diversity in contemporary societies like the United States and Britain.

This book proceeds from the premise that citizenship is a process defined not only by the culturally and historically constituted legal institutions of power politics and the state nor even by what has been traditionally recognized as political participation and civic engagement (Asen, 2004). This more dynamic notion of citizenship emphasizes that questions of subjectivity and affect in the daily struggles, collective analyses, and diverse expressions of resistance to inequality of subordinated citizen-subjects are necessary for a robust understanding of citizenship institutions and practices. The women I interviewed challenged their political marginalization as low-income, non-English-speaking women and the dehumanization of terms such as *illegal* and *alien*. In doing so, they embodied claims against the legitimacy of cultural, administrative, and legal obstacles that prevent full social and political participation of immigrants in U.S. life. Their experiences may be seen as part of the dynamic and contested set of institutions, practices, and ideas that constitute U.S. citizenship. These women recognized the power of the state's monopoly over citizenship as a legal status, and those who had not naturalized never referred to themselves as *ciudadanas* (female citizens). However, they did represent themselves to me, to their children, and to one another as legitimate, if not legal, claimants to the rights, privileges, and obligations of citizenship in the United States. This strength of conviction, gained in large part through the peer support of other immigrant women and political struggle with one another and with other poor and immigrant communities, was striking, and led me to consider in greater depth the role that collective grassroots organization and motherhood played in forging their sense of citizenship.

Considered together, the topics of immigration, citizenship, and motherhood stand at the center of contemporary debates over inclusion and exclusion—who really belongs and is a fully entitled member of U.S. society, and who is not. In this book, I aim to understand the specific social processes through which citizenship and motherhood were mutually constituted in the lived experiences of one group of Latin American immigrant women, the members of the Mujeres Unidas y Activas grassroots community organization in San Francisco, California. While immigrants and women continue to be marginalized with respect to the exercise of full citizenship rights in the United States and in the local community of San Francisco, the members of this immigrant women's organization had a great deal to say about the terms of their membership in their adopted local and national communities. Economic subordination, domestic violence, and racial, cultural, and linguistic discrimination were all issues that the women examined in their stories without dividing them into discrete categories of individual, family, or community issues.

The book can convey only some of what I learned from the women I met in San Francisco. The main focus is what they told me about the individual and collective processes through which they came to claim rights and exercise responsibilities for themselves, their families, and *la comunidad*—by which shorthand they referred to the community of Latin American migrants and their U.S.-born and/or U.S.-raised children, but that other times included all of San Francisco as their community.

Mujeres Unidas y Activas comprised two hundred members and five staff people between 1996 and 1999, when I conducted the bulk of this research. They graciously welcomed me as a student and a collaborator able to provide translation, interpretation, and transportation. When I moved to the East Coast, I maintained contact with the group and with several members through regular visits, letters, children's birthday and holiday cards, and phone calls. Since returning to live in San Francisco permanently, I returned to more regular contact with current and former group members; I keep in touch with those who are no longer active members when we run into one another grocery shopping, at our children's schools, at church, or at other public events. In the fall of 2007, I was honored to be asked to begin a two-year term as part of the member-led *mesa directiva*, or board of directors, which was constituted after the organization became its own 501(c)3 nonprofit in 2006, and which is a remarkable body in and of itself.[8]

Rather than argue that because MUA members were unique individually or collectively (which of course they were), and therefore that their narratives of citizenship and motherhood were exceptional, I found that this group articulated an important and concentrated set of ideas about how the immigrant women came to feel a sense of belonging and entitlement and a positive vision for themselves and their children as members of U.S. society. Their narratives of individual and collective pride constituted a powerful counter-discourse to the derogatory, xenophobic rhetoric historically directed at working-class and poor immigrants. At times their stories also offered critiques of dominant American ideologies of individualism, consumerism, and competition, while making claims based on more universal ideals of social justice and human rights.

Through the experience of collective support, discussion, training, and political engagement that MUA offered, the women I interviewed came to see their individual stories as part of broader collective experiences with political implications. While many of the women I spoke with first arrived at the group with ideas of motherhood centering around the care and nurturance of children, they described how their notions of their duties as mothers had expanded to include advocating for their own, their children's, and other immigrants' interests with respect to health care, social services, the law, and education. This sense of motherhood included a claim not only of belonging in their adopted city, but also a claim that they and their children were entitled to certain rights and services and to respect. These women, their experiences, and their analyses indicated productive ways to bridge feminist theories of the social construction of motherhood (Collier and Yanagisako, 1979; Yanagisako and Delaney, 1995) with the aforementioned new perspectives on the subjective and cultural aspects of citizenship (Hall, 1990; Ong, 1996; R. Rosaldo, 1994).

Although hegemonic norms of race, immigration status, gender, and language excluded them from first-class citizen status, the women's experiences and interpretations of community participation and what it meant to belong and to be entitled to rights and services constituted important examples of the contemporary theory and practice of American citizenship. Their language and collective struggles attended to the gendered underpinnings of the state-defined realm of politics and rights, as well as to the everyday ways in which men and women actively shaped the terms and scope of their rights and their entitlements. This book therefore offers a gendered analysis of how social belonging and political agency, the disciplinary forces of nation-states, and individual women's personal experiences and ideas shape the meaning and content of political belonging in their lives. In particular, stories focus on understanding the changes in their sense of self and their relationships with their local community, friends, and family after joining an immigrant women's organization. In so doing, they foregrounded issues of subjectivity, affect, and trust so often elided in discussions of citizenship and political engagement (Asen 2004; Hardy-Fanta, 1993; Kivisto, 2001; Quayson, 2005). The women discussed in this book, along with their words and actions, do not illustrate social theory, but rather constitute immigrant women as active participants in the remaking of what it means to be a full political and social member of U.S. society.

Citizenship Talk, Citizenship Theory

On-the-ground discourses of subjectivity and personal transformation such as those the women shared with me in this research constitute cultural citizenship stories because they engage women's struggles over and relationships with personal and familial issues and women's political participation and rights. Gloria Anzaldúa regards such narratives as *teorías*, or intersubjective and multilayered social theories that can "reflect what goes on between inner, outer and peripheral 'I's within a person and between the personal 'I's and the collective 'we' of our ethnic communities" (1990, xxv.). The immigrant women cited here, while excluded de jure and de facto from full citizenship, offer examples of the effective mobilization of liberatory aspects of liberal democratic discourse, while maintaining a critical distance from its exclusionary neoliberal roots. Such processes are fraught by the imbalances between official and popular versions of ideas like "human rights" (Merry, 2006a, 2006b, 2006c) and "citizenship." Yet we need to attend carefully to the complex ways Latina speech and silence around politics, sexuality, class, or race represent contestation of, as well as concessions to, dominant groups' definitions and norms (Zavella, 2003).

Considering vernacular discourses of how individuals and collectivities come to feel a sense of belonging and rights as theory (rather than theorizing on top of vernacular examples) offers what Mary Louise Pratt calls "resources for hope" for the rejuvenation of citizenship theory and practice.[9] The women I interviewed identified multiple factors operating simultaneously on individual, household, community and political levels—including peer support, information, training as organizers, and collective political action—as important in their coming to feel a more affirmative sense of themselves. Confronted with powerful ideological limits on counter-hegemonic speech, as well as direct assaults on citizenship embodied in "wars" on drugs, terror, civil rights, and civil liberties, grassroots community activists like those interviewed here continue the work of alternative teoría-building and political action.

In contemporary nation-states, the ideal of citizenship associated with notions of individual, equal-rights-bearing political subjects coexists with pervasive social inequality and emergent social groups struggling to claim full membership as citizens. This raises the question of how citizenship might be reconfigured theoretically and practically to address exclusions from full citizenship and new citizens' claims based on class, race, gender, sexual preference, disability, and immigration status (Hall and Held, 1989). Not unlike earlier feminist formulations of "the personal is political," discourses of cultural citizenship expand the realm of what Evelina Dagnino calls "new citizenship," including the "moral, intellectual and cultural reform within civil society and the transformation of social practices" (1994, 76). However, this view of citizenship and political subjectivity recognizes that not only is the private and intimate realm always politicized, but that public political participation is constrained by gendered and racialized obstacles to the practice of full citizenship by many political subjects (Williams, 1988).

The women of MUA remind us that citizenship involves praxis and contest over diverse social domains and relationships. More than just a state-defined legal status devoid of dynamism or dispute, citizenship includes women's struggles to make a voice and space for themselves in the family, as well as in local communities and the nation. Mujeres Unidas y Activas linked the intimate and public domains of political subjectivity in a process of making claims, learning to speak, acting collectively, and building grassroots institutions that promoted *autoestima* (self-esteem). In the context of legal-juridical and economic forces designed to marginalize and silence them, these women's demands for social and cultural respect challenge us to reconsider not only the scope of citizenship studies, but the very nature of citizenship itself.

Where and When I Enter This Story

My response to the citizenship events I attended at the Masonic Auditorium and the sense of irony I inferred from their location were rooted in my own understanding of very local histories of citizenship and entitlement in San Francisco and, by inference, in California and the United States. For my Irish Catholic family in particular, Protestant Nob Hill with its wealthy mansions, Episcopal Cathedral, and Masonic Temple was a key symbol of upper-class Anglo-American exclusivity that my father invoked in his stories about growing up a working-class, fourth-generation San Franciscan in the "Outer Lands" of the Richmond District. Not so long ago, we would not have been allowed to enter the marbled hall of the Masonic Temple because of our religion, he told me in grade school when a classmate invited me to a dance put on by the Masonic girls' social club.

Like some others with several generations of roots in San Francisco, I grew up with tremendous pride in my unionized, industrial, multicultural city. However, my parents also conveyed skepticism about the nostalgia for the old-time city of some of our co-ethnics. My parents and grandparents bracketed any sense of entitlement with stories of gender, ethnic, and religious prejudice from their own lives and those of our family's previous immigrant generations. More frequently, they told me about how their friends, coworkers, and neighbors of color had to struggle to live with dignity in a city that continued to be deeply racially segregated through the 1960s (and that has been resegregated along new lines in recent years). I learned that my parents bought our family home in 1965 because the liberal Jewish developer insisted that all of his developments be racially integrated; my mother's dream house turned out to be affordable for a teacher and a librarian precisely because not all our neighbors were white. I was also part of the first class of San Francisco kindergarteners to be bused out of our neighborhood in 1970 to promote school integration. Though several of our neighbors chose to send their children to private schools instead, my parents put their firstborn four-year-old on a bus to an all-Latino classroom, where I first began to learn Spanish.

As parenting decisions often do, my parents' choices and accidental circumstances changed my life course in unexpected ways. They prepared me to meet one of the two cofounders of Mujeres Unidas y Activas, Clara Luz Navarro, a Salvadoran nurse and political refugee who became an immigrant advocate and organizer in San Francisco, and who is now very deservedly retired. In 1992, when MUA was a new group, I was the program coordinator for a local solidarity organization, the Committee for Health Rights in Central America. Together we organized community events aimed at educating North American health professionals about conditions facing their colleagues in Central America and making connections between U.S.-backed wars in that region and immigrant health concerns in San Francisco. These experiences inspired me to do fieldwork on women's health in Mexico and later to pursue a Ph.D. in anthropology at Stanford.

Rethinking American Urban Life and Citizenship

The history of San Francisco is a story of mobile and shifting populations and constant renegotiations of boundaries of belonging in the local body politic (Godfrey, 1988; Voss, 2008). Latina/o immigrants in San Francisco today are neither cultural pioneers nor easily assimilated into an identifiable local mainstream. Their nationalities share a history in the region and the city dating back to the eighteenth-century founding of the Presidio and Mission as an outpost for Mexico and Spain and later for nineteenth-century Central and South American gold miners and twentieth-century industrial and service workers. Each era and structural position entailed different avenues for inclusion as well as exclusion and different relationships with the state and with local communities.

The women I interviewed migrated not only to another country but to a locale with cultural and linguistic diversity they never expected. Experiences with migrants from nations other than their own, as well as unexpected opportunities to get to know San Franciscans of different ethnic backgrounds, sexualities, and social classes, had a formative impact on their sense of their own position in the local and national community. San Francisco is the California city with the largest proportion of immigrants and refugees (to whom I refer more generally as migrants and immigrants in this book). Thirty-four percent of San Franciscans, in contrast to 22 percent of Californians and

8 percent of the U.S. population overall, are foreign-born. Despite having a population of less than 750,000, the City and County of San Francisco ranked fifth among U.S. cities in absolute numbers of immigrants during the period of this research (White et al., 1995). One-third of San Francisco's residents were Asian, 14 percent were Latino, and fewer than 10 percent were black. One-third of city residents were non-Hispanic, nonimmigrant whites (U.S. Bureau of the Census, 2006).

Uniform, static notions of culture, identity, and community are inadequate to describe the diversity among and between migrant and native communities in metropolitan areas today (Baumann, 1996). American racial categories mask the extent and complexity of this diversity. San Francisco's Asian/Pacific Islander community in 1990 comprised 60 percent Chinese-, 20 percent Filipino-, 5.7 percent Japanese-, and 6.1 percent Southeast Asian-descended people. By 2000, more than half of the city's foreign-born residents were immigrants from Asia. The Latino population in 1990 comprised immigrants and their descendents from Mexico (40 percent), Nicaragua (11 percent), El Salvador (19 percent), Guatemala (4 percent), and Puerto Rico (5 percent).[10] Immigrant and undocumented populations are probably underrepresented in these 1990 census numbers, with some estimates concluding that the Latino Mission District of San Francisco was undercounted by almost 20 percent (Reed and Krebs-Dean, 1996). Almost 40 percent of San Franciscans speak an Asian language or Spanish as their primary language at home, with another 5 percent speaking other non-English languages (U.S. Bureau of the Census, 2000).

San Francisco presents itself to corporations and tourists as a cosmopolitan Pacific Rim city known for its bohemian past, picturesque views, international cuisine, and support for progressive artists, intellectuals, and political activists. City politics are self-consciously progressive, with only two registered Republicans managing to get elected to any local or state-level office in the last forty years.[11] When Mayor Willie Brown appointed a replacement for the only straight white male on the Board of Supervisors, the powerful African American politician joked about his manifest commitment to affirmative action for "underrepresented groups" when he chose a campaign supporter and young white businessman named Gavin Newsom. Although regressive ballot measures passed resoundingly statewide in the 1990s, San Francisco opposed the anti-immigrant ballot initiative Proposition 187 as well as subsequent initiatives to end affirmative action (Proposition 209) and bilingual education (Proposition 227), defeating each by the highest margins of any California county.

San Franciscans often tell a story of local exceptionalism, referring to their medium-sized town as "The City" and explaining eccentric local characteristics such as perpetual mayoral candidates "Chicken John" and "Sister Boom-Boom" of The Sisters of Perpetual Indulgence with the all-purpose descriptor "only in San Francisco." This self-consciously tolerant, indeed irreverent, atmosphere has helped constitute the space in which immigrant political participation can flourish with some degree of general public support. However, while the progressive local political culture limited conservative electoral power, it failed to slow the larger-scale shifts in deindustrialization, urban development, and social stratification in the 1980s (De León, 1992). Women I interviewed confirmed that working-class and poor migrants to San Francisco experienced tremendous hostility and suffering. They felt the full pressure of statewide anti-immigrant politicking and also limits on their mobility due to local dynamics of gentrification combined with national laws restricting their employment opportunities and protections as workers.

Immigration and welfare reforms coincided with major shifts in the political economy of San Francisco in the 1990s. The coincidence of these shifts and the particular ways the dynamics played out in the local cultural geographies are important for appreciating immigrant women's experiences and narratives. Interviews and events in this book took place during a period of escalating social stratification in the city, with both the extremely wealthy and the extremely poor sectors growing and middle-income people fleeing the city. Since deindustrialization and the decline of the Port of San Francisco in the 1970s, the Manhattanization of downtown in the 1980s, and the collapse of the garment industry in the 1990s, the city's economy has been largely based on professional and service jobs in hospitality, finance, and technology.[12] Beginning in the 1970s, working- and middle-class San Francisco families of all races and ethnicities—especially, but not exclusively, white middle-class families—had begun moving to more affordable suburban areas. This trend accelerated in the late 1970s and the 1980s as the city's industrial base disappeared and rents and housing prices began to climb out of reach for most families. In the 1990s, the high-tech boom and the deregulation and growth of the financial industries further fueled gentrification.[13]

The technology-, service-, and high-finance–based local economy was implicated in growing disparities, with poor public education and systemic racial discrimination making the digital divide between races and classes appear as impassable a border as the national divide between North and South.[14] These divisions mapped onto local geographies in both subtle and stark ways. In San Francisco, as in other regions, African Americans, Latino/as, and Native Americans were twice as likely to live in poverty as whites and Asian/ Pacific Islanders. Poverty numbers were distributed unevenly by gender as well as across races and classes. According to the 2000 census, 13 percent of the children in San Francisco lived below the poverty line, but almost one in five of children in the Mission District and one in three children in Bayview lived in federally defined poverty (Pamuk, 2003). In the 1990s, 46 percent of San Francisco families headed by women with children under five lived in poverty, compared to 16 percent of single-father households and 10 percent of households with children headed by married couples. Given the systematic undercounting of immigrants in most census figures, these numbers are likely higher than reported for Latinos, especially the undocumented.

By the mid-1990s, the Mission District had become a key symbol of the rapid pace of gentrification and the displacement of low- and middle-income residents, Latino/as in particular (Mirabal, 2009; Quayson, 2005). Named for Mission Dolores, the small white stucco structure built on the Camino Real in 1776, the Mission District was a predominantly Irish working-class family neighborhood with its own identity and accent in the late nineteenth and early twentieth centuries. Other than in a few exceptional areas like Guerrero Street and Liberty Hill, where large mansions attest to some old-time gentry presence, most of the district's housing comprised small family homes, modest duplexes, and larger multiunit tenements. Most of the Mission was spared from the fire that destroyed the city after the 1906 earthquake, and many original structures remain. Many families left the area for the East Bay after 1906, while others sought their own homes in the newer suburban developments west of Twin Peaks starting in the 1920s. The Mission became increasingly multicultural and identifiably Latino in the 1950s and 1960s. In the 1970s, the district became home to increasing numbers of artists and intellectuals. By the 1990s, the central location, good weather, historic buildings, and bohemian atmosphere had drawn pricey restaurants and boutiques to serve new residents able to afford such services. Despite rent control, rents increased rapidly, and record levels of "owner move in" (OMI) evictions forced many low-income and long-term residents out (Godfrey, 1988; Menjivar, 2000; Mirabal, 2009). The southeast corner of the city,

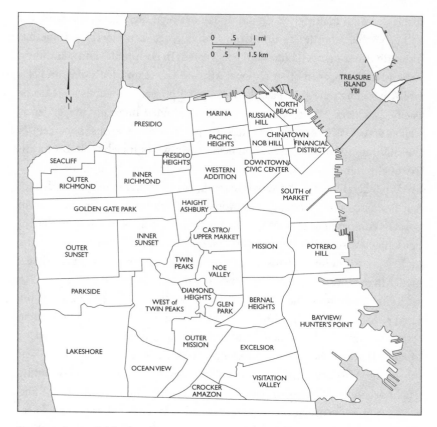

San Francisco neighborhoods

known as Bayview–Hunter's Point, in contrast, has been a largely African American working-class family neighborhood since World War II, when it housed Italian American and African American naval shipyard workers.[15] Since the 1980s, the area has become increasingly Asian and Latino.[16] As in many parts of California, demographic shifts resulting from immigration have coincided with the structural economic changes associated with dein-dustrialization and declining military production to redefine the ethnic char-acter of areas, threatening to exacerbate tensions between immigrants and nonimmigrants, whites, blacks, Asians, and Latinos. In 2008, voters endorsed a plan for the southeastern neighborhoods—promoted by major develop-ment and construction interests, the mayor, and some of the senior black com-munity leaders—that many neighborhood residents and community activists predict will accelerate the already rapid displacement of low- and middle-income black San Franciscans.

The accelerating decline in San Francisco's African American population became a matter of broader public concern and political debate after the release of the 2000 census figures, but Mirabal's oral history of gentrification in the Mission District documents the less-recognized fact that San Francisco was the only major U.S. city in which the Latino population declined in this period (by 10 percent between 1990 and 2000). She links this decline to the same forces pushing out working-class and low-income African Americans, namely, the restructuring of the local economy and the escalating cost of housing, making life in San Francisco unaffordable for most working-class people (Mirabal, 2009). The lives and stories of the women at the center of this book's claims about citizenship need to be appreciated in the context of such political-economic shifts driven by national and transnational forces, and the way these changes map onto historically racialized and classed local geographies like those of San Francisco's neighborhoods.

Outlining an Ethnography of Citizenship

This book examines how one group of immigrant women in a specific locale came to think of themselves as legitimate, rights-bearing members of U.S. society during tense, complex times. Reframing the subject of citizenship studies from a decentered perspective, such as my focus here on immigrant Latinas' narratives of personal transformation as well as collective politicization, is not exceptionalism.[17] This is not a view from the margins of citizenship, but rather a challenge of the co-construction of political margin and center that marginalizes groups based on gender, class, race, or language. If we can better appreciate the citizenship of excluded, marginalized, or subordinated persons today, we can better understand the polity-in-formation as these communities are incorporated (not necessarily assimilated) into the national body politic. Understanding the ways that obvious inequalities are both maintained and contested also challenges us to think harder about the way that other forms of difference and inequality within citizenship might be obscured or erased from our consciousness.

Ethnography, with its attention to personal narrative and the contextualization of particular experiences, offers a strategic point of entry into understanding how personal experiences of transformation and collective processes of political struggle constitute the meanings of citizenship for individuals and groups. The assertion that citizenship is a dynamic, intersubjective, and contentious process is both a rationale for, and an artifact of, my approach to this research. Ethnographies of immigrant communities in the United States have traditionally emphasized localized community, kinship, occupational, and ritual worlds as their objects of study. These frames of reference have separated public political and private family life into discrete, gendered domains while also privileging cultural or ethnic differences over analyses of race and class in migrants' experiences. More recent social theory has suggested the importance of looking at themes, issues, and experiences that span cultural domains previously deemed autonomous, or forcing the juxtaposition of domains in the analysis to advance theory.

The focus of Chapter 1 is on the Mujeres Unidas y Activas organization that these women built together and how their subjective experiences of broader political conditions interacted with their efforts at collective political education, mutual support, and engaged political activism. The *doble misión* (dual mission) of MUA was based on addressing both individual and collective needs for transformation as equally important aspects of the struggle for social justice for immigrant women. This integrated vision for organizing for social change entails a broader vision of citizenship that can account for the diverse terrain of women's citizenship struggles from the home and family to the street and with state institutions.

Chapter 2 situates MUA's work on behalf of migrants, women, and low-income families in the highly fraught political and social context they encountered in 1990s California. This period was characterized by rhetoric and policies antagonistic to immigrants, poor families, and people of color. Latina immigrants in particular were targeted rhetorically and in policy, becoming the scapegoats for Californians' experience of changes due to globalization (Inda, 2007). The legacy of this period continues to shape the politics of immigration today (Jacobson, 2008).

Chapter 3 considers women's stories about how learning the ropes in San Francisco public institutions affected their sense of their rights and position in this society. In learning to maneuver through public entities such as their children's schools, health care, public assistance, and subsidized housing, the women learned specific lessons about motherhood and citizenship in the United States. Motherhood was both an intimate experience and a social role; being a good mother was a private satisfaction, but it also required public acts on behalf of self and children. Women's stories of the mutual constitution of motherhood and citizenship bridged the private-public divide that has falsely defined so much of women's experience as outside the realm of citizenship.

Chapter 4 focuses on how women's stories of personal transformation emphasized a concept of *autoestima* quite distinct from the individualist version of self-esteem more familiar to Anglo-Americans. Women linked *autoestima* to the support they received from peers, the strength they gained from collective political action, and the finding or regaining of their own individual voices. This discourse of *autoestima* reflected not only the group's influence on individual women's narratives, but also the extent to which this shared conversation helped them articulate their claims of rights as immigrants. This chapter also examines the complex and contradictory ways that immigration and welfare laws privilege heterosexuality, marriage, and a certain version of victimhood and domestic violence.

Chapter 5 considers the women's emphasis on "learning to speak (up)" as part of their stories of political and personal transformation. Their narratives illustrate how they have negotiated the multiple forms of inequality and exclusion they face in the United States. The stories reference the specific institutions, relationships, and people *through* and *against* whom the women have come to understand and claim their right to belonging. These people and relationships include the ethnographic encounter in which the subjects sought to enlist me in their collective citizenship struggles and to shift my focus of research into more direct dialogue with their goals. Their demands for voice in my research in turn forced me to consider what I wanted to say as an ethnographer in collaboration with their words, but also in dialogue with broader debates over citizenship in anthropology and in U.S. political life.

Just as studying women's political practice and subjective experiences led me to question the limits of the domain of citizenship, so did women's notions of pan-immigrant coalition and alliances with other marginalized citizenship groups challenge overly narrow definitions of identity politics. Chapter 6 examines a particular powerful example of how Mujeres Unidas y Activas bridged multiple divides within American citizenship with a long-standing collaborative project for women's leadership development carried out with the Chinese Progressive Association of San Francisco's Chinatown.

Chapters 5 and 6 each approach different discursive practices of citizenship in order to deepen our appreciation of the multiple forms and arenas in which women encounter citizenship. Vernacular concepts and women's actions relating to them suggest new directions in citizenship theory that point beyond narrow definitions of political life and issues of empowerment toward an understanding of transnational identities, citizenship, gender, and grassroots political participation.

1 Conviviendo con Mujeres Unidas y Activas

Passing the Time with MUA

THE WEATHER WAS UNUSUALLY WARM and sunny on May 1, 2006, as tens of thousands of white-shirted demonstrators filled the streets of San Francisco's financial district.[1] The synchronized marching of the uniformed honor guard of the Longshoremen's Union elicited cheers. I recalled stories my father told me about how militant longshoremen led the last general strike in San Francisco in 1934. Labor activists and anarchists, among others, keep up the International Workers' Day tradition each May 1 in San Francisco. The marchers wear their union locals' T-shirts or jackets or carry red-and-black banners declaring "Value Labor, Not Capital!"

A celebration of organized labor's contributions to a proudly union city, the 2006 May Day had been recast as "the Great American Boycott." It was distinguished from other years' commemorations not only by its size, but also as one of many local manifestations of a national immigrant work stoppage and consumer boycott. Some Latino demonstrators who had never participated in a U.S. May Day greeted white radicals with smiles and thanks for joining in "their" march.[2] Red, white, and blue signs proclaimed "AMERICA, we are YOUR people!" Immigrant women pushed babies in strollers alongside older children boycotting school for the day and behind banners demanding equal labor protections for domestic workers. Men had draped Mexican as well as American flags around their heads, and the Nicaraguan consular officers hung their flag out the consulate's high-rise window. Signs ranged from the pragmatic "Stop HR 4437" to the pointed "You like our food, why don't you want our people?"[3] The militancy of the marching male and female longshoremen was matched by the lighthearted spirit of protesters who squatted down and jumped up in

May Day 2006, Market Street, San Francisco

concert to make long waves up and down Market Street from City Hall and the
Civic Center to the Ferry Building at the Port of San Francisco.

The first national walkout of this scale for immigrant rights reclaimed the
international celebration of organized labor for a new American workforce. If
the contemporary global order denies the dignity of labor and seeks to define

May Day 2006, Market Street, San Francisco

us by what we consume, these demonstrators embodied the message that not all workers are men, not all consumers are adults, and not all voters are white and native-born. In the words of one banner, "Today we march, tomorrow we vote." The marchers' actions echoed the tradition of each new generation of U.S. immigrants learning to wield influence in electoral politics. However,

May Day 2006, South of Market Street, San Francisco

they also demanded recognition of their difference along with inclusion. By claiming equal rights and democratic protections for all, even for those excised from the body politic by law or by custom, they challenged fundamental assumptions of membership and belonging in this country.

Experiences such as these lead me to a very different conclusion from those who see Americans as increasingly "bowling alone" instead of building civic institutions (Putnam, 2000). Such formulations tend to erase the contributions, indeed the personhood, of the people who may be the most active in building community and social life in many parts of the United States. This book introduces one such group of new citizens—the members of Mujeres Unidas y Activas (MUA)—and the processes through which they came to feel a sense of belonging and entitlement to rights and protections in the United States.

The Myth of the Sleeping Giant

Media coverage of the events of May 1, 2006, focused on the phenomenon of a sudden and spontaneous mobilization of millions of immigrants around the country. Pundits pointed to the power of Spanish-language radio to move people to march, invoking the image or specter, depending on your point of view, of the awakening "sleeping giant" of Latino political participation. However, this book argues that at least for one group of immigrants participating in the May 1 marches, and likely for many others as well, participation was neither spontaneous nor exceptional, nor could it be explained as a "post-9/11" phenomenon.

Activism by noncitizens is one piece of evidence that de jure legal citizenship and voting should not define the scope of de facto political contributions in a liberal democratic society. Understanding contemporary immigrant claims for citizenship, belonging, and entitlement requires an appreciation of the particular forms of grassroots immigrant organizing that have taken place over many years in different parts of the country, and that shape the contours of current events. Latino/a immigrant rights activism today has social and institutional roots in the community-based legalization and refugee-services organizing of the 1980s (Coutin, 2000), as well as in efforts by organized labor to reach out to the new immigrant workforce in the 1990s. Claims based on human rights and workers' rights draw on language from civil rights and women's rights organizing and social movements in the United States as well as in Latin America (Coll, 2004, 2005; Dagnino, 2003). Understanding how this group of women came to identify with and participate in these kinds of efforts highlights the complex processes underlying the dynamic notion of citizenship they laid claim to.

Public acts in the political realm, such as the naturalization ceremony described in the Introduction and the May Day demonstration, have long been understood to be constitutive of citizenship (Young, 1990). However, the women I interviewed focused their stories of politics on profoundly personal and intimate experiences that disrupted the dichotomy between the political/public and the personal/private that is central to cultural logics of racial, class, and gender exclusivity in American citizenship. Iris Marion Young traces the heritage, assumptions, and tensions within American notions of politics and civic life to Machiavelli, Rousseau, Hobbes, and Locke, showing how these tensions are foundational to what otherwise seems like internal contradictions between universal ideals of democracy and discriminatory citizenship laws. She points out that the very notion of a natural dichotomy between the public and private social realms was part and parcel of the suppression of difference within the citizenry and the relegation of emotion, intimate relations, the body, and other forms of identity to the private world apart from the public world of citizenship. Such cultural beliefs about the public and private mean that, even when previously excluded groups are formally admitted to the citizenry, they continue to be "measured according to norms derived from and defined by privileged groups" (Young, 1989, 255).

Collective efforts to bridge the divide between public and private in citizenship ideals and practices challenge the marginalization of certain citizen-subjects along lines of difference such as race, religion, sexuality, and language. Despite the ideological and practical forces aligned against them, the women I spoke with reported that attending protests against public service cutbacks, speaking out at school board meetings, and participating in door-to-door immigrant voter registration campaigns were powerful and transformative personal experiences. Reason and emotion, the intimate and the public, and private and political issues and identities were interwoven in these stories. The women "felt" the changes in themselves and how they "thought" about their rights and social position in the United States as a result of both public participation and the more private processes of peer support and changes in family relationships they were undergoing at the same time.

Claiming Rights

The public claims for rights and recognition of the women I knew in the crowd in San Francisco on May 1, 2006, had roots in struggles in the more intimate domains of the self and family and the intersections between these realms and public institutions such as law and policy. Behind these women's participation, as well as behind the absence of others on that day, were histories informed by experiences of politics and citizenship in their home countries, dynamics within their families of origin and their current households, and subordination as working-class, non-English-speaking Latin American immigrants in the United States. Each woman's story was unique and shaped the distinct ways she came to claim a place and rights in the United States. Through sharing time together and dialogue about their commonalities across diverse experiences, including analyzing some of the historic and institutional reasons for their shared experiences, women came to articulate shared critiques and views on immigration, and also alternative politics of gender, race, education, health care, and labor.

This book tells a particular story about how a group of immigrant women experienced their political capacity, or lack thereof, in different areas of life.

Their view of citizenship changed depending not only on institutional rules and boundaries, but also on the members of the body politic and how they understand their rights, entitlements, and social roles. State policies and traditions may enable or repress certain citizenship identities, but the dissent, struggle, and creativity of women like these have their impact on citizenship as well.

Citizenship processes became visible in these women's actions, but also in the way they told their own stories and the particular language of citizenship that they developed in conversation with one another. What I refer to as their citizenship discourses, or vernaculars of citizenship, reveal the way that intimate, personal, and domestic conflicts and concerns inform the public political actions and identities that we more often associate with citizenship. Key concepts that the women used when talking about coming to see themselves as members of U.S. society, whether legal citizens or not, reflected the multilayered, multileveled nature of their citizenship identities (Yuval-Davis and Werbner, 1999). These narratives highlighted the ways in which citizenship concerns and claims were constituted at the points of intersection, tension, and conflict within or between the domains of the family and the state. Although later chapters focus on the processes that the women called gaining *autoestima* (self-esteem) and *aprendiendo a hablar* (learning to speak), this chapter focuses on some strategies they employed collectively to empower themselves through *buena informacion* (good information). Just as their stories challenge us to rethink what we mean by citizenship, we also need to pay careful attention to the more complex and multidirectional dynamics underlying a seemingly straightforward project of getting informed about services, rights, and other shared interests.

Ethnography, Citizenship, and Motherhood

Studying citizenship ethnographically required bracketing my own cultural "common sense" that citizenship was fundamentally a state-defined legal status, or that it was an issue only when people used the term explicitly. To understand the meaning of citizenship as a cultural, social, political, and historical process, we need to look not only at state power and institutions, but also at other aspects of political economy and history, including individual and collective processes of political participation and transformation in daily life. Liberal multiculturalist visions of democratic political life tend to focus on how excluded groups come to join the body politic over time and, as Bloemraad

(2006) points out, on internal characteristics of immigrants rather than on receiving societies and institutions. This is too partial and unilinear a story (Kymlicka, 2001). In contrast, critics of "governmentality" also may overstate the effectiveness of state efforts to monopolize citizenship and shape political subjectivity (Ong, 1996). Citizenship is both a mode of exclusion and a site of struggle for equality (Holder, 2008). This central tension produces new dynamics and new identities that may be as contradictory as they are productive of new political identities.

I began this research project as a witness and collaborator in conversation with subjects who were themselves social analysts (R. Rosaldo, 1989). While their goals and interests were more immediate and concrete, it was through close attention to Mujeres Unidas y Activas members' stories and beliefs about their position and rights in this society that I came to see that the realm of citizenship included such issues as domestic violence, childrearing, welfare, public health care, and immigration. The state holds and deploys tremendous power that shapes not only institutions and practices, but also our senses of ourselves, who we are, and where we fit into society (Ong, 1995, 1996). Yet we do not always see or conduct ourselves as the predictable subjects of governance desired by the state and described in some social theory (J. Clarke, 2005; Li, 2005, 2007).

Careful attention to MUA's approach to organizational and individual development helped me appreciate what was specific and innovative about this particular group, and also what such community-based participation had to teach about political identity and social practices more broadly. The thirty women interviewed for this book were, among their other personal characteristics, immigrants from Mexico and Central America, non-English-speaking, low-income, and of diverse immigration statuses.[4] Many were also single mothers who had received or were receiving some form of public assistance to support their children. I saw several I knew from 1990s MUA activities again among the marchers on May 1, 2006, ten years later. Others have since moved out of San Francisco in search of more affordable housing, or now have steadier work and so cannot attend regular meetings. While such women often participate in marches or special events with MUA, the organization they helped build has continued to grow with new generations of more active members. "They have us on remote control now," one full-time working mother told me with a laugh when we discussed our new phases of life and relationship to the organization as we waited for our children at their first communion class in

2005. She was pleased that newcomers and other "veteran" activists continued to expand the work, and also that they kept her up to date on events and called on her for public actions.

When Mujeres Unidas y Activas was founded in 1990 with two leaders, a dozen members, and no office, it operated under the auspices of a regional immigrant rights coalition that also raised and administered the small amount of private funding the organization received. By the time I began fieldwork in the summer of 1996, the group claimed over two hundred members and an active core of fifty women, including four full-time paid staff members. Although still operating with the fiscal sponsorship of the larger coalition, Mujeres Unidas y Activas had its own office space in a building with other nonprofit organizations in the Mission District of San Francisco. Most of the funding came from private foundations, but a significant portion of the budget also originated in public funds channeled through nonprofits to offer support, referral, and education services, often in lieu of public services that had been eliminated by previous budget cuts.[5] During the 1990s, California was struggling to come to terms with having become, in less than three decades, home to one-third of the nation's immigrants and 40 percent of its undocumented population (McCarthy and Vernez, 1997; Immigration and Naturalization Service, 1999).

In order to study citizenship among largely noncitizen immigrant women, I needed to pay attention to women's actions as well as to their words, individual stories, and collective discussions. My own identity affected what women were willing to share with me, and I was constantly confronted with the limits of my understanding as a middle-class white American citizen with a supportive spouse, adequate income, and quality child care. As an *amiga del grupo*, I felt in particular that some women's descriptions of racism by other whites may have been more reserved, and that some may have guided conversations to topics of perceived mutual interest, motherhood among them. With these caveats in mind, I hope to convey the content and also the tenor of this group of women, their organizational process, and their political projects. During the time we spent together at immigration offices, elementary schools, public clinics, baby showers, women's group meetings, and public demonstrations, what they had to say about citizenship, personal experiences of politics, and the relationship between these domains was important for understanding both gender and belonging in this globalizing era.

The particular discourse of rights, responsibilities, and citizenship that Mujeres Unidas y Activas members articulated grew out of the political and economic conditions of the United States in the 1990s, along with the specific organizing traditions and programmatic goals of their grassroots group. As I interviewed women about their immigration stories, experiences of work and family, and views about their social roles and rights in the United States, many shared terms and ideas that I had also heard in group meetings and collective discussions at MUA. These ideas related individual experiences to social phenomena, linked personal and political rights, and evinced a shared analysis of equality and social justice. I came to regard this collection of phrases and concepts as vernacular articulations of citizenship, that is, as everyday language and social theory relating rights, equality, and belonging. How was it that a women's support group went about generating "citizenship talk" among women whose primary goals in joining the group were often more instrumental, such as managing personal crises or looking for jobs?

Broad themes soon emerged from my participant observation and interview experiences. I listened as women told stories of how their life changed as a result of *autoestima*, which challenged my own North American pop-psychological understanding of self-esteem, and the *apoyo* (support) and *información* (information) that the women's group provided along with the chance to *desahogarse* (get things off one's chest) for the first time with other women. These narratives of transformation were present in interviews and also group discussions, where women bore witness to their experiences and provided one another with advice and support. In fact, women spoke often of the liberatory and transformative aspects of such speech itself, emphasizing how they themselves "learned to speak" (*aprendieron a hablar*) through their experiences, in some cases regaining their voices after feeling silenced by the psychic as well as the geographic dislocation of migration. Most striking to me were the ways they linked what at first seemed to me to be intimate, highly personal processes, such as developing *autoestima*, with intersubjective and explicitly political processes. Many of them asserted that it was in helping others through community organizing (*ayudando a los demás*) that they came to feel better about themselves and their place in U.S. society and their local community.

In the following description of the group and its practices, I place particular emphasis on the attention paid to women's emotional needs and changing sense of self. This was striking not only in the substance and content of group meetings, but also because it was a major focus of the women's narratives when I interviewed them. Their stories helped me appreciate the complex, multifaceted, and highly personal ways that people experience social inequality. Individual interviews and sustained observation of the group over time made clear the extent to which such grassroots analyses of experiences of belonging, entitlement, and disenfranchisement provided the women with hope for addressing, not just surviving, the challenges they faced as immigrants, workers, and women.

Discussing, Debating, Contesting Citizenship

In the mid- to late 1990s, Mujeres Unidas y Activas was the only non-service-providing, nonreligious organization dedicated to promoting peer support and civic activism among Latin American immigrant women in San Francisco. Other discussion groups were transitory and explicitly nonpolitical, religious, or devoted primarily to service provision. Mujeres Unidas y Activas' political vision and project distinguished it from these other institutions, though they maintained a complementary relationship with service providers (agencias) and other groups, referring women to them as appropriate, and receiving referrals from them as well. For example, MUA received women referred by groups serving women in crisis, such as the well-regarded Homeless Prenatal Project, which continues to provides shelter and instrumental and peer support to battered and/or homeless women, including many immigrants (Ovrebo et al., 1994).

Community groups, nonprofit agencies, private foundations, and the state are inevitably bound together in relations that are at the same time mutually supportive, reactive, and conflicting. When the Immigration Reform and Control Act of 1986 (IRCA) passed, la amnistía (amnesty) not only created unprecedented opportunities for long-term undocumented residents of the United States to legalize their status, but also fostered an increase in services to counsel immigrants about provisions of the new law.[6] Since amnesty was available only to immigrants who met specific criteria, had specific forms of proof of residency, and applied by the deadline, nonprofit service agencies banded together to reach out to immigrants through vigorous legalization campaigns. The Northern California Coalition for Immigrant and Refugee Rights and Services was one such group formed by diverse service-providing organizations in San Francisco. From 1986 to 2000, it supported community organizations that helped seventy thousand immigrants legalize their status under IRCA; educated elected officials and bureaucrats about immigrant and refugee[7] rights issues at the local, regional, and state levels; and held voter registration and education campaigns at naturalization ceremonies and door-to-door to register tens of thousands of newly naturalized citizens to vote.

In 1990, the Northern California Coalition published the results of a large-scale community-based study that initiated a national debate over the specific state of immigrant women's rights (Hogeland and Rosen, 1990). The group surveyed several hundred Asian and Latin American immigrant women about their experiences with immigration, work, and family in order to assess the needs and concerns of a broad cross-section of immigrant women. The two Latin American immigrant women who conducted the bulk of the surveys and interviews, Clara Luz Navarro and María Olea, formed a small support group of a dozen of the women they had met in the course of their research. This was the nucleus of what later became MUA. I never met María Olea, but I came to know Clara Luz in 1992 through our shared interests in Central American solidarity work and immigrant rights and through collaborative efforts between the newly formed Mujeres Unidas y Activas and the Committee for Health Rights in the Americas, where I worked.

The new women's group held regular meetings twice a week at various times of the day to accommodate different schedules, with child care provided. Some women attended more than one meeting a week. Practicing what they called *democracia dirigida* (guided democracy), the group's leaders noted issues of concern that members raised individually or collectively and invited informational speakers on these subjects. The topics ranged from how to get a child into the public school of choice to aspects of recent legislation important for battered women, such as the Violence Against Women Act (VAWA).[8] An important aspect of the skills development program included training workshops on topics such as child development, youth violence, and immigrant rights. The training was conducted in all-day sessions on weekends over the course of six to eight weeks. Participants received small stipends and were required to design and carry out a community campaign relevant to the training's topic after the workshops were completed.

Meeting women's needs for peer support and personal transformation along with developing their political leadership and collective participation became the *doble misión* (double mission) of the group. While MUA was in many ways a product of the specific social and political conditions of California in the 1980s and 1990s, it was also infused from its inception with political practices that owed much to U.S. feminist and Latin American popular movements' organizing traditions. MUA's practice resonated with the approach of contemporary women of color organizations such as the National Black Women's Health Project, which in 1984 grew out of small self-help groups that approached politics from a perspective of care for the "physical, spiritual, emotional, and psychological health needs" of members by creating a "safe, validating environment for us to learn how to come together to share our stories, to be appreciated for the struggles we have participated in, to review our circumstances, and to make decisions designed to change our lives and our health circumstances" (Silliman et al., 2004, 71, quoted in Brodkin, 2007). Political refugees from Central America in San Francisco also contributed their experience and skills to the broader immigrant rights movement that took shape in the 1990s. Clara Luz was a nurse in El Salvador and had to flee her country in the 1980s after being threatened for her oppositional politics and success as a local elected official in her hometown. In the United States, her political leadership guided the formation and development of Mujeres Unidas y Activas in its early years.

However, the story of MUA is not the story of one charismatic leader. Clara Luz retired from MUA more than ten years ago, and the group she helped start has been run by staff and leaders drawn from the rank-and-file membership for the majority of its two decades of existence. Though it was not part of the scope of my research, this small part of Clara Luz's exceptional story reminds us that as much as this book focuses on the common experiences and practices of immigrant women in the United States, immigrants have histories, backgrounds, skills, and capacities developed prior to immigration. Clara Luz's story was exceptional not because it was so different from those of other political refugees from Central America, but rather because most women in MUA were not at all politically active in their home countries in the ways they came to be in San Francisco, nor were most looking to "get political" when they began participating in group meetings and activities.

The early members joined the group in search of peer support, information, and also often a break from the stress and isolation of their home and work lives. The coalition provided funding to pay participants' bus fare, to provide child care, and to offer refreshments during the meetings. The meeting format varied, with informational guest speakers and/or undirected discussions of issues raised by the women who came to the meetings. The group later received additional funds to form discussion groups focused on domestic violence, sexuality, and AIDS/HIV and to develop a home health care training and job development program. MUA soon opened its own office in the

Mission District of San Francisco, which was close to public transportation, where many recent immigrants begin their lives in San Francisco. Many women lived, worked, or had children in school in the area.

As public institutions at the local level had fewer resources to provide services and respond to changing client needs, more public and private funds were channeled through nonprofit agencies, just as nongovernmental organizations (NGOs) in other nations also began to provide more services in response to government cuts. MUA received funding from individual donors, but the largest sources were private foundations and public sources administered by the larger nonprofit coalition. Providing information rather than services was central to the group's collective self-definition, as was the conviction that the women themselves already had many of the skills, knowledge, and experiences they needed, if only they could share them with one another in an ongoing way.

Mujeres Unidas y Activas' organizational stability and accessibility was one key to its success. Since the office was staffed full time and there were various types of meetings (general, self-esteem, sexuality, and home health aid collective) on various days of the week, a woman in a crisis could find a group of peers almost any day. Regular group meetings took place twice a week on different days, one in the late morning and the other in the late afternoon, to accommodate different schedules. The frequency and consistency of meetings allowed for a degree of intimacy and consistency of peer support that no service agency or institution could provide. Children other than sleeping or breast-feeding infants were not allowed in meetings, but child care was always provided in a nearby room. Refreshments were provided for both women and children at all meetings. As the organization developed, peer support and informational meetings were separated into alternate weeks, with visitors or observers like myself eventually asked to attend only general meetings. However, in the early years, the format of meetings was open, though confidential, and included both peer support and informative guest speakers, depending on the week, the availability of a speaker, and the desire of the women present to talk about specific personal issues or concerns.

Instrumental Support and Political Organization

Community organizations like Mujeres Unidas y Activas face the difficult challenge of addressing immigrants' economic needs, which frequently underlie the social and political issues that the groups seek to address. During the early years of MUA, there were few places for immigrant women to turn for employment referrals or support on labor issues. Many women first approached Mujeres Unidas y Activas with the understanding that it was a work cooperative, job agency, or economic development organization. Though the group was clear from the start about its political priorities, it did make forays into micro-entrepreneurship, including one short-lived catering cooperative. In 1994, MUA developed the Manos Cariñosas / Caring Hands program in response to many members' needs for independent sources of income. The group's official history cites in particular domestic violence victims' need for "economic opportunities that would enable them to leave abusive situations or help their families obtain greater economic security" (Mujeres Unidas y Activas, n.d.). Many members were already doing domestic work and were in need of peer support, labor rights education, and professional development. MUA identified home health and elder care as a potential area of job development that could be steadier and more lucrative than house cleaning and private child care, but that required practical nursing skills and education on conditions such as dementia, diabetes, and heart disease.

To be eligible to join the Caring Hands project, women had to have been members of MUA for at least six months before participating in intensive training. Thereafter, they were expected to attend weekly meetings and workshops on topics such as toxics and workplace safety issues for housekeepers, skill building for home health aides, and peer support and education for those working with homebound elders, especially Alzheimer's patients. Not only did many MUA members gain long-term employment through Manos Cariñosas, but many project participants went on to be strong leaders within MUA. By 2006, Manos Cariñosas had developed into what MUA called a "workforce development project and workers' association" and helped form statewide and national networks of domestic workers to lobby for living wages and overtime wage protections for domestic workers and home health aides. According to MUA's official history, "Caring Hands became a site for both job training and placement and for collective action to help Latina immigrants achieve dignified and just employment" (Mujeres Unidas y Activas, n.d.).

It is not surprising that many women who came to MUA for the first time were hoping for job opportunities. However, they also wanted reliable information on immigration policies, referrals to services, instrumental support to help them negotiate life in San Francisco, and a peer-directed space for collective reflection, education, and self-advocacy. Although the group limited participation in employment-generating programs like Manos Cariñosas to members with at least six months in the group, any woman in need could walk into the office without an appointment and receive immediate peer counseling, referral to appropriate social services, or even accompaniment to the police or a hospital. Many of these drop-in visitors subsequently became active members after experiencing the mutually supportive atmosphere and engaging in collective discussions and public actions with the group. Though most initial counseling was provided by staff members, within ten years MUA developed a program of peer-counselor training for these initial visits, and trained members were available in the office to screen visitors, assess their immediate and longer-term needs, provide appropriate referrals to staff or other agencies, and accompany them to the hospital or police station. These peer counselors also sought to involve newcomers by orienting them to the projects and goals of MUA and inviting them to attend group meetings.

Programs and Discourses of Citizenship

Mujeres Unidas y Activas distinguished itself from social service–providing agencies by promoting political education and collective action among immigrant Latinas. Instead of prescribing an evolutionary schema of steps for each participant to follow in order to "progress," the group sought to involve women in civic activism while helping them address their most pressing individual needs. Interrelated programmatic goals included providing quality information and consistent peer support, building self-esteem, and fostering individual claims for domestic rights at home in conjunction with collective claims for political and cultural rights in the public arena.

When women spoke about their changing senses of themselves in interviews and in group discussions, they spoke of a sense of identification with and belonging to a local community of immigrants (*la comunidad*) and also how they came to see themselves as *latinas*. In asserting collective identities as immigrants, Latinas, and MUA members, they staked a claim to a cultural and political space in the United States. Identifying as Latina did not mark a shift away from a distinct national or cultural identity as a *mexicana, salvadoreña*, or *guatemalteca*. Women continued to identify with their nationality of origin, even if they did not intend to return home to live permanently.

Group identity was strategic and coalitional, but was also born of shared experiences in the women's group. In the process of spending time and sharing experiences with one another, the women learned about each other's different cultural and national heritages, and also came to emphasize what they shared as immigrants, women, mothers, and Latin Americans. Group identity also represented a strategic reclamation of a gendered and racialized collective identity that they recognized as imposed by U.S. categories.[9] While the official demographic term *Hispanic* conflates and confuses the diversity among and between people of Latin American and Iberian ancestry, *Latino* and *Latina* come out of community and cultural activism and emphasize rather than flatten this richness and breadth of experience (Dávila, 2001; Pérez, 2003; Ramos-Zayas, 2004; Suárez-Orozco and Páez, 2009).

The Power of *Buena Información*

The politics of information were as important to the internal strength of the organization as to the public or the institutions from which it hoped to garner support and solidarity. Information and the technologies that increasingly mediate its dispersal were of critical importance to community groups like Mujeres Unidas y Activas. In interviews, women repeatedly referred to the importance of the information they gleaned from MUA meetings and programs in shaping their own decisions as well as the decisions of others with whom they shared what they learned. It is not easy to get *buena información* on laws, policies, history, and politics when one is entirely dependent upon commercial media sources, especially if one is Spanish-speaking in an English-language-dominated society. Women complained of the *amarillismo* (yellow journalism) of both English and Spanish mainstream media and how frequently it failed to impart buena información about immigration and welfare reform.

Carolina Jiménez, one of the early members of the group who no longer participates regularly, said that the informational resources as well as the emotional and instrumental support that Mujeres Unidas y Activas provided were the things she liked most about being an active member. "I like the information . . . the presenters who come and speak. . . . When one has problems, being able to speak with the group and get their support. . . . When I was depressed, it helped me a lot. . . . When we moved and I was so stressed because I needed money, they helped me find work babysitting."[10] Carolina had a well-developed ability to gather information and was always willing to talk to many people to be well informed on a variety of topics. "You have to investigate . . . one who investigates suffers less." Carolina is an example of one of the difficult analytical aspects of my research. Did she come to Mujeres Unidas y

Activas because she had nowhere else to get this support and information? Or did she and other women who joined the group find it precisely because of their finely honed information-gathering skills?

Whether the group was their only source of information or one resource of many, buena información drew women to Mujeres Unidas y Activas and kept them coming back. The topics that came up in the open-ended discussions at general meetings became topics of future informational meetings where women could share information and debate their own analyses of issues. Many times, women would distinguish this type of open discussion from the bad information (*mala información*) imparted by commercial media sources and everyday neighborhood gossip.

Perhaps because the great majority of women at meetings were mothers living far from family and other lifelong forms of social support, a great deal of collective energy was directed toward issues of family, parenthood, and child-rearing. Discussions included basic peer advice around parenting and discipline, but also revealed women's fears about raising children in the United States, from the perceived threat of the state taking away their children, to the power and influence of U.S. social values, including consumer ideology and individualism, over their children.

The provision of a peer group with which to openly discuss, clarify, analyze, and assess key areas of cultural concern was another service the organization provided to the community at large. Childrearing and family organization were particularly potent areas of interest addressed in general meetings with child psychologists, social workers, lawyers, and educators who prompted discussion and dialogue among participants. In the process, members understood the history and issues underlying what often seemed to them to be draconian rules of state interference in family life. These discussions often included voicing fears about state interference in child discipline in particular, and how the perceived threat from Child Protective Services (CPS), combined with the cultural shock of migration, undermined parental authority. Loving and firm parental discipline was responsible for the respect and coherence of the family unit central to women's sense of themselves as Latinas. Through these discussions, they also analyzed the power and the limits of state involvement in parenting and reformulated notions of "Latina-ness" to accommodate childrearing practices slightly different from those with which they were raised.

Criando niños bieneducados meant raising children who respected but did not fear their parents; were polite, well-groomed, and well-behaved in public settings; were good citizens in their school and community; and were responsible toward their families, helping their parents and younger siblings. Although women allowed that all kinds of people could and did raise "well-educated" children, women asserted that Latin American cultural traditions were at the root of many of the strengths they identified in their own parenting practices and abilities. They had specific ideas about how to *educar*—to raise, literally, to educate—children in a manner that respected Latin American childrearing practices without violating legal norms. In doing so, they reclaimed a sense of cultural identity that allowed for the dynamism of cultural practices, the new context in which they were raising children, and their understanding of what modern, improved childrearing practice should consist of, regardless of the locale.

In addition to their views on the proper practices and attitudes of mothers in their homes, MUA activists strategically deployed an image of honorable immigrant parenthood, including motherhood, on behalf of the issues or positions they promoted in the larger community. In doing so, they tapped into the political tradition of identifying and lobbying for women's needs in terms of their primary social role as mothers, but also promoted an alternative vision to that of nostalgic social conservatism in order to redefine desirable American family life and values. The honorable immigrant families that Mujeres Unidas y Activas celebrated were neither assimilating nor Anglicizing, but were hardworking, dignified, and law-abiding. In this formulation, many immigrants are forced to enter and work in the United States illegally, but this is proof of their desire to provide for their children by contributing positively to American society rather than evidence of a lack of respect for the rule of law.

Mujeres Unidas y Activas members' invocation of the honor and dignity of immigrant parenthood in their efforts to advocate for their social and political agenda highlighted tensions in their discourses of morality and legality, tradition and change, migration and citizenship. In this formulation, immigrant families had moral rights that should be respected in law, cultural traditions that were worthy of preservation even though they were also dynamic and changing, and political rights regardless of their nationality. In the collective articulation of these concerns, the very definition of family shifted to include one's community (*la comunidad*) of immigrants and the women with whom one shared experiences of collective struggle. As many women repeated in their interviews, "the group is like a family to me," "the group is my family here," and "I can tell the women in the group things I could never tell

C A S T I G O (Punishment)

autoridad (authority)

amenaza (threat)

obediencia (obedience)

¿mal comportamiento? (bad behavior?)

D I S C I P L I N A (Discipline)

enseñar responsabilidad (teach responsibility)

firmeza/sin gritos (firmness, without yelling)

motivar a entender que hay consequencias, no promover sumisión (teach consequences, not submissiveness)

enfoca la acción en el mal comportamiento mensaje al niño: "eres malo" mensaje al niño(a) (focus on the child: message to the child, "you are bad")

se enfoca en el pasado (focus the action on the bad behavior in the past), *el mal comportamiento tiene consecuencias* (message to child: "bad behavior has consequences")

P A C I E N C I A (Patience)

Sugerencias (Suggestions)

• *establezca actividades rutinarias y sígalas* (establish daily routines and keep to them)

• *enseñe a sus niños a que respeten a los demás* (teach your children to respect others)

• *usted es el adulto, no se deje mandar o manipular por su niño(a)* (you are an adult, don't let yourself be manipulated by your child)

• *no prometa lo que no va a cumplir* (do not promise what you will not carry out)

• *juege y platique con sus hijos* (play and talk with your children)

• *felicite a sus hijos por sus logros/éxitos* (congratulate your children for their successes)

• *cuando sus hijos prometan hacer alguna tarea o mandado, ellos deberán cumplir* (when your children promise to do a task or errand, they should carry it out)

• *tenga expectativas realistas, de acuerdo a la edad de ellos* (have realistic, age-appropriate expectations)

Transcription and translation of a collectively generated chart from a MUA discussion on childrearing. In July of 1997, there was a hand-drawn poster written in Spanish with colored markers and hanging in the MUA office. The poster was the product of facilitated group discussion about childrearing issues and principles and represents the type of negotiation of meaning and practice discussed in this chapter.

my sisters." This last theme of "chosen" families as an immediate source of support that was sometimes superior to one's own kin was reminiscent of Kath Weston's observations about gay and lesbian life in the Castro District in the 1980s (Weston, 1991). Transnational migration led to a more expansive notion of family for many women. In the words of Elsa Camacho, a thirty-two-year-old mother of two who shared a four-room flat with a single woman, another family, and her own alcoholic husband, "When I am feeling desperate and I want to run home [to Mexico], I go to a meeting and I feel like I'm with my family."

While the group's purpose and program included facilitating immigrant women's access to government services and institutions, there remained an undercurrent of fear and distrust of what too much state access to one's family might entail. The topic of the difference between child abuse and discipline eventually developed into a theme for women's leadership training workshops, with the goal of clarifying the difference between the two in ways that felt authentic to the participants and also educated them about legal standards and definitions of abuse in the United States. In 2008, MUA participated in coalitions of immigrant rights groups protesting Mayor Gavin Newsom's decision to reinterpret the local City of Sanctuary ordinance to allow federal immigration officials to intervene and remove unaccompanied (often trafficked) minors without clear legal immigration status, private legal representation, or families to advocate for them. Unlike earlier American Progressive Era notions of "social mothering," however, MUA's support for incarcerated youth saw their demands for respect for these young people's rights in the context of the rights of all San Francisco youths to the special legal protections as minors, regardless of immigration status.

Building Citizenship Through Contest and Collaboration

The particular collective identities that the women developed together in MUA were complex and shot through by experiences of race, class, and language, as well as gender. The women sorted out their position in U.S. society in collective discussions that involved debate and critique, and also in direct experiences of conflict and contestation with other groups with relative advantage, due to class, race, or institutional location. Together they waged political struggle at many levels, with a balance of attention to individual concerns, often the concerns of mothers, and collective analysis and action. In doing so, they show how citizenship is also constituted in realms and struggles that may appear insignificant to others, but are of immediate importance to women's developing political skills and social identities.

The leaders of Mujeres Unidas y Activas organized diverse allies of local professionals, effectively affirming the importance of their solidarity and bolstering their identification with the group. MUA provided a major service to police, health, and educational officials by facilitating the orientation and support of women with great social needs that these other institutions were not equipped to help in an ongoing way. At the same time, women in the group pushed service-providing professionals to engage their social critiques, including those of their own institutions and colleagues. They managed to "organize up" the status hierarchy by cultivating strategically positioned allies in the health, social services, educational, and legal professions and bringing them to group meetings to provide information from their areas of expertise. Often, guest speakers would arrive with their own agendas to find the group willing to listen to their presentation. On other occasions, the women present would reorient the topic of the meeting during the discussion period following a presentation, in order to convey their political messages to speakers.

Clara Luz Navarro, the now-retired cofounder of MUA, explained that this was part of her vision of organizing for immigrant rights and social justice among diverse social sectors. She believed that to improve the situation of all poor people in the United States, not just immigrant Latinas, all different classes and interests needed to be politically educated and united around the justice of their demands. Organizers recognized that appealing to professionals and other allies to give educational or informational talks gave these individuals and their institutions a sense of being appreciated by and accountable to the immigrant community. Such meetings provided a means of collectively representing the immigrants' needs and critiques to the institutional representatives on the immigrants' own turf, rather than in a clinic or school building. The meetings were also a means by which more experienced participants in the group modeled strategies of speaking truth to power to newer or younger group members who might be reticent about asking questions or posing challenges to speakers.

To deepen allies' understanding of immigrants' position, MUA challenged middle-class and nonimmigrant authority over issues and concerns ranging from health care to education, from violence to childrearing. The strategy of bringing in an institutional ally to provide information, then shifting the discussion to ask for her support on a related issue, helped make weekly meetings stimulating, but also deepened collaborative relationships with service providers while challenging vertical power relations. The women turned a set of social relations in which they might have been configured as the deficient party needing orientation into productive exchanges that were mutually informative and educational, even when the guests did not themselves acknowledge the mutuality of the encounters.

The group had an ongoing relationship with a Latina social worker at the county human services department who felt particularly committed to the group, because, as she regularly reminded her audiences, "I am an immigrant woman, just like you." She strongly identified as an advocate for immigrant women and Latino families within her agency. At one MUA meeting, she promoted foster care provisions among immigrant families, noting the dearth of Latino homes in which to place foster children and challenging the women present to consider becoming foster parents. Though she did not address this issue directly, many of the women knew that they were ineligible to be foster parents, no matter their desire, because of their immigration status. Instead of disengaging from her presentation, however, they pushed their guest to answer their questions about when and how the state could take a child from his or her parents and the rights of parents of children in foster care and incarcerated minors. By the end of the meeting, the audience had shifted the topic of discussion to their own critiques of child protective services rules, their ideas about the rights of immigrant parents, and a series of complaints about "disrespectful" and "abusive" treatment at the hands of other social workers at their guest's agency. The guest who had come to impart information became the recipient of her audience's own educational and orientation program for service providers.

On another occasion, three non-Latinos—a senior pediatrician, a nurse, and a medical social worker from the county hospital—were invited to answer questions about how to maneuver through the clinic's administrative systems. The women soon shifted the focus to let the health workers know about the bureaucratic obstacles to care they had faced, including naming specific eligibility workers and caregivers who had impeded their access to care in the past. They engaged their guests to go above and beyond the topic they had been invited to discuss in order to consider more critically the politics of health care encounters for immigrant families. One teenage mother, Alejandra Llamas, with a toddler named Haydée, who toddled a bit differently than her peers, managed to have the pediatrician examine her daughter's crooked leg and unstable gait after the meeting concluded. Her daughter's pediatrician was a medical resident at the time, and she had not managed to arrange a consultation with an orthopedist. Shortly after the MUA meeting, the guest speaker made sure Haydée was referred to an orthopedist as well as to an eligibility worker to enroll her in the state's disabled children's health care program. I attended several medical appointments with Alejandra and Haydée in the following months, during which time Haydée received physical therapy and a series of custom-made shoes and braces to correct the problem. Years later, when she was older, with two younger children, and separated from her husband, Alejandra told me that the experiences advocating for Haydée helped her feel confident about her capacity to advocate on her own for her family's needs within public institutions.

The guest speakers from the county hospital, in turn, left that particular informational session with a deeper understanding of the challenges to health care access for immigrants. Like other allies who engaged the group collectively in discussion, they were better prepared when asked to speak to the media or to lobby policy makers about public health issues for immigrants. Since San Francisco's county hospital is a teaching facility for diverse health professions, the impact of this type of work on professionals who go on to work in other regions and states is not insignificant. One Latina pediatric resident exemplified the political leadership development that MUA offered its allies. After she gave a talk at a meeting, MUA called upon her to speak at press conferences about the importance of preserving primary care access for immigrants and their children. When she completed her training in San Francisco, she moved to a state with fewer established Latino/a community advocacy groups, and started a pediatric public health program for immigrants and a Spanish-language radio call-in show on children's health.

Organizing allies, educating them politically, and then calling on them for support proved to be an effective strategy that I observed (and occasionally experienced) during my fieldwork. Together the women developed their capacity and sense of entitlement to set the agenda in discussions with teachers, principals, doctors, and others (including anthropologists) who, even from a position of solidarity, often ended up dominating or misinterpreting conversations and conflicts. After a particularly tense meeting with a high-level Latino school district administrator in which the women raised concerns about the impact of anti-immigrant politics on local schools, one staff member described to me how the administrator subjected them to a speech she considered very patronizing. According to the staff member, the women listened as he lectured until he said that "we Latinos do not vote and that's why we have so many problems in this society." She related how she had interrupted him at that point to describe the group's voter education, registration, and get-out-the-vote activities and to remind him that "Although I cannot vote myself, behind me are hundreds of people who can, and they ask my opinion." After that, she felt that the administrator, who was an elected official, listened more carefully as other women spoke up and offered opinions.

Mujeres Unidas y Activas emphasized helping women immigrants stand up individually and collectively against discriminatory behavior from individual and institutional sources, whether due to gender, race, language, or class. When the women had problems they could not resolve at their children's schools, for example, they could call upon the MUA education committee to accompany them to meetings with the principal and/or teacher until the issue was resolved. Often such initially tense meetings led to an ongoing relationship between the woman and the official. I was fortunate to observe several such meetings as a witness and as a translator.

In one case, I was both an observer and a translator when a white, non-Spanish-speaking elementary school principal was initially on the defensive when Patricia Gutierrez, a single mother from Mexico, came with members of MUA's education committee to complain about her daughter's teacher. The teacher, who had disciplined her child for misbehaving by forcing her to clean a school restroom, had been unresponsive to the mother's complaints, even though both were able to communicate fluently in their native Spanish. "She is very old fashioned, and reminds me of the way some teachers in Mexico are. She was not respectful to me," Patricia said. "She needs to understand that it is not the right way to treat her students." By the end of the meeting, Patricia and the education committee members had convinced the principal to be an advocate for the family, to facilitate the transfer Patricia wanted for her daughter, and at the close of the meeting to ask for materials and information about MUA "so that I can tell other parents about you." Despite the tense meeting, he seemed genuinely pleased to have another community resource to offer his students' mothers.

Women relished the autonomy of the group's office space and the opportunity to discuss their pains and frustrations openly and safely. At one MUA meeting, a broader discussion of anti-Latino stereotypes became personal as women shared their experiences of racism in the United States. Heads nodded in understanding when staff member Ana Gómez, a thirty-year-old former nun and mother of two from Mexico, related something that had happened to her earlier that week. She described walking down a narrow sidewalk as a white woman walking her dog approached from the other direction and literally forced Ana into the gutter. With her voice shaking with anger, Ana said, "For some, we are worth less than their dogs." In the context of contemporary anti-immigrant politics, history, and their structural subordination as Latinos in this country, group members agreed with Ana's interpretation of this event, which others might perceive as a more generic form of urban rudeness. Sharing such personal experiences while getting "good information" about policy, learning about immigration history, and carrying out community political education was the framework in which the women built solidarity and collective identity in resistance to the racism and xenophobia they experienced as Latinas in the United States.

These are just a few examples of the impact of the group's practice of cultural citizenship beyond the lives of its members and the immigrant community. In a myriad of ways, a stable community group with good infrastructure and consistent administrative support and leadership strengthened the effectiveness of publicly and privately supported organisms such as social service, health care, and educational institutions. Whether working with battered women, at-risk youth, renters, domestic laborers, or undocumented immigrants, social service agencies face difficulties establishing and maintaining consistent relations with clients. Mujeres Unidas y Activas's emphasis that it was not a social service agency was meant to limit newcomers' expectations of the groups' resources and the support it provided members, and also to underscore the existence of such social service agencies and to direct women and families to the appropriate institutions. In this way, the women directly educated the community about and promoted the work of such agencies, thereby increasing the agencies' popular legitimacy and expanding their client base.

By sharing the buena información they acquired from one another, from guest speakers, and from contacts with public service and social service institutions, women also directly supported the work of doctors, nurses, teachers, and social workers by repeating and reinforcing many of their public messages, sometimes adapting others to make them more appropriate to community members. When the immigration laws changed radically in 1996, MUA members rewrote their street theater piece, a short drama about the impact of the laws and anti-immigrant politics on the lives of a family and its neighbors. Performances emphasized the main aspects of the law's change and people's rights if detained by the INS, and appealed to people to be calm and rational, to learn their rights, and to avoid the confidence schemes of "lawyers," "paralegals," and "notaries" who came forward in the Spanish media to charge people for consultations and often provided them with poor information and advice. By performing the play at churches and in schools throughout northern California and conducting discussions afterwards, often with community legal assistance groups' support, MUA provided a valuable public outreach and peer education service. It complemented nonprofit legal services, recruited clientele for them, and generally raised public understanding of the laws, thus reducing the potential for scam artists to take advantage of the rising anxiety among immigrants at that time.

The process of articulating and claiming an alternative vision of citizenship was at once unique to MUA members' collective process and appealing to other peers who were themselves not politically active. The leadership and much of the political style of the group grew out of Latin American popular and women's organizing (Dore, 1997; Stephen, 1995, 1997, 1998, 2001), infused with a strong North American antiracist influence that emphasized the significance of racism and cultural resistance to struggles for equal rights in the United States. The focus on the needs and issues of women, children, and low-income immigrant families attracted women of all Latin American nationalities as well as diverse allies, and spoke to the broad appeal of Mujeres Unidas y Activas' discourse and activities. New women were constantly joining the group as others moved away from activism after many years of participation. Yet the group was not simply a transitional support, nor did its members speak of their purpose as helping one another to adjust (in other words, to assimilate) to norms of motherhood and citizenship in the United States. The group provided support, information, crisis intervention, and political education for women with young children, survivors of domestic violence and/or depression, newcomer immigrants, and others who enjoyed both the camaraderie and the mutual support they could contribute to and experience in the group.

In focusing on women, and limiting discussion of men and masculinity to issues raised by women themselves, I do not mean to indicate that men are marginal to women's experiences of citizenship, nor present only as antagonists to female autonomy, though that is how they frequently appeared in women's narratives. The ways that women's changing visions of their position in society affect men's understandings of their own rights is an important area of theory and ethnography that scholars of masculinity and migration have begun to address. This new scholarship indicates the need for understanding the mutually constitutive nature of gender roles and the active participation of both men and women in cultural processes of gender no longer seen as synonymous with women (Guttman, 1996, 1997; Quayson, 2005).

Through their participation in Mujeres Unidas y Activas, the women I interviewed developed ways of talking about their rights and their social position that demanded a more expansive vision of who fully belongs in the United States than can be encompassed by the narrow or legal formulation of citizenship. Their discussions of the bases for political and cultural entitlement emphasized their sense of each person's responsibility to others, including but not limited to their own families, and highlighted the relative importance of social participation over nationality in making claims to belonging in the United States. Women's status as low-income Latina immigrants; their relationships with public health, education, and immigration institutions; their household organization and relations; and their participation in the women's community group all played major roles in shaping the way they analyzed what it meant to be a positive participant in and contributor to U.S. society.

The women's experiences and interpretations of community participation, of what it means to belong and to be entitled to rights and services, constitute important examples of contemporary theory and practice of American citizenship. Their language and collective struggles attend to the gendered underpinnings of the state-defined realm of politics and rights, as well as to the everyday ways in which men and women actively shape the terms and scope of their rights and their entitlements. A gendered analysis of cultural citizenship therefore considers social belonging and political agency in the context of the disciplinary forces of multiple nation-states, but also through the consideration of citizens' gendered experiences of locale, domestic life, and subjectivity. The women discussed in this book, along with their words and actions, do not "illustrate" social theory, but rather should be seen as constituting it, of being active, resourceful theorists of American citizenship in their own right.

2 Law, Politics, and the American Dream

Te atacan como mujer.
[They attack you as a woman.]

—Cristina Rodríguez

"JUST YOU WAIT AND SEE. Soon they'll come after legal residents and then even for the naturalized citizens. That's just how they are," said Iris to Anabel, Anabel's daughter Rosa, and me as we drove to the Bayview District of San Francisco.[1] Nine-year-old Rosa and I listened as Iris and Anabel discussed the precariousness of citizenship rights and the danger posed to the civil rights of all groups when one marginal group is targeted the way immigrants and the poor were then being scapegoated in the United States. Iris's and Anabel's stories and the particularities of their discussion illustrate how issues of law, politics, and motherhood converged in their life experiences to prompt their sharp critiques of immigration and welfare reform in California at the end of the twentieth century. Women's experiences of the fierce anti-immigrant movement of the 1990s and the way macro political-economic shifts played out locally are instructive for understanding the legacy of the period in their lives, and the continuities as well as the changes in this context more than ten years later.

That day in August 1997, we were on our way home from a women's group meeting in San Francisco's Mission District, where recent federal and state cuts in welfare and health care funding were the subject of collective worry and discussion. Then-governor Pete Wilson, a prominent leader of the California anti-immigrant movement, had signed welfare reform legislation for the state two days earlier. Among other things, that law cut state funding for prenatal care for undocumented women. It was dark when the meeting ended, and I offered the three a ride home to the southeastern neighborhoods of the city.

Anabel González was in her mid-thirties, married with two children; she had emigrated from central Mexico in 1992. She and her family of four rented a damp in-law apartment in the basement of a modest older home in the Bayview District, where they were part of the recent influx of Latino and Asian immigrant families to that historically African American neighborhood. They sublet one room to another young Mexican immigrant family, a couple with one baby. Iris was a single mother of two in her late thirties. Iris, her sixteen-year-old daughter, and her nine-year-old son lived in a two-bedroom public housing unit in a complex located between Bayview and my own home in the Excelsior District; she sublet one room to another Salvadoran single mother with one child.

Iris Hernández's analysis of the United States had changed radically in the eighteen years since she and a woman friend arrived from San Salvador "llena de sueños y esperanzas" (full of dreams and hopes). I had met her the year before when I interpreted for her at a press conference that was part of a lobbying campaign against then-pending federal immigration and welfare reform legislation. That day, she had spoken publicly about how Aid to Families with Dependent Children (AFDC) payments and public housing were two key supports that allowed her to leave her abusive husband of twelve years.[2] Federal and state welfare reforms threatened these benefits and prenatal care for immigrants, making it even more difficult for immigrant women seeking to leave violent relationships. She felt strongly that the "anti-illegal" politics of the times were a thin veneer over a more general political animosity toward immigrants, the immigrant poor in particular.

Iris was clear about the ambivalent and frequently hostile attitude toward newcomers she had encountered in this "nation of immigrants." When Anabel and Iris spoke about American citizenship, they recalled both past and current exclusivity in immigration laws as conditioners of their efforts to define a place for themselves in the civic life of the United States. Their stories of exclusion emphasized the righteousness of their claims for inclusion for themselves and their children, who they knew were paying attention to their mothers' words, as nine-year-old Rosa was that night in the car.

Xenophobia and Immigrant Citizenship in 1990s California

The fieldwork for this book spanned a period of increasing antagonism toward immigrants and people of color embodied in the passage of statewide referenda seeking to eliminate affirmative action, public services to undocumented migrants, and bilingual education programs in California. Although "moves to restrict immigrants and immigrant rights form a long tradition in California history" (García Bedolla, 2005, 26), the final decade of the twentieth century was nonetheless remarkable for the level of anti-immigrant activism by both popular initiative campaigns and the state government. In 1993 alone, the state legislature considered twenty-three pieces of legislation aiming to take away rights and services from undocumented immigrants (García, 1995, 130). On the national level, major reform legislation altered the shape of welfare and immigration law, reversing the decades-old emphasis on family reunification and financial support for poor families with young children. Immigrant families and poor mothers in particular were drastically affected by these changes.

Conservative political forces gained momentum in 1990s California when voters passed three ballot initiatives aimed at further marginalizing immigrants and citizens of color. Women spoke frequently about how they and their families experienced such politics in profound and personal ways. The day after the passage of anti–bilingual-education Proposition 227, participants in a somber Mujeres Unidas y Activas general meeting shared their fears. One woman spoke of how she had coaxed her second grader to go to school that morning, reassuring him that he would be neither scolded nor expelled for speaking Spanish with his friends or teachers. She quietly but angrily related how he asked her, "Mom, can't we speak Spanish anymore?" By sharing her story, not only was she mourning her child's pain and loss of innocence, but she was also protesting the violation of her rights and resisting discrimination. The 63 percent of Latino voters in California who opposed Proposition 227 recognized the attacks on bilingual education as more than a civil disagreement over how to best educate immigrant children. As Juan Andrade noted at the time, Proposition 227 was really "about re-institutionalizing discrimination and legalizing the deprivation of knowledge and educational opportunity. This proposition sanctions the rejection of Latino culture and our language in society and in the public schools."[3]

Immigrant women's citizenship struggles in California have implications for, as well as were influenced by, larger structural and political struggles over who truly belongs and is recognized as a full member of U.S. society. While discrimination against Latinos is a national phenomenon, these state-level electoral battles over immigration illustrate some of the regional contours of racialization and Latinidad (De Genova, 2005; Dávila, 2001, 2004; Pérez, 2004; Ramos-Zayas, 2003). History and context matter to both the structural characteristics of second-class citizenship and its impact on individual sub-jectivities and collective identities. Factors ranging from California's history as a Mexican territory until 1848 to the specific tone and character of the anti-immigrant ballot measures affected the ways that the women talked about injustice and racism. However, the national discourse around immigration was also affected by California's pitched battles (Chavez, 2001, 2007; Inda, 2002, 2005), and low-income women nationally also experienced the tremen-dous pressure and anxiety felt by immigrant women in California due to se-vere cuts and changes in welfare. The "tired, . . . poor, . . . huddled masses yearning to breathe free," in Emma Lazarus's words, were as central to the national melting pot story as they were targets of laws designed to keep them out (Boswell, 1995; C. Chang, 1997). Contrary to popular perception, current levels of immigration are not at a historic high, and neither do immigrants appear to be assimilating any more slowly in measurable terms (as hard as such a comparison may be to quantify) than their predecessors (Vigdor, 2008). In 1990, 7.9 percent of the U.S. population had been born in other countries; the number had risen to 10 percent by the 2000 census (U.S. Bureau of the Census, 2003b). We have still not matched the 15 percent foreign-born popula-tion found in the United States from 1890 to 1910 (Portes and Rumbaut, 1996, 6). The complexion of the immigrant population at the beginning of the twen-tieth century was different than it is today. Laws limited Asian / Pacific Is-lander immigration from 1882 to 1965 (Lowe, 1996; Ngai, 2004). In 1910, the great waves of refugees from the Mexican Revolution had not yet begun in ear-nest. However, during this period of heavy southern and eastern European im-migration, the newcomers were seen as racially and culturally inferior as well as unassimilable.

Women, Marriage, and Citizenship

U.S. immigration law historically treated migrant women's citizenship as sub-ordinate to men's, with marked biases toward heterosexuality and marriage. This reflected the centuries-old doctrine of coverture, according to which "a woman's legal identity ceased to exist after marriage, when she became her husband's chattel" (Lilienthal, 1996).[4] Alien wives of U.S. citizens and lawful permanent residents were exempted from exclusions based on health or oc-cupation, tying immigrant women's positions in this country inextricably to their husbands (Bredbenner, 1998; Calvo, 1991). In 1922, the Act Relative to the Naturalization and Citizenship of Married Women further codified gender inequality by preventing women citizens or legal residents from sponsoring their foreign spouses.[5] This act of Congress threatened women who tried to sponsor their husbands with the loss of their own citizenship. Even though a congressional act on July 11, 1932, recognized a woman's right to sponsor her husband's residency application (provided they were married before the bill's passage), both the tradition of coverture and the exclusion of those considered to be potential public charges in effect doubled the burden of most women who were forced to rely on male sponsorship for immigration.[6]

The War Brides Act of 1948 allowed male veterans who were U.S. citizen to sponsor foreign-born spouses and children, codifying the family reunification principle that came to guide post–World War II immigration policy until 1997. The patriarchal assumptions embedded in the family reunification policy of the Immigration and Naturalization Service was a two-edged sword as far as women immigrants were concerned. Specific changes in immigration law in 1986 (the Immigration Reform and Control Act, or IRCA, and the Immigration and Marriage Fraud Act) and 1990 (the Immigration Act, or IMMACT) and aspects of the 1994 Violence Against Women Act (VAWA) formed the context in which marriage, immigration, and domestic violence framed new legal identities for battered undocumented women.[7]

IRCA contributed to an increase in the numbers and the marginalized status of undocumented immigrants and the feminization of undocumented Latinos as a class of immigrants (Johnson, 1996; Hondagneu-Sotelo, 1994). While the amnesty provision of the law allowed more than two million previously undocumented residents of the United States to legalize their status if they could prove continuous residency since 1982, many who could not qualify for amnesty were women. After 1986, there was an increase in women, children, and first-time migrants crossing the border. Some estimates held that women made up the majority of Mexican undocumented immigrants in the United States by 1990 (Woodrow and Passel, 1990). The increase in female Mexican undocumented migration resulted from a variety of factors, including the normal maturation of migration networks, which tend to include increasing numbers of women and children over time, fear that "the door was closing" for future immigrants, and the disproportionate impact of employer sanctions on men employed in the formal sector as compared to women employed in domestic work (Hondagneu-Sotelo, 1994, 26). In short, as men legalized under IRCA, their spouses and children joined them in the hope of later legalizing their status (Cornelius, 1990). Additionally, the U.S. economy began expanding in the mid- to late 1980s, while the Mexican economy contracted and the wars in Central America escalated, creating increased demand for laborers and driving working people, peasants, and other political refugees northward.

In the 1970s and 1980s, surveys of immigrants entering the United States under family preference visas as spouses or immediate family members of citizens or lawful permanent residents (LPRs) found that about 70 percent had lived in the United States at some point before being granted visas. In 1993, 93 percent of legal Mexican immigrants were granted legal residency under family preference or as immediate relatives of U.S. citizens (Portes and Rumbaut, 1996, 15). Thus the traditional roots of immigration patterns in chain migration and family ties directly diminish any woman's ability to legalize her own status later on. In 1996, national efforts to repress gay and lesbian equal rights claims culminated in the Defense of Marriage Act (DOMA), which reinforced the legal privileging of heterosexual marriage in civil life, social welfare, and immigration laws (Lubhéid, 2005).

Unscrupulous employers further victimized undocumented men and women who did not qualify for *la amnistía*, the colloquial name for IRCA's amnesty provisions. Since the law required workers to present their documents to begin new jobs, and threatened to fine employers of undocumented workers (rarely enforced), some employers took advantage of workers' fears of losing their current employment (Mahler, 1995). Whether they married in the United States after immigrating without documents or crossed the border illegally to reunite their families in the United States, many women remain undocumented, even though they are eligible for permanent residency by virtue of their proximate relationship to a lawful permanent resident. They may live in legal limbo for five or more years while they await the processing of their residency applications. The length of time to process such applications varies by nationality, due to large numbers of applications from specific nations, with Mexico having the longest backlog by several years.[8] The fact that Cristina Rodríguez waited three years to submit her papers after marrying her husband has slowed the process further, but others with whom I spoke found themselves in the same situation because of the time it took them to trust the institutions enough to reveal their undocumented status and risk deportation.

The two landmark pieces of legislation passed by the U.S. Congress under the banner of immigration reform and welfare reform during this period—the Personal Responsibility and Work Opportunity Reconciliation Act of 1996

(PRWORA) and the Illegal Immigration Reform and Immigrant Responsibility Act of 1996 (IIRIRA)—changed what had been the course of national social welfare and immigration policy for most of the twentieth century.[9] Together with DOMA, "these laws importantly reconstructed the regulation of contemporary legal immigration" (Lubhéid, 2005, 70). Immigration reform tightened controls at the border with Mexico, increased deportations, and made legal immigration and naturalization more difficult for the families of immigrants already in the United States. Though President Bill Clinton removed the provisions regarding legal family-sponsored immigration from the final version of the law, families are now obliged to sign a legally binding affidavit of support for sponsored family members and must themselves earn at least 125 percent of the federal poverty guideline figure for the petition to be granted. On April 1, 1997, the law's new expedited removal procedures took effect, leading to more than a thousand summary expulsions from the United States per week, sometimes within hours of an undocumented person's arrival and mostly taking place along the U.S.-Mexico border and at the Los Angeles and San Francisco international airports. Before the 1996 reforms, a person facing exclusion (a process affecting those awaiting deportation or those barred from entering the United States) had the right to a hearing before an INS judge whose decisions were subject to appeal. After the new law took effect, individual border agents were also newly empowered to summarily deport migrants with no due process.[10]

"They Attack You as a Woman"

Political debates and legal reforms shaped experiences of migration and resettlement. At the time of our interview, Cristina Rodríguez was a twenty-eight-year-old immigrant from a small town in Jalisco and an eloquent analyst of popular political discourse. Although her son was a citizen and her husband a permanent resident, Cristina remained undocumented. Like many thousands of women in her position, she had the right to permanent residency because her husband was a lawful permanent resident.

Cristina's husband gained legal residency under the amnesty provisions of the 1986 Immigration Reform and Control Act. IRCA had five basic provisions: (1) the legalization of undocumented immigrants residing in the United States continuously since 1982, (2) sanctions for employers hiring undocumented immigrants, (3) reimbursement of state governments for the costs of legalization, (4) the screening of welfare applicants for immigration status, and (5) special programs to bring in agricultural workers. Of an estimated 2.5 million eligible undocumented migrants in the country, 1.7 million were legalized under the amnesty program.

Two perhaps unintended consequences of IRCA were a crippling shortage of agricultural workers for the 1997 summer harvest and the feminization of the undocumented population of Mexican migrants (Sandino-Glasser, 1998, 79, note 38; Hondagneu-Sotelo, 1994, 26). Like Cristina, many women came to the United States without proper documents and later married or rejoined partners who had received legal resident status. While U.S. immigration law allows for the almost immediate granting of legal status to the foreign spouses of U.S. citizens, lawful permanent residents must petition for residency for their spouses. After IRCA, because of the high number of applicants and the limited number of visas allocated to this purpose, many women faced the choice of waiting for years in their home country for their visas to be approved or entering the country illegally to reunite their families. Those who migrated lived in the peculiar limbo of undocumented people who are legally eligible for permanent residency by marriage but cannot achieve it because of the backlog. Other undocumented women were married to men who for a variety of reasons never submitted petitions for their wives' residency.

When I interviewed her in early 1998, I asked Cristina how long she had been waiting for approval of her residency. This question elicited the longest uninterrupted narrative of any interview. Cristina criticized the changes in immigration law pertaining to the elimination of Section 245(i) of the U.S. immigration code and cutoff of services to the undocumented (prompted by Proposition 187).[11] She spoke continuously and moved from one topic to the next without prompting, connecting her status as an undocumented person eligible for legal residency to the change in immigration policy that tried to get people in her position to return to their home country, to the general assault on immigrant families, to the Proposition 187 initiative campaign, and to the explicit political focus on pregnant undocumented women.

Cristina related these issues to her *desilusión*—the breaking of her dreams about the United States, the humiliations she faced and that others have continued to face due to their legal status, and the racialized conflations of immigrants with Latinos in current political debates. "When they talk about immigrants, we know they are pointing with all their fingers at us." She gave voice to the sentiments of many women about what it feels like to be "under attack" as immigrants, wives, and mothers, responding directly to the daily polemical assaults of the media and the state. Her *testimonio* wove politics, emotion, state discipline of immigrant families through immigration laws, and analysis of antifemale and anti-immigrant discourse. Her narrative was a continuous flow of thoughts and associations:

> The thing is that I already have been waiting for three years [for residency]. When we turned in the application, they told me, "It'll be three or four years." At the minimum I've been waiting three years, but I think it'll be a while. The problem isn't waiting so much as the laws and how they are attacking us. I have defended my residency like you wouldn't believe. All the laws they are making . . . they are attacking me, they are touching me. So I have had to give testimony, I have had to go to ask, to beg that they cease all this that they are doing against us.[12]

Cristina did indeed give testimony at public meetings, at informational forums, and on Spanish-language television and radio news programs, where one seemingly obscure aspect of the 1996 changes in immigration law began to get a great deal of attention in the summer of 1997. Section 245(i) gave undocumented people with pending applications for residency a date by which they had to return to their country of origin to wait for their applications to be processed. The penalties for not leaving the country by the deadline (which Congress extended to September 30, 1997) or for trying to reenter after leaving the country included a fine, a delay of several years on the residency process, or the barring of their legal reentry to the United States for from three years to life.[13] For many undocumented Mexican women who might have been able to return home temporarily for a family emergency, this aspect of law made such trips even more perilous; if the INS caught them reentering the United States after having overstayed a previous visa or previously living here without documents, they could be barred from reentry for life. Even women like Cristina, who are entitled to live in this country as spouses or children of lawful permanent residents or as parents of minor citizen children, were required by law to choose between separating their families or jeopardizing their applications.[14] Immigrant families faced very difficult personal decisions, and most with whom I spoke chose, as Cristina did, to stay in the United States despite the risks:

> Because with this [section] 245 (i), I already had bought my ticket to leave. And without even consulting my husband, because it wasn't his place to say I

could go or not. It was a very, very personal decision, that I couldn't ask any-one's opinion about, well, their opinion, yes, advice, sure, but no one could tell me "go" or "stay." So in a moment of desperation, I went to a travel agency and said, "reserve me a ticket for this day." But I didn't just sit and wait. Every in-formational meeting, every thing that there was about this, I was there. Even though I heard the same thing day in and day out, that there was no solution, it was like I just wouldn't give up. And then came the day, the last chance be-cause it was a Wednesday and the law was up on a Friday. And I had a ticket to leave Friday morning. And the lawyer [at one forum] was so fair. . . . He was also desperate and told us, "I can't tell you all to stay or to go because later you're going to tell me, 'But you told me to stay and look what happened to me!'" But he said, "Weigh and consider, what will happen if I go and what will happen if I stay?" I can only tell you that in your own country, no one will pay you any attention, and since you are in your own country, the United States will have nothing to do with you. And your case will be at greater risk, since they are consulates and if you are missing a paper or they deny your application for any reason, you will not have any right to appeal but here you do. . . . So I thought about it, I weighed the issues and considered it. Well, I may have to wait there four, five more years. And in four or five years, who's going to guar-antee me that when I return here I will still be with my, that my husband will still be here waiting for me? The law will be the same. There [in Mexico] I'll be alone, and I mean, what am I going to do? My family will be here. How can I take my son's father away from him? How can I tell him that because some man makes a law, I am going to take away his right to grow up with his fa-ther? In six years the boy will be grown and every time he asks, "And where is my daddy?" what will I tell him? "We had to come here because a law sepa-rated us." So I thought about that, that I didn't want to take away my son's father from him. And I didn't want to be without my husband because that's why I got married, in order to be with my husband, not so that someone could decide for me, would tell me that "You'll have to leave him for five years."

Cristina's experience with what might seem a minor clause in a huge piece of immigration legislation made clear that the primary effect was to limit the liberty of women in her position rather than to deter new immigrants. She continued to experience an enormous amount of stress and anxiety as a result of what Menjívar (2006) calls the "liminal legality" of her standing, as well as the uncertainty of how new immigration laws are eventually applied in practice. After attending numerous informational events and acquiring the best possible information about her options, she found that the law required her to either remain illegally in this country or risk her marriage, her family, and her residency by returning to Mexico for an indefinite period. Such experiences highlight how immigrant women's position and rights in the United States are not solely defined by laws and legal relationships, which, women learn through experience, are ambiguous and uncertain, but also through the interpretation and actions of the subjects of the laws.

Cristina's husband was already a lawful permanent resident when they married in the United States, and they had been awaiting the decision on her immigration petition for three years when I interviewed her in 1998. One particularly harsh provision of the 1996 Immigration Act called for the elimination of section 245(i) of the Immigration and Naturalization Act, which had allowed a woman in Cristina's position to remain with her spouse and/or children while awaiting the approval of her petition. The 1996 law placed undocumented women married to residents in an untenable position. On the one hand, eliminating 245(i) called for undocumented spouses of legal residents to divide their families and return home to wait for visas, possibly for years. On the other hand, immigration reforms threatened anyone proven to have resided illegally in the United States with a lifetime ban on reentering the country or legalization. The paradoxical results of these policies discouraged return trips to home countries and increased the pressure on women and children to immigrate illegally to reunite their families.

Psychological Warfare

Women in MUA noted the "psychological warfare" waged against them via public policies and political discourse that aimed to silence them socially and politically. Cristina's migration experience was shaped directly by the politics of the times. In 1994, she was pregnant with her son when supporters of Proposition 187 (the so-called Save Our State ballot initiative) sought to exclude undocumented immigrants from public services, including prenatal care and public education.[15] The initiative obliged service providers, including teachers, doctors, and social workers, to verify the status of any "suspected" undocumented person requesting services, including the parents of public schoolchildren, and to report suspected undocumented people to federal immigration officials.[16] It passed overwhelmingly statewide, though it failed in San

Francisco. Although the courts blocked Proposition 187 and later declared it unconstitutional, "it exemplifie[d] the marginality of poor, undocumented women of color . . . [and its] provisions, if implemented, would have an especially adverse impact on poor, undocumented women of color" (K. Johnson, 1995).[17]

The rhetoric surrounding the initiative was horrific for Cristina, who was far from her home and family and expecting her first child in an environment that "gave license to discrimination and intolerance. . . . [Proposition 187] resulted in heightened discrimination against Latinos of all backgrounds" (Cervantes, Khokha, and Murray, 1995, 2–5). This rhetoric also contextualized Cristina's use of images of warfare and violent attacks to describe her experiences as an undocumented Latina:

> I was pregnant during the [Proposition] 187 [campaign], and I didn't know whether to leave or stay. "Where will my child be born?" And when I had this huge belly, I was overcome by depression and said, "I'm going to go." But because I was at the point of delivery, I couldn't get on a plane. So, well, it's really hard that they are attacking you and your child who's not even born. Like, [the child] can't defend himself, can't even yell, "At least let me be born in peace!" As a couple, expecting your first child, they don't even let you enjoy it. Instead of me feeling, when they told me, "Yes, you're pregnant," I didn't know, well I was glad because I was going to be a mother, and it was the news that my husband and I had been hoping for since we had gotten married. It took me three months to get pregnant and it seemed like forever. And I said, "And now what am I going to do? With this war they are waging against us? No, no, well, what should I do? Have [the baby] in my house?" And since it's your first pregnancy, in a strange country, it's like, they have you completely confused.

Proposition 187 blamed and punished undocumented immigrants for generalized economic and political problems; Latinos were the explicit target of the rhetoric. By blocking access to public health, education, and social services for "suspected" undocumented immigrants, supporters argued, the proposition could stem the tide of immigration altogether. The very cornerstone of Governor Pete Wilson's reelection campaign that same year was combating the "flood" of illegal immigration (García, 1995, 130). In one letter to the editor in the *New York Times*, the campaign media director for Proposition 187 sought to promote this xenophobic agenda on the national level, essentially declaring California on the verge of a *reconquista* by Mexico:

Proposition 187 is . . . a logical step toward saving California from economic ruin. Illegal aliens collect welfare payments through post office boxes in San Ysidro, just a 15 minute walk from Mexico. They receive free medical care and flood schools with non-English speaking students. By flooding the state with 2 million illegal aliens to date, and increasing that figure each of the following 10 years, Mexicans in California would number 15 million to 20 million by 2004. During those 10 years about 5 million to 8 million Californians would have emigrated to other states. If these trends continued, a Mexico-controlled California could vote to establish Spanish as the sole language of California, 10 million more English-speaking Californians could flee, and there could be a statewide vote to leave the Union and annex California to Mexico.[18]

Such rhetoric contextualized Cristina's use of images of warfare and violent attacks to describe her experiences as an undocumented Latina in 1990s California. In her case, the support and information provided by her sister and other women in Mujeres Unidas y Activas allowed her to continue seeking prenatal care and to give birth to a healthy baby at San Francisco's county hospital.[19] But soon after passage of Proposition 187, at least two deaths were attributed to the fears that kept undocumented patients and their families from presenting for care at public facilities in the state.[20]

Even though Proposition 187 never took effect, it did set the political tone for the decade, creating a context in which immigrants feared claiming the rights and services due them, while additional regressive ballot initiatives could be passed and enforced. In 1996, supporters of Proposition 209 generalized the attack on immigrants to Latinos, African Americans, Native Americans, and Pacific Islanders by eliminating government affirmative action programs and overturning affirmative action at the University of California, the country's largest public university system. In 1998, Silicon Valley entrepreneur Ron Unz, who had shown no previous interest or experience in educational issues, bankrolled Proposition 227, which sought to eliminate bilingual education in the state's public schools.[21]

Cristina reported feeling the psychic sting of anti-immigrant policies such as cuts in public benefits, even though she herself has never received welfare. The rhetorical attacks on immigrants were part of what disillusioned her with political life in the United States. She was careful to distinguish between the people and the policies of the state in our interview, however, perhaps in deference to me. She also emphasized that attacks on immigrants are not just anti-Mexican, but more broadly anti-Latino:

One arrives with the, with the illusion, because it is pure illusion, that this country is the country of marvels. The land of dreams. And you arrive and find such sad things that you are forever disillusioned. For me, day after day, month after month, year after year that I have lived here have been one continuous disillusionment with this country. Maybe not with the country, but with those who govern it. It's like with welfare. What is it that they say? "Oh, but the immigrants!" But when they refer to immigrants they are almost always talking about Latinos. Even though one might like to play dumb, that the word is immigrant, you realize that they are pointing with all their fingers at Latinos.[22]

Though diverse immigrant communities felt the impact of these politics and policies, the predominant xenophobic imagery of the times highlighted the southern border as the source of the "illegal" problem (Coutin and Chock, 1995). At the time of Cristina's interview, conservative official estimates were that 41 percent of undocumented immigrants actually arrived by plane and overstayed visas (Immigration and Naturalization Service, 1999). Yet middle-class, air-traveling, and visa-carrying Canadians and Europeans were not identified as problem immigrants by the INS or media sources. Cristina also called attention to the fact that supposed reformist attacks on welfare-consuming undocumented immigrants are disingenuous, given that such migrants did not previously qualify for public benefits such as cash assistance, food stamps, or nonemergency health care (K. Johnson, 1995). Yet the rhetoric invoked "the stereotype of large Latino families 'draining' the welfare system" (Cervantes, Khokha, and Murray, 1995).

Histories of Exclusion

The history of U.S. immigration and nationality law has been as much about exclusion as about including newcomers in response to changing geopolitical interests and domestic ideals of the citizenry (Ngai, 2004; Lowe, 1996). Citizen-subjects feel the weight of these political forces and values differently depending on their positions in the dynamic contests over power and social position. As early as the Articles of Confederation, the young state excluded "paupers, vagabonds and fugitives from justice" (Neuman, 1993, 1846).[23] In contrast to Lazarus's poetry, Europe's huddled masses did not fit the ideal of the honest, hardworking stock the founding fathers hoped for. The image of the desirable new citizen was further racialized and codified in the 1790 Naturalization

Act, which limited citizenship to free white persons (Haney-López, 1995). Exclusions based on poverty and other attributes such as criminal activities, mental illness, and infirmity were reaffirmed in additional immigration legislation in 1875, 1882, 1891, and 1903.[24] In addition to excluding potential public charges based on class, the government also enforced political and racial exclusions, particularly directed against Chinese (1875, 1882, 1885), Japanese (1907), and Italian (1903) migrants. In 1917, to further limit the entry of those with inadequate cultural capital, and also virtually banning new Asian immigration, legislation enacted a literacy test for immigrants. In 1921, 1924, and 1927, the government responded to ever-increasing racism and xenophobia by enacting a system of national origins quotas designed to conserve the general racial and ethnic characteristics of the population and limit especially non-Northern European immigration. Insisting that the problems of today's immigrants and their reception in the United States are somehow related to greater racial or cultural difference between them and the receiving society than was the case during the eras of large-scale European migration is to imagine that Irish, Italian, and eastern European Jews were welcomed, or that they overcame their subordination because today these groups are "white."

Anti-immigrant sentiment and political organizing has been as much a part of post-1848 California history as the gold rush and the railroads. Just as the San Francisco Bay still remains polluted with the mercury that drained down the Sacramento River from nineteenth-century Sierra gold mines, the state's politics are infused with the 150 years of antagonism toward non-European migrants and their children. Californians ranging from mainstream politicians like Governor Leland Stanford to populist nativists like Dennis Kearney stoked the fires of late-nineteenth-century xenophobia.[25] Although his co-ethnics were the primary targets of the anti-immigrant vitriol of the original East Coast "Know Nothings," Kearney and other California Irishmen assumed the status of white male citizens and led the charge against Chinese immigrants. Californians led the national efforts to pass federal immigration legislation in 1875 barring convicts, prostitutes, and Chinese contract laborers from immigration, and to pass the even more restrictive Chinese Exclusion Act of 1882 (Ngai, 2004; Takaki, 1990).

California's particular history with respect to migration from the south began before the occupation of the Mexican capital and conquest of its northernmost provinces in 1848. Despite provisions in the Treaty of Guadalupe Hidalgo protecting the rights of Mexicans in the newly annexed U.S. territories,

Mexican Americans had been deprived of political, civil, and property rights by the end of the nineteenth century. By 1910, the Mexican Revolution prompted new flows of war refugees to California and coincided with federal legislation that cut off new farmworkers from Asia, creating dependence on Mexican agricultural labor that continues to this day. Agricultural interests later succeeded in winning special waivers from the literacy and head-tax requirements of the 1917 Immigration Act for Mexican migrants (García, 1995, 127).

Almost immediately, Mexican migration and use of public services became points of political contention in California, resulting in the redefinition of racial and ethnic terms to reflect the social ambivalence toward Mexican Californians. In 1916, the Los Angeles County health department began distinguishing "Mexicans" from "Whites" and "Others" (Negro or Asian) in such health statistics as birth and death records. When popular resentment against Mexican migration accelerated, public health data were racialized, defining Mexicans as nonwhite, and unprecedented mass deportations of Mexican Californians began taking place (Molina, 2006). According to some estimates, half a million people were forcibly placed on trains and sent to Mexico in 1930, and another three hundred thousand were deported between 1931 and 1934, including U.S. citizens and legal residents (Cervantes, Khokha, and Murray, 1995, 2). Although wartime labor shortages led to the recruitment of Mexican agricultural workers through the Bracero program, soon the U.S. government was organizing mass deportations again. In 1954, Operation Wetback deported over one million Mexicans and Mexican Americans to Mexico and "included a relentless media campaign to characterize the Operation as a national security necessity, and a tightening of the border to deter undocumented immigration" (García, 1995, 127). Given this historical hostility, the xenophobia of the 1990s can be viewed as a contemporary resurgence of a long-standing statewide hostility to migrants from south of the border (García Bedolla, 2005).

Refugees and Asylum in the 1990s

Although Cristina's experiences were congruent with those of many MUA members, immigration law and policies affected other women differently. The women's life stories were tremendously diverse, and part of their challenge was to represent their stories in ways that legitimated their continued presence in the eyes of the state. Of the women I knew or had heard of in the women's group, only two were petitioning to change their undocumented status to that of political refugees. Most knew that an asylum petition was a risky route to legalization. They frequently spoke of desperate immigrants they knew, sometimes encouraged by scurrilous immigration attorneys, paralegals, and notary publics, who had submitted asylum applications to get temporary work permits even though they had no chance of obtaining asylum, thereby increasing their chances of removal or deportation.[26]

Central to a successful asylum case was a petitioner's ability to represent herself as an upright and moral person with a "well-founded fear of persecution" were she returned to her home country. The determinations are made by INS judges and involve the participation of attorneys on behalf of both the INS and the petitioner. Central Americans have had a notoriously difficult time gaining political asylum in the United States. Coutin (2000) charted the collective journey of Salvadorans from staking their claims based on refugee status in the 1980s to a transformation in collective rights claims as immigrants after political conditions in El Salvador changed and achieving asylum status became even more difficult. Successful Mexican and South American asylum cases are even rarer than those for Central Americans.

Like applicants for residency under VAWA, petitioners for political asylum have faced particularly rigorous attention to their narrative and self-representation skills. The law demands evidence that a petitioner meets its criteria for legal admission to the U.S. polity, and this evidence is presented in the form of a story that must be clear, credible, and compelling to judges and attorneys on all sides. Not only did immigration law reinforce certain norms for desirable immigrants, but the mainstream media in the 1980s constructed certain Latino immigrants as suspect or threatening and others as worthy and virtuous, especially young, single, childless women workers (Coutin and Chock, 1995). These norms were profoundly heteronormative, reflecting the particular history of coverture and sexuality in U.S. immigration history (Bredbenner, 1998; Park, 1995).

Daniel Guzmán's story illustrates a different set of challenges facing asylum applicants when sexuality and sexual identity become the grounds for their petitions. Daniel was a twenty-five-year-old female-to-male transgendered member of MUA. He and his partner, Isabel, represented themselves as lesbians in the group before his public claiming of a transgendered identity. Although Daniel used his female name in the group, he told me that he preferred to be addressed as a man and said that this was one of the first steps he needed to take in preparation for sex reassignment surgery. Daniel was one of the few MUA members who identified as middle class in origins, having left

Ecuador while in college in order to pursue a new life in the United States. He had traveled by ground from South America to the United States, often walking or hitchhiking, and told harrowing stories of his experiences on the road, including the rape that produced his beloved only daughter. He met Isabel in San Francisco, where she and her two children were living in a shelter after she left her abusive husband. Daniel, Isabel, and their three daughters now shared an apartment in the Potrero Hill public housing project. Daniel applied for asylum under immigration law provisions recognizing institutionalized forms of sexuality-based oppression as potential grounds for asylum. He was able to convince the immigration judge that conditions in Ecuador precluded life without persecution there as a transgendered person. Daniel petitioning for asylum as a transgendered person rather than a lesbian made a critical difference to his chances of approval, since lesbians have had a far more difficult time gaining asylum than have gay men or transgendered persons (Neilson, 2005). He eventually won his case, obtained refugee status, enrolled in a training program for the skilled trades, underwent surgery, and stopped coming to MUA, as did Isabel.[27]

Anabel Ibañez was a thirty-five-year-old home health worker who lived with her husband, a ten-year-old daughter, and a fifteen-year-old son when we first spoke at length in 1997. We got to know each other well in the course of my interpreting during her conflicts with her daughter's teacher and principal. After many meetings and trips to plead her case at the central school district office, Anabel managed to transfer her daughter to another elementary school. It was painful and humiliating for her to break down in tears in front of each of the officials, but in the end she had the intense satisfaction of finding her daughter a school and teacher they were both happy with. Anabel subsequently invited me to join her for her medical visits for hip surgery and later for her legal appointments and trips to the INS offices. After seeing her engage in different levels of struggle for her own and her children's rights in San Francisco, I was not surprised to learn about her political history in Mexico. Of all the women I spoke with, only Anabel and Clara Luz reported having engaged in political activities in their home countries.

Anabel was a community leader in her small town in the state of Mexico, near Mexico City. She explained that she was an officer in a civic organization backed by the PRI (Partido Revolucionario Institucional), the ruling party. The civic organization supported the PRI's political hegemony through patronage and clientelism; its job had been to help people with their problems to gain their loyalty to the PRI. After she came into conflict with corrupt party bosses in the municipal government, she experienced disillusionment, harassment, and fear. Her home was taken by cronies of the party boss; federal police attempted to kidnap her husband; and her family fled to another state. In 1994, two years after the problems began, Anabel and her family fled to the United States after the appearance of suspicious-looking men who they feared were sent to harass or hurt them.

Asylum determinations depend heavily on the political relationship between the United States and the government of the country of origin, as well as on the individual proclivities of the immigration officers, attorneys, and judges, who are appointed and employed by the federal immigration agency and are not members of the independent judiciary. These officials, the immigration lawyers working on behalf of petitioners, and the agents, clerks, and lower-level government administrators make up an "empire of bureaucrats" who earn their living processing immigrants' paperwork and enforcing immigration laws' discipline over individual and family lives (Dummett and Nicol, 1990, 20).

In the cases that I followed closely through the INS judicial process, I was impressed by the extent to which the personalities, politics, and private interpretations of immigration policy of the individual hearings officers, INS attorneys, and judges shaped their rulings and the petitioners' life courses. The judge has the final authority to accept the claim and redefine the applicant legally as eligible for asylum and legal residency or decline the claim and begin the process of "voluntary departure" ("removal," meaning deportation, is the alternative). The power of judicial authority, even of a judge working for the INS, normalizes a petitioner as legitimate or illegitimate according to the judge's evaluation of the case. Referring to criminal and penal cases, Foucault observes that the court itself is an activist institution, not just a source of judgment and sanctions.[28] Petitioners, their attorneys, and the INS staff all seemed to acknowledge the extent to which the chance for favorable disposition of one's case relied on the "luck of the draw" in that first allocation of a hearing officer.

Anabel knew that she, along with her husband and children, would face removal if the INS denied her application. A community lawyer who made frequent informational visits to the women's group first referred her to a private attorney specializing in asylum claims, who offered to handle her case for $5,000, win or lose. Over the course of the two-year process, she met with attorneys, INS claims officers, and INS judges presiding over what usually seemed to be a prosecutorial process in which Anabel stated her claims as a political refuge and the INS mainly sought to refute them.

The task of an asylum applicant is to normalize her or his story, honing it to be both true to experience and convincing to the INS hearing officers, and then to the judge and attorneys. Anabel's story required elaborate explanations of confusing political details and intra-party intrigue that seemed illogical and confusing to the questioners, including her own attorney. The INS strategy was to try to establish that even if Anabel rightly feared returning to her hometown, she could live safely elsewhere in Mexico. Anabel was the first Mexican in recent history to be awarded political asylum at the San Francisco federal immigration offices. Even her own lawyer seemed surprised, though joyous nonetheless, at her victory.

Anabel had copies of local newspaper coverage that detailed her personal struggle with corrupt local PRI party officials and how she had lost her land and home. What she had no documentation for, despite her sharp and precise recollections of dates, places, and names, was the subsequent harassment and threats that forced her family to move to her natal village and eventually prompted her and her husband to flee the country with their two children. When in Mexico during this process, I was able to meet with a nongovernmental human rights organization that provided documentation of a woman PRI activist who had been "disappeared" in Anabel's home state after a similar conflict over property and local corruption, so we added this material to her file as well.

In our discussions away from the INS offices, Anabel did not distinguish herself from other Mexican immigrants as somehow more deserving of residency as a refugee. Rather she saw herself as fortunate to have won her asylum case and wished that her friends and acquaintances could also have the opportunity to legalize their status, since few planned to return home permanently. Anabel was indeed fortunate to have had her petition approved when she did. By July 2000, the PRI was ousted from power in the Mexican presidential and congressional elections. Had she been assigned a different judge or waited longer to submit her petition, the INS might have been able to argue that the local officials and institutions that persecuted her had been driven from power.

Anabel's and Daniel's stories reveal the extent to which state power seeks to shape persons' subjectivity and their self-representation in legal narratives of their identities and life stories. However, Anabel and Daniel and their advocates responded with strategic choices in the face of such discipline. They also understood that the application of laws and policies is often unpredictable and depends in part on which individuals serve as the face of the state in any given encounter.

Anabel's and Daniel's cases illustrate how specific norms of family, sexuality, and other "private" concerns continue to influence the content and application of immigration law and public policy. The persistent power of a cultural dichotomy between "masculine" realms of politics and "feminine" domains of family and sexuality undergirds interpretations of asylum law that privilege the kind of public political activism and state persecution that Anabel was able to document and favor the types of masculine identities that fit officials' ideas of who is more likely a potential victim of public persecution (Neilson, 2005). As difficult as the road to asylum was for these two MUA members, it continues to be an impossible route for most immigrants, even when they have similarly well-founded fears of persecution in their countries of origin, but are unable to produce the forms of evidence or embody the victim-subjectivities that immigration officials demand of refugees and asylum seekers.

Conclusions

Cristina's, Daniel's, and Anabel's stories reflected some of the tremendous diversity of personal trajectories and identities of Latina immigrants I met in San Francisco. Their narratives also conveyed the extent to which specific citizenship traditions embodied in history, law, and policy, as well as their experiences in a grassroots organization like MUA, contributed to their sense of shared interests and identity in the United States as Latinas. Daniel's ambivalent relationship to the group and his ultimate departure, along with his partner, from MUA signaled some of the tensions that emerged, along with the solidarities, from this process.

Despite tremendous political, economic, and social pressures whose combined effects should have prevented the emergence of a group like Mujeres Unidas y Activas in the 1990s, MUA not only grew locally, but also became a resource for immigrant rights advocates in other regions as well. MUA members promoted civic debate and action in other regions and states by consulting with fledgling women's groups, sharing their experiences and advice, performing educational theater programs in churches and schools, and preparing materials, such as an organizing manual in Spanish, to share with others trying to build similar groups. Such community work, whether funded publicly or privately, played a valuable role in creating spaces in which politically marginalized people could join together to resist the marginalization of their communities, issues, and political positions.

These achievements also raise the question of how activists were able to sustain and expand their work under the tremendously hostile conditions described in this chapter. Chapter 1 addressed some of the collective strategies and social resources women used to engage public institutions and advocate for their needs. This chapter has provided further examples of how women came to an analysis of the institutional discrimination they experienced as low-income, non-English-speaking women of color in order to challenge their social and political marginalization. Chapter 3 examines one strategy the women employed in mobilizing their personal experience in service to collective political organizing, namely their *testimonios* about "learning the ropes" of social services in the course of coming to feel themselves entitled to such services and to recognition.

3 Learning the Ropes
Stories of Motherhood and Citizenship

IT IS A COMMON ASSUMPTION THAT IMMIGRANT WOMEN, particularly those who cannot speak English or are undocumented, live on the margins of society and have few social connections outside their domestic or family networks. Becoming a mother in the United States can be an isolating process if it decreases a woman's participation in the workforce, keeps her physically more tied to home, and/or increases her dependence upon her child's father. Most significantly for understanding the multilayered and dynamic nature of women's citizenship, these stories weave analysis into narratives that have collective resonance but also present diverse personal experiences that resist falsely universalized claims about "immigrant Latinas" as a monolithic group.

Paying close attention to both the women's stories and their actions reveals how they both bend to and resist the power of the state and the social expectations of them as low-income immigrants, as women, and as mothers. The dynamics and conflicts between immigrant women and their families, their peers, and public institutions like welfare, public education, and health care produce new citizenship forms and practices. Such tensions play increasingly powerful roles in women's day-to-day lives as they parent children in the United States. Women's relationships with Mujeres Unidas y Activas and the collective analyses and campaigns they developed also responded to and reshaped members' normative ideas and aspirations about the relationship between motherhood, rights, entitlements, and politics.

Feminist anthropology has focused on how motherhood became associated with a private social sphere under industrialism and the modern nation-state (Delaney, 1995; Reiter, 1975), but immigrant San Franciscans provided different perspectives on how domestic–public relations shaped their citizenship. Their stories of motherhood were filled with politically charged negotiations with health institutions, social workers, immigration officials, and community organizations. At the same time, their "private" family lives were the focus of public debates over immigrant childbearing, single motherhood, and the causes of poverty among families with young children. As scholars of Latina activism have documented in other U.S. cities, motherhood led to the politicization of some women not only because it forced them to engage state institutions that they might otherwise have avoided, but also because of the common ground and politics of solidarity forged among women as mothers in MUA meetings (Hondagneu-Sotelo, 1994; Pardo, 1990, 1991, 1995; Ruíz, 2000). This was problematic for some women without children, but the group's staff members also tried to avoid maternalization of their politics and struggled against any effort to reduce their political status to that of mother-citizens. Along this line, discussion facilitators asked questions that led to discussions about whether certain rights derived from motherhood, from contributions through labor, or simply from one's humanity. They would also draw out the opinions of women without children and women long past childbearing years to enrich and broaden the discussion.

Women's stories of adjustment to life in San Francisco after immigration made clear the extent to which motherhood and citizenship were mutually constituted in their experiences of "learning the ropes" in the United States. For many of the women of MUA, the complexity of their position as local mothers, long-distance mothers, sisters, and daughters, and/or as paid care providers for the children of other working women infused their stories about how they understood their position and rights in the United States. Though this practice has changed, in the early years of MUA, a woman usually introduced herself at group meetings by offering exactly three facts: her name, her country of origin, and the number of children she had. At the same time, women resisted conflating womanhood with motherhood. Rather, they acknowledged work and family, including but not limited to parenting, as key shared social experiences that were profoundly shaped by their position as immigrants. This chapter offers the stories of three women about how their experiences as mothers shaped their sense of citizenship in the United States. Together the stories describe a shared set of strategies and orientations toward encounters with state and private institutions, and a set of collectivized analyses of them.

Even as the women related to issues of motherhood from very different subject positions, they shared a view of Mujeres Unidas y Activas as part of what they now considered to be family. This was as true for the women I interviewed who were not parents as for those who had children with them in San Francisco. Several women had left children in their home country in the hope of being able to reunite with them in the future, and others had experienced such separations in the past.[1] Many were unmarried or separated from their children's fathers. One couple included Daniel, a transgendered MUA member who was beginning the presurgical social transition from female to male identity, and also from motherhood to fatherhood, when I interviewed him (see Chapter 2). Other women did not have children at all, but several of them went on to have children in the years since our interviews.

Given this diversity with respect to parenting, it was striking that most of the women I interviewed made their claims for rights, recognition, and dignity in the United States as mothers and parents of future citizens. Motherhood was a defining feature of their relationships and experiences with public institutions, particularly health care, public education, and social services, and the women felt the political shifts in these areas as deeply as they did the immigration reforms discussed in Chapter 2. Many were very anxious about any type of contact with the state, regardless of their immigration status, and were glad to be able to evade the state or its representatives as much as possible. However, motherhood made evasion not only difficult, but also undesirable.

Just as national debates and policy changes referred to as immigration reform dominated women's stories in Chapter 2, so the massive changes in policy and politics embodied in welfare reform affected mothering, health, and social services. In 1996, the Personal Responsibility and Work Opportunity Reconciliation Act (PRWORA) set lifetime limits of five years total (not necessarily continuous) for welfare benefits.[2] The law shifted thousands of families off the welfare rolls in exchange for some additional child care, English, and job training programs. These provisions created an officially sanctioned for-profit poverty industry by allowing for-profit entities access to federal funds that previously only nonprofit service providers and foster families could utilize.[3] Welfare reform adversely affected all poor people, whether born in the United States or abroad, by placing lifetime caps on the receipt of cash benefits and tightening eligibility requirements for food stamps, Medicaid, and Supplemental Social Security (cash assistance to the blind, disabled, and aged). PRWORA denied "virtually all legal immigrants access to sixty federal programs" (Tamayo, 1995, note 103). Although President Bill Clinton managed to reinstate these programs for legal immigrants one year later, the law struck terror into the hearts of elderly immigrants and their families, prompting massive naturalization campaigns by state and local governments to protect access to aid to at least those immigrants eligible for citizenship (C. Chang, 1997).

Women's experiences and relationships with the state were complex; some rejected cash benefits on principle. However, all had to learn to navigate public services and institutions and make a place for themselves in the United States. Reading women's stories about learning the ropes of caring for their families as low-income immigrant mothers challenges us to consider the way specific identities are both enabled by and resistant to dominant discourses of both motherhood and citizenship.

The Local Institutional Terrain of Immigrant Motherhood

Learning to navigate institutions and services in San Francisco reflected the force of the social context on women's sense of citizenship, with service providers embodying the institutional forces constraining women's social identities, and others serving as key conduits through which women came to know community resources and organizations, including MUA. Most of the women I spoke with had given birth at the county public hospital in San Francisco (SFGH), and they and their children received outpatient care at SFGH, its neighborhood satellites, or the Mission Neighborhood Health Center—"La Shotwell," as they called the private nonprofit clinic on Shotwell Street. Upon diagnosis of a pregnancy, a woman was referred to an eligibility worker to enroll in the free prenatal care program through Medi-Cal, California's Medicaid program.[4] Then she was assigned a social worker, who arranged for other benefits, such as Women, Infants, and Children (WIC) food subsidies, food stamps, and cash benefits, if she had citizen children and met low-income guidelines.

Each of these programs and the prenatal medical regimen as a whole entailed a disciplinary regimen for the pregnant woman and new mother. WIC supplements offered options such as a choice of free infant formula or additional food supplements for mothers who chose to nurse. Neither WIC nor food stamps were accepted at every retail outlet, so poor families' consumption patterns were to some degree prescribed by the programs. Prenatal care visits included regular meetings with social workers, nutritionists, and nurse-practitioners who intervened in social or mental health conditions, prescribed healthy diets, and kept in close contact with women in precarious socioeconomic situations. As one OB/GYN at the SFGH Women's Clinic told me, "Most prenatal care visits are really for social rather than medical purposes." This physician, who had trained at SFGH and was now an attending physician, felt that although the visits were well intentioned, they needed to have more medical content to encourage women to present earlier in their pregnancies and more consistently attend their appointments.

Some women reported refusing cash subsidies on principle. "Vinimos a trabajar, no a recibir," was a frequent refrain: We came to work, not to receive [benefits]. Other women who were undocumented feared that such subsidies might jeopardize future petitions for permanent residency. At the time of my fieldwork, the stated policy of the San Francisco INS office was to not hold previous receipt of welfare benefits against a petitioner for residency, on the grounds that the benefits were for citizen or legal resident children, not for their adult parents. However, ten years later the politics of implementation and interpretation were changing in that office and elsewhere, making women's fears about this possibility seem prescient rather than paranoid.

Rather than acting as a barrier to immigrants' utilizing necessary services, certain provisions of the 1997 Immigration Act discouraged undocumented immigrants from leaving the country, even when they wanted to. The law threatened sanctions including a lifetime ban on reentry to the United States for any "out of status" migrant apprehended while leaving or reentering the country after having lived illegally or overstayed a visa while in the United States. These sanctions placed a particular burden on women without proper documents who have received public benefits on behalf of citizen children or while pregnant because they would have been registered for hospital or public health care, meaning they had a record of having received public benefits in the past. By the fall of 1997, most of the women I spoke with were familiar with the sanctions, and several had canceled trips to their home countries out of fear that they might never be able to return.[5] Crossing the border without papers was expensive and risky enough without the added threat of a ten-year to lifetime ban on reentry. Women sobbed as they described, for example, what it was like to say goodbye to a dying parent by phone instead of in person because they could not risk apprehension by immigration officials on a trip home.

The decision whether, when, and what public services to accept was tremendously fraught for many reasons. Whether or not a woman chose to avail herself of public benefits at first, the social worker's role would typically become more involved over time as the woman might chose to later accept benefits she had at first declined. Perhaps a mother would decide that she wished to work outside the home but needed subsidized child care. Or maybe she decided to apply for public housing in order to leave an abusive partner. Both the Women's Clinic and the Pediatric Clinic at San Francisco General had their own benefits eligibility workers and social workers, whose job was to step in and address patients' nonmedical needs.

Raising One's Child, Raising Oneself: Alejandra Llamas

Though I know her now as a confident and outgoing, thirty-year-old single mother of three, a self-employed cook and child care provider, and a lover of dancing and parties, Alejandra Llamas was a nineteen-year-old Mexican mother of one toddler when I first met her. She had emigrated from Yucatan, Mexico, with her then-boyfriend and had become pregnant soon after arrival. She now lived in a small three-bedroom apartment with her husband, her child, and six single men. At home she was responsible for most of the cooking and cleaning, but her male roommates usually paid her to do their preassigned chores when they weren't able to. She felt unsupported by her husband and in-laws, who, she said, criticized everything from her housekeeping to how she cared for her daughter. She felt the need to conceal any earnings from her husband.

In the course of her daughter's encounters with health care, social services, and then-publicly funded child care, Alejandra developed into an effective and decisive advocate for her child and herself. During the course of my research, I observed Alejandra's change from a scared and withdrawn pregnant teenager into a more outgoing and self-confident young woman. Though she continued to struggle for her voice in her household and for a viable economic role for herself as a worker, Alejandra's understandings of her role as mother and citizen were clearly constituted through sustained interaction with state institutions, mediated by the support and advice she received from her *compañeras* in the women's group and her own ideas about what it means to be a good mother to one's child. "Es una niña criando a una niña" (She's a girl raising a girl), said one woman in her thirties, explaining the special attention the women in the group paid to Alejandra and other young women with no extended families in San Francisco. Older women supported her in her experiences at the hospital, encouraged her to save her earnings for herself and her future, and tried to warn her about the pitfalls of consumerism peddled by local merchants whose cheap clothes, toys, and household goods tempted many recent immigrants.

After having her daughter, Alejandra learned to ask for more help and utilize the services available to her. At one point, she told her pediatric social worker that she needed to earn some money of her own, so the social worker got her daughter into a publicly funded day care, and Alejandra found a job washing dishes. Several women spoke about this particular social worker and how she had gone out of her way to address maternal as well as child needs. Anabel Ibañez's son's social worker asked about Anabel's pronounced limp from her childhood hip dislocation, arranged for an orthopedics consultation for her, and helped her enroll in emergency medical insurance so as to have her hip surgically repaired.[6] Tomasa's story (below) illustrates how a savvy social worker can make all the difference in helping a woman utilize available resources to become independent of an abusive partner. Still, women had many complaints about the paperwork, bureaucracy, and obstructive social and health care workers with whom they had come into contact.

Alejandra had both positive and negative experiences within the bureaucracy and with its representatives. When her toddler was diagnosed with an orthopedic problem, she needed to be enrolled in the California Children's Services (CCS) system, which would reimburse the county for care related to her condition. Even though her Medi-Cal social worker was bilingual and bicultural, and Alejandra felt she was efficient, approval of eligibility took more than six weeks. As a result, the hospital orthoticist was unable to give her the special orthopedic shoes that he had had fitted for her child, and he worried that they would no longer fit her properly by the time the paperwork went through. Both he and Alejandra were visibly frustrated with each other at this point, although both agreed that the problem lay in the eligibility process. Still, the orthoticist asked me again if I was sure she had filled out the proper forms, and Alejandra asked me again why, if the shoes were already there, he couldn't just give them to her. Wasn't this an unnecessary delay of her daughter's treatment?

These sorts of health care interactions are not foreign to anyone in the United States, whether we use public or private medical insurance. Institutional structures discipline us all into various roles—the caring (or cold) professional, the compliant (or troublesome) patient—at the same time that they remove us from the site at which decisions about resource allocation are actually made. For undocumented and other immigrant poor women like Alejandra, the act of coming forward to request services is infused with political and personal tension. How will she and her child be treated by staff? Will her status be reported to the INS? Will her children's services be affected by the parents' immigrant status? What if she is risking future hopes for legalization by using such services?

Before her daughter was two years old, Alejandra had to learn the ropes of the medical, social services, employment, and child care systems. With a primary school education, she waded through paperwork in English, arrived at appointments on time only to wait for hours, and kept track of her daughter's medical history after her pediatrician completed residency and she was assigned a new resident physician. Alejandra was undocumented, but that information was not relevant to eligibility workers, who focused on her economic status, her citizen daughter's needs, and how to fill out forms to ensure that the county would get properly reimbursed for the care. Alejandra was a petite and friendly young woman. She managed all these interactions with as much good humor and smiling as possible, but she was also extremely tenacious. After many months of being told by the orthopedic residents to "wait and see" if the problem corrected itself, Alejandra took advantage of a visit to a Mujeres Unidas y Activas meeting by a senior pediatrician from the hospital to ask his opinion. He examined her daughter on the spot and spoke to the orthopedist on her behalf, after which an order was placed for the corrective shoes and brace. Through these interactions, Alejandra learned that she needed to advocate very actively on her child's behalf in medical and, soon after, in child care contexts.

In each case, Alejandra was overtly deferential to the institution's representatives and made good faith efforts to follow the rule and procedures, but she never blindly put her faith in what she was told. She ultimately trusted her own judgment in pressing for what she thought her daughter needed and in both the medical and child care cases, she felt that the outcome justified her concerns. This type of behavior characterizes a citizen with self-confidence and a strong sense of entitlement, yet I did not observe Alejandra advocate for her own interests in her home or elsewhere in a similar fashion until several years after these events.

"Poniendo Todo a Mi Nombre": Tomasa Hernández

Tomasa Hernández described learning to make demands on the state as a gradual and often conflicted process, with the same agencies providing support, exercising discipline, and/or causing her fear at different moments in her life in San Francisco. Welfare institutions have been central to her experiences of motherhood and marriage in the United States, playing both positive and negative roles in both her and her children's lives at different points. Tomasa was thirty-eight years old when I interviewed her in 1998, and she had lived continuously in San Francisco since migrating from Mexico in 1965.[7] When her children's father, her common-law husband, was incarcerated on drug charges, she feared being alone but soon found that she was better off. Her husband had always cashed and kept the welfare checks, even though they arrived in both their names for the children's benefit. Once he was in jail, she confided in the welfare caseworker how her husband had threatened her, and the caseworker reissued the application in her name only. "He would threaten me, and since I didn't know my rights or anything, he would say, 'If you don't give me the money, I'll go to the social worker and tell him to take it away from you.' And I said, 'If they take that from me, what will the children eat? It's better to just give it to him.' And he'd grab the money. One day a man, a social worker, inspired my trust and I told him what my husband was like."

At the time the family lived in a two-room apartment in an old building in the Mission District. As Tomasa began paying her own rent, she changed the lease and all of the utility bills into her own name. Several women cited this process of claiming legal and economic responsibility for one's affairs, or "poniendo todo a mi nombre" (putting everything in my name), as central to gaining a sense of their own ability to function independently in the United States. In Tomasa's case, as well as in other cases, a sympathetic social worker helped greatly, changing her children's welfare benefits checks from her husband's name to hers. However, peer support and information networks helped her take the social worker's actions one step further. When Tomasa went to the next Mujeres Unidas y Activas meeting and told her compañeras what she'd done at the welfare office, they told her she could also change the telephone and utility bills to her name:

Oooh, I felt so happy when they told me that! But, then he got mad. "You think you're something because you put everything in your name!" After I trained myself to be like a father to my family and a mother at the same time. But it really was very heavy burden. I would say, "I have to pay the rent!" Since he had never let me go anywhere, I didn't know how to pay anything. Yes, I knew which street it was on, but the first time I went to pay rent, I was so scared. Trembling! I said, "And what if they ask me why I am the one coming?" And besides that, I even put the apartment in my name alone. Besides that. Everything was in my name . . . he could no longer say to me like he used to, "Turn off the light! It's not in your name! . . . and you have no reason to be talking on the telephone," and he'd tear it out of my hands, because he said it was in his name.

For survivors of domestic violence with whom I spoke, their children's eligibility for cash welfare benefits, public medical insurance, and nutritional supplements were critical for their ability to establish some economic autonomy, even in the context of a dependent relationship to the state. While welfare before 1996 allowed low-income single mothers to receive cash benefits indefinitely, these sums were generally inadequate for dignified living, precluded the acquisition of paid employment, and involved rigorous surveillance of the most intimate details of their lives, including whether they had male partners who regularly stayed in their homes.

In general, the women and their families eschewed cash benefits whenever possible, preferring to work. Contemporary studies have estimated that Mexican immigrants, for example, have contributed more than they received in services (Hondagneu-Sotelo, 1994). Many of the women also cited the broadly held conviction that previous receipt of welfare benefits might endanger future efforts to gain legal residency status in the United States by indicating they were potential public charges and/or by tarnishing otherwise good moral character.[8] Women attached less stigma to receiving noncash benefits linked to children's basic needs, such as public health insurance and nutritional programs, including prenatal and perinatal health and nutritional care for themselves. When I asked why they thought it was undesirable to receive cash benefits, women generally said that they had come here to earn their living as workers, that they knew that many Americans believed immigrants were taking advantage of such benefits and resented them for it, that they also believed that some welfare recipients were taking advantage or were too lazy to work, that the benefits were not worth the control the state gained over them, and that receiving such benefits might *perjudicar* (prejudice, work against) future attempts to legalize their status. One woman reported that she and many of her friends firmly believed that the act of registering their children for cash benefits meant that their sons would automatically be drafted into military service when they turned eighteen.

The overwhelming majority of the women I interviewed were Mexican, and their familiarity with children's entitlement programs in Mexico may also have played a role in these attitudes. In Mexico, there are no cash benefit programs, but there exists a broad network of nutritional supplementation and support programs targeting women and children and guaranteed free state health care for the poor. There is also a mandatory military service obligation for eighteen-year-old men in Mexico, who are chosen for or excused from service by a lottery that is widely viewed as corrupt, favoring more privileged or well-connected youths.

Tomasa understood the reticence that many people feel about accepting cash subsidies from the government in exchange for the "humiliation" of intimate scrutiny such as "searching your closets for men's shoes." The couple and her four youngest children had lost the room they rented in a three-bedroom home in which each room and a basement unit were rented to different families. The tight quarters and live-in landlady who insisted on charging Tomasa extra every time her teenage daughter took a long shower were too much to bear. When her baby was born, the family had been living on the living room sofas and floors of friends for several months. After the baby's birth, since Tomasa was eligible for some cash support for the baby and was enrolled in nutritional support (WIC) and public medical insurance (Medi-Cal) during her pregnancy, a hospital social worker asked her and the baby's father if they would like to enroll the child in welfare. When the father insisted that he did not want welfare for his child, the social worker notified the social services department that Tomasa's other children should also be disenrolled to comply with federal guidelines that either all of or none of the children in a household be enrolled, regardless of paternity. The guiding principle, also underlying the state's empowerment to police intimate relationships, is that if an able-bodied man is present in the household, all the children present become his economic responsibility. Tomasa reported her disenrollment from welfare to me with some anxiety but made clear that she wanted to honor her partner's sense of paternal responsibility, even though it ended up making her and her other children even more economically reliant on him. She was also somewhat relieved to be free of that particular part of the state bureaucracy's involvement in her already complicated life.

Tomasa's understanding of the honor of responsible paternity and maternity is in line with the women's group's demands for dignity and respect. The women I interviewed upheld the traditional family structure of male as breadwinner and female as homemaker, each playing equally important roles in the maintenance of the household and the creation of a loving family, and each showing one another respect in public and in private.

To a great extent, this division of labor reflected the economic facts of life in the United States as much if not more than a commitment to cultural traditions of family organization. Where buying child care and other domestic tasks is too expensive relative to women's entry-level salaries, their participation in full-time employment is effectively limited by economic rationality as much as by traditional divisions of labor. In addition, the higher number of undocumented women married to or living with men with legal papers also reinforces gender inequality with respect to income.

Considered collectively, a fairly coherent, though certainly not uniform, vision of appropriate gender roles emerged around a few key points of agreement in the stories of the women I interviewed. They spoke of good women as adept housekeepers and cooks; loving mothers of well-behaved and happy children; supportive, attentive wives; and frequently, depending on household structure, dutiful daughters-in-law. A good man was sober and hardworking, devoted to work and family, economically responsible for his household, and supportive to his natal family, especially his mother. Women did not report disagreements with their husbands on these points but did complain when their male partners failed to live up to the expectations of sobriety, industry, and respect to their wives. They also reported that their husbands' main complaints about them were that they spent too much time on community activities rather than remaining in their homes, and that they disrespected their husbands by not acceding to their authority. Although the women I talked to did not seek to overturn the family division of labor, they did expect autonomy and respect in return for fulfilling their own expectations of themselves as good women, which they saw as in accordance with their family and cultural traditions.

Rather than representing such negotiations over gender roles as the result of immigration or cultural change due to North American influence, the women identified the impetus for shifting relationships in the home as the effects of their participation in community organizing, sharing their experiences with other women, and familiarity with politics, laws, and other social issues. The difficulty in creating more equal and mutually respectful gender roles in the context of traditional patriarchal family organization was also apparent to many of the women I spoke with. In this respect, Mujeres Unidas y Activas members and their dilemmas and ideals about motherhood seemed more similar to than different from other North American mothers from diverse social classes and cultures (Bassin et al., 1994; Rich, 1995 [1977]).

Many women offered a vision of continuity and change with respect to their childrearing practices as well as their family labor as wives. Although they felt that Latin American cultures generally promoted loving and affectionate relationships with children, even more than what they observed among North Americans, they frequently distinguished their own practices from those of their own parents, especially in regard to ideas about discipline, personal autonomy, and sexuality. In individual interviews and group discussions, many MUA members spoke of how they had been physically disciplined as children, or forced to remain silent or otherwise defer to adult authority, even when it was unreasonable. Frequent group discussions about children's rights touched on everything from the right to refuse to kiss strange adults or distant relatives in greeting (which many women remembered disliking as children), the right to speak up and be heard at home and in school, and the right to good nutrition, a safe home, health care, and education. Some women regretted that their families had prevented them from studying beyond elementary school because their parents had feared for the honor or safety of adolescent girls on the way to or from school.

In one particularly memorable group discussion, the women related how they first learned about sex and pregnancy—frequently at the time of their first experience. I admit to feeling sheepish when the facilitator insisted that I share my own story. I related how I asked how babies were made when I was five years old, and my mother, who was very Roman Catholic but also a nurse educator, answered my question with a brief but anatomically correct account of intercourse. Many women nodded vigorously in agreement with her approach. After I added that it was not until almost ten years later that I figured out that a woman did not get pregnant every time she had intercourse, the group broke out in laughter at the evident success of my mother's teen pregnancy prevention subterfuge. The general tone of the discussion on that day and on other occasions was that most women hoped to be more open and helpful to their own children about sex, sexuality, and reproduction than their own parents had been, and several mothers of older children shared how they had already spoken with their children about the issues. Again, rather than read this as an evolutionary post-immigration cultural change, I interpret it as a generational shift also reported by working-class women in both rural and urban Mexico, and certainly not uncommon among poor and working-class North Americans as well.

Achieving Motherhood: Carolina Jiménez

Carolina Jiménez's difficulties with infertility, motherhood, and depression led her to join the nascent women's group that later became MUA. During her first years in the United States, the group was her main source of peer support

and information on topics ranging from childrearing, to household maintenance, to how changing immigration laws would affect her and her family.
Drawing strength from her supportive spousal and peer relationships, her experiences as an independent worker in Mexico, and her commitment to advocating for herself and her children in the United States, Carolina learned when
and how to get good quality information and the resources she needed.

Carolina traced her own process of learning the ropes of life in the United
States to two main experiences after immigration: bearing children and joining the women's group. She was forty-one years old at the time of our interview in 1998 and had lived in San Francisco since emigrating from Jalisco,
Mexico, with her then-new husband in 1990. She was from a small town (about
two thousand people, she estimated) and had only five years of primary school,
but she had worked for many years selling fine decorative lace and crochet
work before meeting her husband and getting married.

On the day of our interview, Carolina's six-year-old daughter was at the
neighborhood elementary school. Her three-year-old son played at our feet,
alternately entertaining himself and trying to take control of the tape recorder.
The two-bedroom house was sparkling clean and neat, smelling of vinegar,
which had become Carolina's cleanser of choice since attending a presentation
on the dangers posed by cleaning supplies. She had spent the morning cleaning
in preparation for my visit, taking evident pride in her excellent housekeeping
and sighing in relief as she sat down on the sofa next to me, finally having a
chance to get off her feet. We had not met before the interview; it had been a
long time since she had participated in group activities. Although she no longer attended meetings, she was proud to be among the founding members of
Mujeres Unidas y Activas.

Carolina lived just over the southern city limit of San Francisco, two
blocks off of Mission Street, or the northernmost portion of El Camino Real—
the road laid by Franciscan missionaries in the eighteenth century. The area
was virtually indistinguishable from the outer Mission District of San Francisco. The political divide between San Francisco and Daly City was significant because her address was part of what made the 1950s' "junior five" (five
rooms, usually ranging from one thousand to twelve hundred square feet total) affordable for this janitor's family. The family rented rooms in the basement to another couple from Mexico and their infant son to help cover the
mortgage payments. Carolina was one of only three women I interviewed who
owned their own home.[9] The overwhelming majority of the women whose

homes I visited not only rented but also shared smaller spaces than Carolina's with three and sometimes four other households, typically with one family in a dining room, one family in the living room, and one family in each bedroom.

Despite her relative comfortable current conditions, Carolina's initial immigration experience was one of isolation, depression, and displacement after moving from small-town Mexico to San Francisco.[10] Her tale resonated with those of other interviewees in her emphasis on how ongoing peer support helped her through depression, tense economic times, and difficult decisions about her immigration status. "The city seemed very ugly to me. I didn't like it."[11] Carolina's reaction to her immediate environment was understandable. Her first home in San Francisco had been in a one-hundred-year-old tenement in the middle of the most run-down, deindustrialized, and drug-filled parts of the Mission District. The neighborhood had been struggling to maintain its working-class family atmosphere since the 1950s, when subsequent generations of Irish and then Latino families moved through and out of the area, and the 1989 Loma Prieta earthquake had a profound negative effect on the northern Mission District.

When Carolina moved to that area shortly after the earthquake, it had become the new home for many displaced residents of the inner-city Tenderloin neighborhood, where single-room-occupancy hotels had been seismically damaged and where landlords were pleased to be able to evict their tenants. After 1989, the drug-, prostitution-, and homelessness-related activities that had been based in the Tenderloin moved with the earthquake refugees to the closest affordable neighborhood—Carolina's. Her particular address also straddled the borderline between two rival factions of the Sureños gang's territories (in general terms, the dividing line between the Mexicanos and the Salvadoreños factions) and was less than five blocks from the edge of Norteño territory. For a woman from a town of two thousand in rural Jalisco, the atmosphere must have been quite brutal. It also explained the determination with which she and her husband worked on buying their own home, just three miles south of their first apartment, on the same Mission Street corridor but a world away in terms of urban stresses.

Carolina met her husband when he came from the United States to visit relatives in her hometown. Until they married, she had lived with her parents and worked selling handmade baby clothing and doilies. In February 1990, one month after marrying, they moved to San Francisco, where her husband had been living and working for several years. After she struggled for over a year to get pregnant, a friend referred her to a private Mission Street doctor who prescribed fertility drugs. She was pleased when she finally conceived her first child at age thirty-six. But instead of enjoying her first pregnancy as she had expected she would, Carolina was isolated and depressed. She hated her living conditions and felt homesick and worried about problems her family was having in Mexico.

When Carolina's husband mentioned that he had seen a familiar face from her hometown in their apartment building, she asked him to invite Marta Cordero over to visit.[12] Carolina marked this as a turning point because from then on, she had a friend and confidante. "I didn't suffer a lot because when I was feeling lonely, I'd call her and she'd support me." Through their proximity, frequent contact, and consistent emotional support for one another, they built a relationship of trust.

Marta invited Carolina to participate in the nutritional survey focus group that was the founding core of what later became the women's group. This group of eight women provided a forum to air individuals' stress and depression, and also to discuss the collective social concerns underlying their stressors. These charter members developed the meeting format of holding peer support discussions, bringing outside speakers in to provide information on specific issues, and trying to help members utilize the instrumental supports available to them. The small but growing group of women met Marta's needs for peer support and an outlet for the stresses of her domestic life. Despite their very different domestic relations, the group helped her by providing a place to *desahogarme* ("unload" or "get things off my chest"). "Sometimes one feels depressed and you get to the group and you relax a lot. . . . You feel pressured by your kids, by the house, by your spouse."

When I asked Carolina more specifically how group meetings helped her deal with stress, she spoke of a confluence of activities and resources that other women had also mentioned: information from peers and from presenters from other agencies and groups, peer support and a chance to talk about problems, access to economic opportunities, and personal skills development. "I like the information . . . the presenters who come and speak. . . . When one has problems, to be able to speak with the group and receive their support. . . . When I was depressed, it helped me a lot. . . . [w]hen we were moving and I was really stressed because I needed money, they helped me with work providing childcare."

Although Carolina initially sought out the group for peer support, she became more involved and committed to it when it provided opportunities for personal growth and development as well as paid employment. The combination of emotional and instrumental supports solidified her commitment to participating. Many women I interviewed said they first attended a group meeting because they were under the impression that the group was an employment cooperative and would help them find work. While the group has an economic development project training and placing women as home health aides and domestic workers, this project is accessible only to women who have been active in the group for six months or more.

The group founded a collective to provide child care at its own and other community group meetings and decided that it needed to train the providers, beginning what became a tradition of organizing workshops called *entrenamientos* or "trainings" on topics ranging from babysitting safety to child discipline to community leadership and organizing.

Carolina had the opportunity to care for members' children during meetings, where child care was always provided. These infrequent opportunities were helpful to her, and at least as important was the chance to take child care training workshops sponsored by the group, where she learned child discipline techniques, activities for groups of children, and safety measures such as CPR. Carolina reflected on how helpful learning child care techniques has been to her as a mother, particularly ideas about combating poor behavior with affection rather than physical discipline and providing children with stimulating activities for their development and to help them keep on their best behavior. Carolina gave equal importance to the political leadership skills she acquired, even though they have no economic application for her:

> I began to do childcare and earn a little and learn things. . . . I participated in two trainings, on leadership and childcare. . . . The leadership training dealt with the theme of immigrants . . . how to speak in public. . . . I got over my fear of speaking in public. . . . I learned that in a campaign, you have to do things rights or it's better not to do them at all. . . . In the childcare training they taught us to be very affectionate with [the children] . . . to not hit them, how to treat them well . . . to have patience so that they will not become even more rebellious.

Carolina, like many other women I interviewed, continues to regard *información* as among the most important benefits the group provided her. "I like the information . . . the presenters who come and talk. . . . When one has problems, being able to talk with the group and receive their support. . . . When I was depressed, it helped me a lot. . . . When we moved and I was really stressed because I needed money, they helped me find work taking care of children."

Reliable information on a variety of subjects—from social services to welfare and immigration policies—is notoriously difficult to come by for monolingual immigrants. Women frequently spoke of the misleading information proliferating in the Spanish-language media and the popular rumors that spread and mutated rapidly. A common complaint involved businesses that advertised on Spanish-language broadcast media and charged gullible clients for services or advice available for free elsewhere in the community, or that gave clients false information to continue to charge them for more and more services.[13]

This peer support and the access to quality information and referrals was a large part of what initially attracted Carolina to the women's group, but opportunities for economic and personal advancement also kept her participating over a period of years. First, the group offered English tutorials by volunteer female native speakers. Two to three students met weekly in one another's homes, which was attractive to those intimidated by or otherwise unable to attend the neighborhood adult school's free classes. Most of my subjects spoke little or no English, and they all seemed to share Carolina's conviction that it was important for them, and even more important for their children, to learn English without losing their native Spanish skills. "English is so very important for everything, to go to the store, the doctor, the children's school."

The combination of economic and training opportunities she received from the group gave Carolina confidence in her own community organizing and childrearing skills, helping her earn her own income and proving useful daily in her own home and with her own children. They also gave her the sense that she had something important to say in public, that her knowledge and skills were valuable to others in her community.

Being able to talk to strangers and to search out the correct information have served her well, as has her mutually supportive relationship with her husband. He and Carolina both were unhappy in their first apartment and neighborhood, especially after having their children. Together they set the goal of buying their own home in a safer area. He took a second job, while she investigated first-time home buyer loan programs. She proudly noted that he was able to find a unionized job as a janitor and that he handed his checks over to her to manage the household and save for the down payment. Although he likes to say that "primero son los niños" (the children come first), meaning that her first responsibility is as a mother, he has never strongly opposed her participation in the group and recognizes how it has helped their family. Carolina considered her marriage emotionally fulfilling and mutually supportive, with both sharing responsibility for major decisions such as prioritizing their work and savings. She also emphasized that they were mutually respectful of one another's contributions to the family division of labor.

Motherhood as Organizing Identity

Just as early-twentieth-century U.S. women reformists mobilized around relief benefits for single mothers and their dependents, rather than economic and political rights for all citizens, the women of Mujeres Unidas y Activas employ a risky strategy, especially regarding the symbolic and political capital of the motherhood role. Early women reformers reshaped the notion of motherhood in the context of the strains that developing industrial capitalism placed on the family and women in particular.[14] The women of immigrant rights groups are reshaping the notion of motherhood to include the impact of migration, cultural and linguistic discrimination, and changing notions of human rights at the turn of the twenty-first century.

Much of the discourse of immigrant rights activists in the 1990s utilized human rights as a universalized, moral position from which to defend immigrants' claims for social and political personhood in the United States. "Immigrant Rights Are Human Rights!" proclaimed the Northern California Coalition for Immigrant Rights' T-shirts in English, Spanish, Chinese, Tagalog, and Vietnamese. Closer to the Mexican border, the nonprofit Arizona Border Rights Project sponsors the Derechos Humanos Coalition, which organizes public rallies against border militarization and immigrants' rights violations (Martínez, 2000). Although the categories of rights and human rights are highly contested, and seen as packed with liberal assumptions about the autonomy of rights-bearing individuals in anthropology and cross-cultural studies of law and politics, the notion of basic, universal human rights provided the women a sense of legitimacy in making demands on the state.

In the context of transnational migrations, international standards for human rights provide a framework in which the women critiqued the political logic that formulated immigration as a problem and excluded the undocumented from basic public services. During the summer and fall of 1997, the state of California debated whether county hospitals would be reimbursed for providing prenatal care to undocumented residents. After decades of public health outreach efforts aimed at gaining immigrant women's trust and publicizing the availability of free or low-cost prenatal and preventive health care, the governor of California enthusiastically advocated eliminating public prenatal care to the undocumented. Cristina Rodríguez, whom we first met in Chapter 2, emphasized that her critique of U.S. policy was to some extent a product of her consciousness as a Mexican citizen who saw the state as the proper guarantor of health care. Even though the quality and availability of such care varies widely, every Mexican state and region has public health care facilities to serve the poor at little or no cost. "[A]s a woman, as a man, and as a child, you have the right to your health, to care for your health. And I believe that even in the poorest nation, they don't deny you this, yet in the richest nation, they are doing this."

Cristina related political rights, gender, maternity, health, belonging, and happiness in a world in which increasing numbers of people must cross national boundaries to subsist and provide for their families. She had specific conceptions from late-twentieth-century Mexico of the role of the state in providing for people's needs through public services. She also insisted on her own right to respect as a person, not just a source of labor alienated from other human relationships and possibilities. These ideas and principles were powerful foundations on which to build collective claims for belonging and entitlement for all immigrants, including the undocumented.

Economic policies in both first and third world nations increased women's need to work outside of the home. Whether working as nannies in upscale households or caring for one or more working-class children in their own homes, immigrant Latinas provide a huge yet unrecognized benefit to the California economy through their services (G. Chang, 2000; Hondagneu-Sotelo, 2001; Parreñas, 2001; Romero, 2002). Cristina herself moved to the United States to live with and care for her sister's children so her sister could return to paid employment. Until she married and had a child of her own, Cristina then cared for the child of another working-class immigrant mother. Cristina later realized that her employer paid her significantly less than the minimum wage, but she knew that her boss didn't earn much herself, treated her respectfully, bought her a monthly transit pass, and always made sure she felt at home and was getting enough to eat during her workday.

Transnational Experiences and Interpretations of State Services

Cristina's discourse on rights revealed her active interpretation and application of legal issues regarding her status and her analytical connection between law, motherhood, and citizenship. Growing up in Mexico and as an immigrant in the United States, she learned of the ambiguous or internally contradictory natures of law and the state. Just as the U.S. immigration laws promoted "family reunification" and the U.S. welfare laws supported "families with dependent children," Mexican social programs promoted specific patriarchal kinship ideals and domestic organization. The twentieth-century Mexican state focused on developing and solidifying client relationships with its subjects through the conditional provision of services. Cristina and other immigrant women arrived in the United States with a clear set of hopes, fears, and dreams shaped through years of interaction with their original home states and its bureaucratic representatives. While their skills in negotiating modern bureaucracies were useful, they were not strictly transferable, and women started over learning the ropes of institutions they were accustomed to accessing differently in their home countries.

Through her experiences of collective discussion and struggle in MUA, Cristina came to articulate a sense of citizenship rights that transcended national boundaries or legal status. Cristina asserted the right of women to prenatal care, the right of children to health care, the right of families to live together, and the right of children to be raised with both parents as paramount to any immigration laws. She did not base her claims for rights on her legal status as the wife of a permanent resident. Cristina reported a loving and satisfying relationship with her husband throughout the several years I had regular contact with her, yet she recognized the conjugal bond, as well as immigration policy, to be both dynamic and unstable. Since she had immigrated and settled in San Francisco on her own and had local siblings and friends of her own, she also had a view of her place in this country as independent of her relationship to her husband:

And as I said in the beginning, who's going to guarantee me that in five or six years, umm, my husband will still be here waiting to give me residency? Then I'd be left with neither husband nor residency. Then my scale weighed in favor of staying. I'm staying with my husband, and if they don't give me my residency, I will be with my husband, my son will be with his father. The laws are changing every day. Maybe by the time I get my residency, these penalties won't even be applied. That's why I stayed. But I am still not at peace with it. Instead I'm waiting. "And now what are they going to come up with?" Sometimes I say, "Ay, no, I don't even want the residency, I don't want anything." But in any case, it's just that I feel that all this is affecting me very personally.[15]

Law, policy, and political rhetoric were real and concrete forces in Cristina's life. These institutions and correlating ideologies shaped her physical and emotional experiences of motherhood in the United States. Cristina described the intersection of motherhood and immigration in corporeal terms, outlining how state discipline undermines both mental health and a positive physical experience of maternity. Her outrage built as she explained how these policies and politics combined to attack the most voiceless, disenfranchised party in decisions and discussions about immigration—the child not yet born to a pregnant immigrant woman.[16]

Cristina spoke against the image of scheming Latinas crossing the border to bear citizen children and receive welfare. In doing so, she resisted the rhetorical conflation of Latina identity with illegitimate maternity and an exploitative relationship with public welfare institutions. Cristina insisted on reframing the discussion of immigrant womanhood and motherhood as one of universal morality and human rights. She asserted both the right and the reality of women bearing children where and when they wish to, regardless of the legal demands of states and their institutions. Since the United States continued to need and attract immigrant women and men workers who lived here for extended periods, there needed to be a recognition that bearing children and forming families would be part of the lives the people made here. As she put it, women don't come here to have children, but children are part of their lives, and their lives are now in the United States:

> And I have always heard that Latinas, especially, that we come here to have children, and lots of them. That that's the only reason we come, to have children. But why wouldn't we have children if we are here with our spouses and our families are here? I don't know a single woman who comes and has a child and then goes! I mean, we have them here because we live here. So, I believe that we women, and even the men, are now aware that one can't raise/educate a lot of children. Right? So, we are educating ourselves, becoming conscious that a happy marriage isn't only so many children, so we are trying to plan our families, right? So it's not that we just come to have and have and have and have [children], what happens is that our life is already formed here, if one can put it that way. Because our children are born here, not because we want our children to be citizens.

Cristina protested the conflation of her identities as a woman, worker, Mexicana, immigrant, wife, and mother in dominant discourses on immigration and welfare policy. Rather than defining motherhood as an intrinsic part of women immigrants' life experiences or social identity, she reframed representations of childbearing as part of the broader reality of women's lives. In doing so, Cristina echoed Anna Lowenhaupt Tsing's call for balancing recent feminist efforts to re-value mothering with a critical stance toward the context in which women's choices about motherhood are made. Instead of celebrating a maternity that essentialized or naturalized motherhood, conflating it with womanhood, Christina joined Tsing's call to "attend instead to the social and historical circumstances that both create expectations for what it means to be a 'woman,' and constrain women's choices about whether and how to bear or raise children" (1990, 297).

There were no simple answers or motives to be found in trying to understand whether immigrant women were choosing to bear children in the United States, why they brought or left other children in their country of origin, or even to what extent individual choice could be implicated in their decision to immigrate in the first place. Cristina pointed out that women and men together made many decisions about their own and their families' lives, including where and under what conditions to bear children. Both the Mexican and the United States governments promoted their own specific model of planned parenthood, which Cristina articulated to emphasize her own understanding of what constituted responsibility and how men and women are raising their consciousness of these issues together. But by emphasizing that their lives are formed in the context of immigration and residence in the United States, she highlighted how even the most intimate personal choices were structured and options limited by forces beyond one's control, such as arbitrary and unpredictable actions by public institutions. By emphasizing the corporeal nature of her experiences as an immigrant woman, Cristina signaled how female bodies were political ground on which anti-immigrant politics are played out. Their bodies were invested with both labor power and reproductive power. Women can produce new low-wage workers for a racially stratified economy, but they also bear and educate new citizens.[17] Political rhetoric targeted Mexicanas and their childbearing power as cultural, linguistic, and political threats to the non-Latino power structure (Inda, 2002). The extent to which state initiatives such as Proposition 187 and federal policies such as welfare and immigration reform aimed to control women's bodies and structure family life bore out a Foucauldian view of immigrant Latinas as "biopolitical subjects" (Ong, 1995). In turn, groups' claims on the state that emphasized the social importance of motherhood represented a reclamation of discursive and symbolic authority over how their image should be spun politically and culturally.

Much of the contemporary academic literature on citizenship focuses on macro processes of legal and state-generated definitions of who is a citizen and what the legal entitlements and social obligations of citizenship should be (Barbalet, 1988; Dummett and Nicol, 1990; Hansen, 1995; Turner, 1993). Feminists have critiqued the liberal assumptions about public versus private social spheres and the resulting institutions and practices that gender a first-class citizen as male (Pateman, 1988, 1989). Feminist ethnographies of kinship have emphasized that private relationships are also constitutive of public identities: "the private is also political." While it would be wrong to assert that a women's primary political identity was that of mother, it was also true that becoming a mother in the United States and/or the experiences women were subject to as mothers played a significant role in their politicization (Collier and Yanagisako, 1987; Yanagisako and Delaney, 1995).

These women, their experiences, and their analyses indicate productive ways to bridge feminist theories of the social construction of motherhood (Collier and Yanagisako, 1979; Yanagisako and Delaney, 1995) with new perspectives on the subjective, cultural aspects of citizenship (Hall, 1990; Ong, 1996; R. Rosaldo, 1994). When mediated through the experience of collective support and information-sharing found in a community organization, the women's institutional work as mothers bore directly on their sense of their social position and political rights in the United States. As they learned to navigate health care, education, and social services bureaucracy—what I mean by the "institutional work of mothering"—they encountered obstacles, learned about systems, and found ways to gain individual access for their families, while working with peers to lobby for broader reforms. Although many of the women I interviewed arrived with ideas of motherhood centering around the care and nurturance of children, they also said that their notions of their duties as mothers expanded to include advocating for their own, their children's, and other immigrants' interests with respect to health care, social services, the law, and education. This new sense of motherhood included a claim not only that they belonged in this new community but also that they and their children were entitled to certain rights, services, and respect, and in turn that they themselves, and their children, bore a responsibility to contribute positively to their new locale and society.

Conclusion

Tomasa's experiences show the significant role that public assistance programs can play in women's day-to-day lives, and how she learned through her contact with these institutions and their representatives to make a place for herself in the United States independently of her husband. At the same time, the liberatory aspects of these programs are tempered by the control and surveillance they exercise over every aspect of her life in exchange for small amounts of public assistance, and rules that end up making her dependent on another male partner. Cristina explained how immigration law and political rhetoric infused and affected every aspect of her experience of life and family in this country, shaping even the most intimate and corporeal experiences of maternity and motherhood. Carolina's story emphasizes the importance of a supportive spouse and peers to her ability to master her new surroundings for herself and the benefit of her children.

In each case, the women shared accounts of both being shaped by and resisting the complete control that public institutions and political discourses exert over their subjectivity and social identities. As they recognized how they developed as mothers and political subjects in the United States, these women bore testimony to the powerful ways that motherhood and citizenship are mutually constituted in the lives of many women. Each woman's reflections on her own experience was mediated by the discourse of the women's group, from the emphasis on the importance of quality information, to the conviction that women have the ability to understand and analyze their situations and needs, to the commitment to a linkage between individual and community well-being. Participation in the group provided members with a sense of collective strength and support, validation of their concerns, strategies for agency on their own behalf, and a collective framework that emphasized shared responsibility. This all contributed to a sense of belonging to a community of parents, immigrants, and working-class people struggling together for their place in a city that is increasingly childless, wealthy, and high-tech in its landscape and power structure.

While belonging to a long tradition of immigrant mutual aid societies in the United States, MUA's discourse and organizing strategies provide a clear alternative to either assimilationist or isolationist approaches of previous generations of such organizations. Mujeres Unidas y Activas emphasized language, cultural traditions, and collective experiences of racialization and discrimination as Latino/as in the United States to forge a group identity. However, the group approached issues and struggles from a position that roots itself in the multicultural reality of San Francisco, the concerns its members share with other communities, and the insistence that maintaining one's cultural identity was necessary to be able to integrate and function effectively in society and with other communities.

The members of MUA expanded the domain of citizenship while neither ignoring nor privileging the state and its practices. The result is a practice of participatory citizenship that challenges society to recognize new political actors on their own terms, with their own sets of concerns, issues, and social identities. Their collective efforts to improve their own lives and the lives of their children and the broader community of immigrant and working families in San Francisco presented a direct challenge to popular cultural notions that see the realms of family, subjectivity, and citizenship as separate domains. Women's stories of immigration and parenting instead emphasized the interrelated power of community institutions, social services, laws, the economy, peers, and collective political action as implicated shaping their understanding of their positions, roles, and rights in U.S. society.

By linking community well-being to individual progress, the group expressed a communitarian sense of responsibility in resistance to the hyperindividualism and entrepreneurial atmosphere of the new economy. I remember clearly the combination of pride and irritation with which one member spoke at a general meeting as she described a complaint she had made to school district officials over problems her daughter was having at her elementary school. "They gave me what I wanted, but then I didn't go away. I asked them, 'What about the next woman who comes with the same problem? We need to change the whole policy, not just make exceptions.'" On the one hand, Mujeres Unidas y Activas transnationalized Latin American popular organizing strategies and their focus on basic human needs to an American immigrant context. On the other hand, its members were claiming a place in the North American tradition of citizens who believe in and fight for the proper functioning of public institutions and officials. Such belief in the possibility of achieving a just outcome for oneself as well as for the community at large by making one's needs and critiques known to public and private institutions is, after all, a very American faith in the system.

Central to MUA's political vision was an elaborate processual approach to the transformation of women's subjectivity, that is, how to get women to value and see themselves as legitimate bearers of rights, worthy of respect and dignified treatment in a variety of social and economic relations. The women had to navigate the rough seas of welfare and immigration reform as part of coming to claim these rights and social recognition. What sorts of personal resources as well as narrative strategies and collective support did women have to call upon, and how did MUA help them develop such capacities? Chapter 4 considers in greater depth one key part of this process that women emphasized over and over again in their individual interviews—what they referred to as gaining, learning, or building *autoestima*.

Autoestima y la Doble Misión del Grupo

Self-Esteem and the Dual Mission of the Group

GIVEN THE TENSE AND FRAUGHT political context described in Chapter 2, I was not surprised to find MUA members picketing Governor Pete Wilson's office, speaking out to the Spanish-language media, and performing popular-theater productions to inform other immigrants about the new laws. Yet more than seeking equal access to dominant political practices, MUA members also wanted to change the rules of the game. They challenged the legitimacy of state control over the boundaries of political membership and redefined deserving citizenship in terms of dignity and justice rather than legal status or economic value.

In centering political work on women's concerns as immigrants, workers, wives, and mothers, MUA enacted a vision of politics that both recognized and mobilized the intimate and affective aspects of citizenship. Central to MUA's political practice was the *doble misión*, or dual mission, of developing women's political skills and addressing members' pressing personal and emotional issues. The group emphasized the importance of engaging in collective political action, but the urgency of many members' concerns meant that their needs for social and instrumental support demanded attention in order for them to engage at all with politics and politicization. The balance between the activity-oriented leadership of the staff and the grassroots nature of the member-led meetings created a dynamic dialogue between big picture and individual struggles, legislative, electoral, and personal, as well as local community-level concerns.

The following stories focus on how women came to believe in the potential for community change, valuing their own interests and those of their children over connections to men and other family members, gaining trust in others, and overcoming personal and collective obstacles to full participation in American political and social life. In particular, these narratives examine the notion of *autoestima* that women developed to encompass personal transformational processes, collective identities as immigrant Latinas, and community social and political concerns such as domestic violence and immigrant rights. *Autoestima* was both a resource to help women stand up for themselves in the home and in close social relationships, and a collective process through which women came to fully articulate their claims for respect and a voice in the community and their full rights in national politics and public institutions, regardless of their gender, language, income, or immigration status.

Dialogue and Intersubjectivity

Fifteen women sat in metal folding chairs in a circle, drinking coffee, eating pan dulce (sweet bread), and making small talk as we waited for the meeting to begin. Sun streamed in the windows, through which we could see the neighboring rooftops in the heart of San Francisco's Mission District. On that fall morning in 1997, the immigrant women's peer support group had no agenda other than to allow those present to talk about issues on their minds and to solicit collective discussion or advice. As other women dropped off their babies and toddlers in the adjacent child care area, the women already seated introduced themselves one at a time, giving their first name, country of origin, and the number of children they had both in the United States and remaining in their home countries.

In many ways, this was a typical *autoestima* meeting. After the women had introduced themselves, the meeting's facilitator met Esperanza Solórzano eyes and held her gaze for a moment. "Esperanza," she asked, "is there anything you'd like to talk about?"

A tall, physically powerful woman in her early forties, Esperanza had lived in San Francisco since emigrating from Mexico City with her husband and three young sons in 1986. She was usually quiet and reserved in group meetings, but that day Esperanza nodded, indicating that she needed to talk. As she began to discuss what she called her *estrés* (stress) and *depresión* (depression), her eyes reddened and her voice shook. This mother of five shared her experiences of physical and emotional abuse by an alcoholic husband, her pain at being ignored and disrespected by her three teenage sons, and her feeling of being overwhelmed when her sixteen-year-old son brought his pregnant girlfriend to live in Esperanza's home. Her main preoccupation was how to protect her preschool-age daughters from what she saw as a very unhealthy atmosphere. "I want to break the cycle for them. It's too late for my sons. I need to become independent in order to be able to leave my husband."

Many women at the meeting that day had known Esperanza for over a year and had seen her emotional state rise and fall repeatedly despite peer support, professional mental health intervention, job training, and employment. Mariana Quiñones, a mother of three in her late twenties from Michoacán, told Esperanza that she had left her husband only two years earlier, at a point when she had no money or work at all. Like Esperanza, Mariana and many of the other discussion participants spoke little if any English, had completed less than a few years of elementary school in their countries of origin, and were undocumented. They were clear about the structurally disadvantaged positions they occupied and the bankruptcy of American bootstrap notions of the self-sufficient individual, yet they urged Esperanza to not see herself as powerless and to have confidence in her own ability to survive and raise her daughters. "If I could do it, so can you," said Mariana.[1] At a time when the state was withdrawing support from women in Esperanza's position, especially undocumented women, by cutting welfare and public housing benefits, such peer support would be an important resource if she chose to separate from her husband. Whatever her decision, the women would provide the emotional support she was asking for.

Two other women present, who were also unhappy with their domestic situations but did not plan to leave their partners, spoke of the importance of *autoestima*. They knew that Esperanza was familiar with the public resources and services available to her and her citizen daughters and that, as one of the few homeowners and small businesspeople in the group, she was far better off in material terms than the vast majority of them. Her fragile emotional condition also factored into their disinclination to tell her or any other woman that her only good option was to leave her husband. Several spoke up to tell her that she needed to focus on her own *autoestima* to make sure her daughters would be able to break the cycle of violence and low self-esteem.

Autoestima meetings like this one were without specific agendas beyond having members raise issues for discussion, ask for advice, or respond to a question posed by the day's facilitator. The group's vision of what was encompassed by *autoestima* was much broader than the direct translation of *self-esteem* and could not be appreciated by an analysis that posited women as passive recipients of neoliberal ideals of the self. Discussions ranged from parenting and discipline, in-law relationships, work problems, and media and consumer pressures to specific economic or personal crises. At one such meeting, members might critique commercial culture or the social messages of *telenovelas* and popular music. At another, they would discuss their problems with and objections to aspects of their children's experience with school busing and neighborhood versus magnet schools. Another meeting would consist of women's sentimental, ironic, and occasionally ribald reminiscences of how they met their husbands or the fathers of their children.

In this conversation, women were clearly deploying something similar to a North American vernacular notion of self-esteem as an individualized process of developing a positive self-concept.[2] They also were operating in North American and Latin American feminist organizing traditions of consciousness raising and dialogic peer support. However, *autoestima* in this context also encompassed personal transformational processes, the shared identity as immigrant Latinas that they forged in dialogue and *convivencia* (shared experiences and time), and their work together on community social and political concerns ranging from immigration reform to domestic violence. They outlined a notion of *autoestima* tied to peer support and dialogue about social issues and how to address them collectively. Talking about their personal problems in a politicized support group helped the women situate and analyze intimate personal issues in a broader social context. *Autoestima* was dialogic and nurturing of women's individual and collective voices, in contrast to the immigration experiences that many women described as silencing and disempowering. Thus, *autoestima* was both a process and an outcome, a means and an end in the ongoing struggle for a richer and more empowered sense of citizenship.

Identity, Dispute, and Difference

Autoestima constituted cultural citizenship on the most intimate levels—between women, among kin, and within the household, especially with husbands and children. To feel entitled socially and culturally, the women, as wives and daughters and mothers, needed to be able to claim the space and power to practice citizenship.[3] They spoke of themselves and various cultural domains in distinctly relational terms, with ideas of self, family, and community always infused with public, political, private, and intimate concerns. This corresponds to what Lynn Stephen has described in Latin America as "[a]lternative cultural discourses of motherhood" that are "multidimensional and both public and private" (2001, 59).

Women's analyses related the transformations in their subjectivity, conjugal relationships, and approaches to parenting after immigration to their changing experiences of motherhood, marriage, and citizenship. The diversity of social identities and experiences embedded in these categories also revealed that tensions and conflicts were as much a part of the group process and dialogue as was the supportive conversation with Esperanza I observed at the *autoestima* meeting described earlier. Women who were not mothers and LGBT members often had to struggle to assert their own contributions in the heteronormative dialogues. Differences in religion, class, or educational backgrounds also caused occasional tensions that were themselves productive in that they allowed for counter-discourses of citizenship within the group itself.

MUA members' shared language both reflected and enabled a multiplicity of subject positions within the group. This process of discursively constituting complex citizen-subjects was neither straightforward nor free of conflict. Group leaders reinforced a politics of unity across differences of nationality, religion, marital and motherhood status, age, immigration status, and sexual orientation. Yet group members' articulation of *autoestima* was usually related to a subject positioned as both heterosexual and parent. Lesbian members or members without children noted in interviews that they sometimes felt a lack of sympathy or collective support for their own issues of *autoestima*, with this eventually driving some women farther from the core of the group's activities. Other terrains of conflict or division were products of group participation itself, with some members gaining more personally and/or economically in terms of skills development or even being hired by the group as staff. Despite the realities and challenges of forging an inclusive group identity and solidarity, what was remarkable was the extent to which these tensions and intra-group differences were neither ignored nor elided in the theory and practice of *autoestima*.

Autoestima encompassed personal transformational processes, a shared identity as immigrant Latinas forged in dialogue and convivencia, and community social and political concerns such as immigration and domestic violence. The term clearly resonated with a North American vernacular notion of self-esteem as an individualized process of developing a positive self-concept. So, I initially had a difficult time understanding women's use of the term *autoestima* as anything more than a strategic use of a problematic concept, or as shorthand for talking about the pride they gained through activities in the organization. Yet in paying closer attention to how women used the term, *autoestima* emerged as a narrative opportunity through which women performed or manifested their cultural citizenship as immigrants, women, and mothers.

To understand how different women understood *autoestima* both conceptually and concretely in their lives, this chapter focuses on how three women— Esperanza Solórzano, Marta Cordero, and Tomasa Hernández—contextualized their experiences of having, losing, and gaining *autoestima* and the relationship between their sense of self and their husbands, their families of origin, their children, U.S. society, and their home countries.

Seeing Herself as a Contributor: Marta Cordero

MUA member Marta Cordero's story linked peer support, personal transformation, and the public collective acts associated with the participatory aspects of citizenship. At the time of our first interview in 1996, Marta was twenty-five years old and had been living in San Francisco since emigrating with her husband, Juan Manuel, from their hometown in Jalisco, Mexico, in 1986. They had two young daughters. Juan Manuel's sister and her family also lived in San Francisco, but local extended family relations were more a source of stress than of support. Marta had felt lonely and depressed for most of the time she had lived in the United States: "I felt really empty inside." At one point several years earlier, she and her daughters had returned to Mexico to visit her parents and ended up staying for six months, returning only after her husband came to bring them back to the United States.

A friend of Marta's learned about the women's group after seeing a group member give a talk on AIDS/HIV at a neighborhood park. Her friend was curious and wanted to attend a meeting, and she asked Marta to accompany her. Marta was not only reticent, she was dubious and embarrassed at the idea of attending a women's support group meeting. "Frankly ... I didn't want to [go]. I was embarrassed." At the very first meeting, however, she recognized that the issues being discussed—*autoestima* and domestic violence—were her concerns. "The first time [I went to a meeting], I was really embarrassed. With everyone. I felt really self-conscious, especially because of the problems I'd been having ... with *autoestima* ... frankly, I didn't know what that word meant. I didn't know that that was my problem at that time. ... [At one meeting the women were discussing domestic violence.] 'That is what is happening to me,' without my knowing it, that I was suffering from domestic violence with my husband."[4]

Marta learned a new vocabulary for talking about her experience when she was invited to participate in an eight-week-long leadership training workshop. The participants decided to carry out educational campaigns about the immigration and welfare law changes they had studied in the training, as well as to lobby local social services department heads and county supervisors about protecting immigrants' access to public services. For Marta, the overall impact of the experience directly linked collective action on issues of concern to an improved sense of her own worth. She talked about her sense of *autoestima* in terms that were instrumental, relational, and dialogic: "It was the greatest thing I have done in my life, because after this training, I feel *useful* [her emphasis]. I feel that I can do something for us, for Latinos, that I am doing something positive. I don't feel this anxiety when I begin to speak. Also, in my family I feel, as a mother, I feel useful."[5]

This discourse of service and voice is where *autoestima* and citizenship meet for many women. "One feels so good when you do something for others." Marta did not mean that her self-worth was defined only in terms of her service to others, but rather that positive changes in her subjectivity were in turn helpful to her children and the broader community. Marta appreciated the skills and knowledge she acquired about resources available to her and the fact that she could now share this information with others. She also specifically located her pride in this knowledge in her relationships with the broader Latino immigrant community and within her own family. It was not surprising that Marta also emphasized her new sense of her "usefulness," with connotations of capacity and skill, in her role as a mother. The women in these workshops were specifically concerned with issues of health care and education under welfare and immigration reform, and they built consensus around their shared concerns as immigrant mothers.

Economic, Social, and Domestic Violence: Tomasa Hernández

The impact of different forms of violence was in the foreground of many women's stories and bore directly on their capacity for bodily and emotional integrity and therefore their citizenship practice. Tomasa Hernández's story is a powerful illustration of these sorts of personal and political transformations and the complex way women reconfigured notions like *autoestima*. Tomasa was a petite and vivacious woman whose youthful physique and penchant for tight jeans and hip urban sportswear belied her status as a mother of six. After finishing elementary school in her small hometown near the lake called Chapala in Jalisco, she had worked for several years to help support her family, and she migrated to California when she was a teenager. Tomasa shook her head and laughed ruefully at her youthful hubris at having jumped on a bus with a girlfriend to make their way north. They eventually found work in sweatshops and restaurants in San Francisco and settled there. Tomasa was one of the founding members of Mujeres Unidas y Activas.

At the time of our interview, Tomasa was pregnant with her seventh child by her boyfriend, whom she described as a wonderful partner to her and a wonderful father to her younger children. She told me a story of personal and political transformation in which she framed herself as having been an emotionally unstable victim of domestic violence whose initial interest in participating in the group was the two dollars she received for attending. The idea of the stipend was to promote participation among women who would not have enough money for bus fare, but to Tomasa's own surprise, she continued to attend after the grant money for the stipends ran out.

Tomasa's emphasis on *autoestima* and its importance in changing her own sense of self did not diminish her critique of the extent to which structural forces limited her options. Her husband, who abused alcohol, played on her fears and insecurities as an undocumented, monolingual, small-town woman with little education. He abused her emotionally and physically:

It was a fear that I lived with, it was a sadness, a . . . because of everything that happens to a woman, umm, who is suffering from domestic violence, I didn't have interest in anything, in anything. I felt so ugly. . . . [T]he father of my children would say to me, "It's just that you are so ugly. Who would love you?" . . . He humiliated me in the worst way, in the very worst way. "You are even uglier than one of those women who walks the streets and charges ten dollars!"[6]

Tomasa reported lying awake at night in their rented room, surrounded by children, waiting for her husband to come home in a drunken rage. He had repeatedly threatened to kill her with a baseball bat, and she believed that he would do it one day. As Tomasa told her story, she shook her head, marveling at his rage. She did everything she was supposed to do as a good wife and mother. At several points in the interview, she returned to this unresolved contradiction. How could he have treated her so badly when she was living up to all her responsibilities in the home and with their children? She had been raised to believe that it would be enough to care for her children, husband, and home, yet no matter how clean her home, how well-groomed her children, and how good her meals, she was unable to win her husband's affection and regard.

Tomasa explained that the women's group's discussions and political work provided a conceptual framework from which she could analyze her own sentiments and experiences in the context of economic and political factors (Hardy-Fanta, 1993). This perspective also allowed her to analyze her husband's abusive behavior in light of his own individual difficult life experiences, as well as contemporary anti-Latino, anti-immigrant politics. Though she never excused his abusive behavior, Tomasa spoke with compassion of how difficult it was for men like her husband, who had little education and English, to maintain a positive sense of themselves in a society that regarded them only as inexpensive laborers. She suggested that economic and psychic stresses on men drove some to alcohol and substance abuse, and that the men and their families suffered as a result of this self-abusing behavior. When we were speaking about her hopes for her children's futures, she returned to the topic again:

> Well, [I hope] that they go to school, that they have a better future, that they don't go through what I have, or what their father has. Because I think that that also . . . leads us, I think, to violence. It may not be that, but I think that economic problems also bring domestic violence into family life, that this desperation, that I think this also influences family disintegration. Because one is already thinking, "Oh, God, I don't have anything to pay the rent. I'll just have another beer to forget." . . . And I haven't just heard this from myself, but from many other people, that family problems are also rooted in all the laws that we have here now that are attacking us. So I also think that there is a great deal of desperation which they [men] are feeling.

Although intimate partner violence occurs in all racial, ethnic, and socioeconomic sectors of U.S. society, empirical studies appear to bear out Tomasa's analysis that poverty, social isolation, poor extended family supports, discrimination, and substance abuse are all associated with increased risk of domestic violence.[7] The desperation that Tomasa blamed on political and economic pressures experienced by immigrant Latinos was exemplified by the escalating economic marginalization of immigrant families at the end of the century.

One finding of the U.S.-Mexican Binational Study on Migration found that the proportion of recent Mexican immigrant families with household incomes under $5,000 doubled from 5.5 percent to 11 percent between 1990 and 1996 (Davis, 2000). Tomasa expressed compassion for so many immigrant men due to the structural violence they experienced. She later went on to join the staff of a local agency that serves day laborers, and mainly male clients, whose tremendous social suffering even in liberal San Francisco has been well documented by Quayson (2005).

It is clear from studies of women's empowerment programs around the world that the certain ways of addressing violence against women and empowerment may constrain as well as enable new political subjectivities and transformations (Cruikshank, 1999; Merry, 2006b; Sharma, 2008). Tomasa was able to harness empowering aspects of feminist critiques of violence against women while maintaining a critical stance toward universalized solutions for complex individual situations. Immigrant and undocumented women in MUA were acutely aware of the double-edged potential of engaging state forces to address family violence. Tomasa rejected stereotypes of Latino men as macho or violent. Without excusing batterers, she emphasized the economic and social forces that help shape family violence. Such commentaries as Tomasa's challenge the conflation of Latin American cultural traditions with violence against women. They also engage the broader debate over how to use law, including immigrant and refugee policy, to combat violence against women without invoking racialized stereotypes of hyper-patriarchal traditional cultures that ignore geopolitics and other structural conditions in which domestic violence occurs (Ong, 2003; Ramos, 1987; Razack, 1995, 1998).

MUA leadership and members walked a difficult line between strategic appropriation of liberal discourse and the power of this same discourse to transform their objectives and, indeed, their very sense of themselves. They recognized that the state was an occasionally strategic but not entirely trustworthy ally of immigrant women victims of violence and their families. Group discussions involved weighing options, evaluating available resources, and choosing among unattractive options.[8] MUA policy was to support the victim of violence and her children, but also to recognize the complexity of every situation. In some cases, out of concern about possibly losing any hope of child support, women feared reporting husbands with prior criminal records who might then be deported. In other cases, women were concerned that reports might lead to investigation of their own immigrant status or intervention by state Child Protective Services. Some feared homeward migration more than remaining with their spouses because they felt they would be unable to support their children, much less have access to adequate legal protection from their husbands, in their country of origin.[9] In general, many of the women I interviewed, whether they were domestic violence victims or not, expressed a desire to return to Mexico to live at some point in the future, but most neither thought this would be economically feasible nor believed that their children would be willing to move back with them.[10]

In urban working-class Mexico City (as in the United States), domestic violence is "generally a proscribed activity" that continues to be commonly practiced and experienced (Guttman, 1996). Institutional support and intervention to end violence are even less extensive than the meager services available to Spanish-speaking women in the United States. But the women's perception about domestic violence may also be understood in terms of their migration to the United States during a period when domestic violence had begun to be addressed in both nations in popular women's organizing and by the state. Given that "[e]conomic dependence of women upon their abusive partners is one of the primary reasons they remain in violent relationships" (Jang, Marín, and Pendleton, 1997, 137), battered women seek to stay in the United States after leaving an abusive partner because of greater economic opportunity and more extensive public assistance in the form of cash, subsidized housing, and medical insurance than in Mexico or Central America.[11] At the same time, the centrality of economic issues to ongoing domestic violence makes the 1996 welfare reform legislation's reduction in benefits and services a particularly powerful concern for battered immigrant women (Goldfarb, 1999).

The women of MUA and other feminists who advocate for domestic violence victims find themselves in uncomfortable alliances with the state in their efforts to empower women to change their situations in part through legal means (Merry, 1995). Engagement with official discourses on domestic violence can lead to the identification of certain women as subjects worthy of state protection due to their victimization (Osanloo, 2006) and certain men as deserving of surveillance and punishment. The shifting legal discourse on domestic violence reflects increased feminist influence on the state and a corresponding denaturalization of gendered violence in domestic relationships. The problem, as Sally Merry clearly poses it, is that such governmental attention may blame "poor women for their failure to take responsibility for themselves while ignoring the economic restructuring which displaces both male and female workers, minimizing the government's responsibility to provide these families with a viable mode of livelihood, and legitimating new systems of surveillance and control of working-class and poor men and women" (Merry, 1995, 69).

The concept of *autoestima* helped Tomasa Hernández establish a position from which to defend her interests as an immigrant, a mother, and a woman. Thus she began transforming her sense of herself, her rights, and the conditions of her life:

I took a few trainings and learned what *autoestima* means. I didn't even know what *autoestima* was. It was here that I learned . . . the *autoestima*, that one has to value oneself first before, before helping another person, first one has to have good *autoestima*, because if not, one can't do anything. And I took a training workshop where we talked first about *autoestima*. That workshop was about migrant rights. . . . [It] was very intense and it was there that I took my first step towards feeling better about myself. Afterwards, I took other trainings, but even though I continued to suffer domestic violence, I already was feeling better. I knew that I was a woman and that I was worth a lot . . . that first came me, and my children, and after came everyone else, and after that, came him. So it was there that my life completely changed. . . . I was like a plant that is drying out, that nobody waters. And when I took those trainings and I saw more women with problems and I saw that I wasn't the only one suffering. So I said, "Here I have to change because this doesn't have to continue like this." So it was like that little plant that when you give it some water, when you water it, you are giving it life, you are giving it the opportunity to flower, to grow, like a guide that keeps growing. So that's how I see my life since I started coming here until now. Because now I am a woman who, with all my problems, has moved forward with my six children. Although we have gone through many things, problems, they have given me trouble and many things have happened, but I think that if I weren't here in the group, if I didn't have all the information that I have now, I think I would be a ruined woman.

Tomasa framed the metaphor of herself as a little plant with themes that arose in other women's narratives of personal transformation. *Autoestima* was one of several concepts they used in representing their experiences, along with self-worth as women, overcoming domestic violence, activism for the rights of immigrants, and access to information and skills development.

Many mentioned the importance of feeling useful, that is, that they came to believe that they had something to contribute socially and politically. They related the ideas of *autoestima* and *utilidad* in their narratives through specific experiences in their families and in community organizing, and in their reflections on their own subjectivity. There are many points in these narratives where *autoestima* and "learning to speak" (*aprendiendo a hablar*) meet to configure a vision of citizenship that demands recognition of their rights as individual persons, and also in relationship with others.

Even though the women's narratives often referred to self-esteem as a received category that invoked the image of a neoliberal and self-governing subject, their practice embodied a more challenging form of political opposition and identity. *Autoestima* conveyed both liberatory notions of democratic possibility and recognition of the constraints of self-discipline and subjection emphasized in anthropological formulations of cultural citizenship. As nonprofit organizations increasingly rely on both public and private funding sources with neoliberal agendas, and as social movements are increasingly articulated through NGOs and nonprofits, developing the capacity to tack back and forth between liberal discourse and democratic practice is a necessary survival skill for political progressives.

The centrality of domestic violence to so many women's discourse on rights may also be traced in part to the emergence of human rights ideals and methodology in women's rights organizing. For the last two decades of the twentieth century, violence against women was a strategic area of issues around which to mobilize transnational networks of activism for women's equality and also networks within the United States. Framing women's politics in terms of human dignity and the right to not be subject to many different forms of violence allowed Mujeres Unidas y Activas to build alliances among diverse women across class, race, and cultural barriers. While the issue of violence against women by the state, by individual strangers, or by intimates was articulated initially by women's organizations in the developing world, it resonated with women's groups in the United States and with others who subscribed to the human rights framework (Jonas and Thomas, 1999).

The power of the concept of *autoestima* stood in for much of the challenge faced by groups like Mujeres Unidas y Activas in mobilizing liberal democratic discourse toward more fundamentally transformative ends. MUA articulated a clear program for empowering immigrant Latin American women and their families seeking to assert their needs and rights. Its practice put it in dialogue with NGOs and foundations in different parts of the world, many of which referenced a transnational discourse of women's empowerment that took on different meanings in localized practices (Sharma, 2006; Merry, 2006a, 2006b). Barbara Cruikshank (1999) forcefully argues that concepts and terms like *empowerment* and *self-esteem* may be "techniques of self-governance" designed specifically to discipline participants in such groups into the logic of neoliberal political subjectivity. She notes that the state government of California, influenced by sociological work that has blamed low self-esteem for social ills from poverty to violence to dropping out of high school, made grants to community organizations doing self-esteem work during this period. Some of these funds may have trickled down to Mujeres Unidas y Activas.

The challenge of studying the movement of discursive references like "self-esteem" across borders of nations, cultures, languages, and social movements is to be able to recognize both the disciplinary power of neoliberal empowerment discourse and different subjects' capacities to critically rework and use terminology in service to their own collective liberatory projects. In some narratives, *autoestima* is a critical tool that helped women link their personal struggles to a more politicized analysis, and has also occasionally verged on becoming a thing in itself, a fact or aspect of women's personhood that they "discovered" in the course of participating in the group.

Even though the women's narratives often referred to self-esteem as a received category that invoked the image of a neoliberal and self-governing subject, their citizenship practice conveyed a much different and more challenging form of political opposition and identity. The problematic concept of *autoestima* is important not only because of the frequency of its citation in the women's narratives, but also because of the way it included both liberatory notions of democratic possibility and limiting practices of self-discipline and subjection emphasized respectively in divergent anthropological formulations of cultural citizenship (R. Rosaldo, 1994; Ong, 1996).

Women's own versions of *autoestima* are important contributions to the elaboration of a notion of cultural citizenship that can embrace both the process of gaining a sense of belonging and entitlement in a given society and the process of producing new subjects in dynamic relations with the state and political economic forces (R. Rosaldo, 1994; Ong, 1996). The grassroots immigrant activists cited here focused on issues of gender and subjectivity as part of their efforts to claim their place as legitimate members of U.S. society and empowered agents in their families and community. Citizenship entailed struggles that required profound changes in participants' sense of themselves and their social roles. Considered as theoretical interventions on the relationship between subjectivity, migration, gender, and politicization, their perspectives offer ways around the gender, class, linguistic, and racial exclusivity of past assumption of that which constitutes politics, agency, and citizenship (Dagnino, 1994, 2003, 2007).

This renewed notion of citizenship is multilayered and multifaceted, involving overlapping and mutually constituting realms of experience and subjectivity as well as political economy.[12] The women described daily struggles about their claims to bodily sovereignty and social autonomy that defined their capacity to even attend peer support group meetings, much less lead political demonstrations. They waged these struggles simultaneously at home, on the street, and in the workplace, with family, peers, neighbors, employers, and the state. Immigrant women's experiences manifested the importance of a more fundamental challenge to the public–private divide in social analysis, a more politicized and historicized understanding of subjectivity, and a deeper appreciation for the importance of intimate realms in collective political life and citizenship practice. Collective struggle to make public claims for citizenship rights is intrinsic to these more private processes while also addressing more explicitly public political goals.

The new citizen-subjects forged in MUA were "constituted discursively," yet this discourse was located in specific political and economic conditions, key among them their experiences as working-class and working-poor Latinas, many of whom had been or were currently undocumented immigrants.[13] This collective and historicized experience of dialogue, peer support, activism, and convivencia not only distinguished self-esteem from *autoestima*, but also demanded that *autoestima* be considered as part of a gendered analysis of cultural citizenship for the women. *Autoestima* was not a substitute for improved legal-juridical status, but it provided women with an empowered position from which to critique and act against state structures and cultural practices that excluded them.

By sharing personal experiences and collective struggle on behalf of one another and the broader community of immigrants, the women gained the strength to speak up for themselves both in and outside the home, with their husbands and with their children's teachers. Together they identified forces undermining their (and their loved ones') *autoestima* as personal and psychological, and also as economic, linguistic, cultural, and political, ranging from violence in the family to the psychological war they felt was under way against immigrants in late-twentieth-century California. These transformative processes were neither inevitable nor inexorable, as Esperanza Solórzano's unresolved problems make clear, despite her extended participation in the group. Theirs are not simple progress stories of life after migrating to the United States, but rather complex narratives of diverse, complicated, and sometimes contradictory experiences. Considered together, however, the stories suggest important avenues toward understanding subjectivity and transformation in the lives of economically, socially, and politically marginalized women.

Although access to legal status and full enfranchisement are of critical importance and highly desirable for immigrants, full citizenship is more than the bundle of rights conferred by the formal legal status.[14] Political belonging is a subjectively experienced and vernacularly expressed social identity that is inseparable from race, class, gender, language, and systems of social inequality. The intimate and personal realms of life are as much a part of these citizenship stories as are macro political and economic forces. As the women's own accounts indicated, the capacity to engage in public expressions of citizenship assumed a basic degree of *autoestima* and personal liberty that they had to assert in their homes and among their peers before they could make public claims for rights and belonging in the broader society. This process of transformation of one's sense of self as a political subject was neither unilineal nor evolutionary in the modernist liberal sense of political development. Instead it entailed understanding how women's roles as mothers, wives, workers, and political actors overlapped and influenced one another.

Chapter 5 examines the process of learning to speak up for oneself and one's community, a process that women described as necessary to articulating their claims for rights. As they did for the notion of *autoestima*, the women's narratives denaturalized learning to speak up and citizenship's assumptions about people's capacity to articulate claims. In doing so, they underlined the significance of subjective factors and the diverse, sometimes intimate processes of struggle that were part of their experience of citizenship.

5

Desahogandose y Aprendiendo a Hablar

Speaking Up and Speaking Out

FROM MUA'S INCEPTION IN 1991, discussion and dialogue about personal stories and experiences were central to the group's approach to personal transformation and collective political development. Scholars working with the Puerto Rican women of the El Barrio Women's Literacy Project in New York noted the link between women's *testimonios* and an emancipatory vision of Latina/o cultural citizenship (Benmayor et al., 1988; Torruellas et al., 1991). Women's life stories were unique and individual, but were also shaped in dialogue with other women as part of a shared project of claiming rights and dignity as Latina immigrants (Benmayor, Torruellas, and Juarbe, 1992; Torruellas et al., 1989). Being able to speak with other women and articulate one's story was part of being able to claim rights and demand recognition as political subjects. Giving women the space and time in which to tell their stories, including testimonios, was an organizing method, a transformative personal experience, and part of a broader struggle for social justice that was rooted in Latin American social movements and adaptable to the immigrant context in the United States (Beverly, 2004).

The women I met in San Francisco said that the opportunity to get outside their usually cramped living quarters, to be in the company of supportive women with similar concerns and experiences, and to have the security of trustworthy child care nearby were important reasons for their early participation in Mujeres Unidas y Activas. The most common word they used in interviews was the need they had to *desahogarse*—to get things off their chests. The choice of this phrase by so many informants evoked the many levels on which women can feel trapped, choked, and burdened by poor domestic relations, economic stress, and substandard living conditions. The process of *desahogandose* was both dialogic and intersubjective. Women reported feeling relief at the opportunity to articulate not only their feelings, but also their ideas and opinions about a variety of topics and to hear the experiences, information, and analyses that other women had to share. Regaining voice, discussed in terms of learning to speak or getting things off your chest, was therefore both a goal and an organizing methodology for the women's group. Desahogandose was a key first step for women in *aprendiendo a hablar,* learning to speak out or speak up. The ability to desahogarse was critical for those trying to change their lives individually, as well as for those hoping to speak up for their children, their families, and their communities. Women came to speak out from this collective experience and on behalf of community interests as well. Adela Aguirre's physical symptoms after meetings ended were dramatic but also telling about the physical impact of political silence and disenfranchisement: "During the two hours that I'd spend here with the group, oh, I'd feel so happy. But just as soon as those two hours were over, how awful. My stomach would start churning from my anxiety about returning home."[1]

Adela was not the only one to use terms of embodiment to describe her loneliness and relief. In 1996, when Luz Salinas was in her early twenties, she moved to San Francisco from the central Mexican city of León with her husband and their one-year-old son. Luz described spending her first fourteen months in the United States "shut in the house, isolated and lonely." She felt trapped in her own home not by her husband, with whom she had a good relationship, but by her lack of confidence in her language skills and her ability to get around the city on her own. When she began getting severe headaches, her husband took her to the public health clinic. The doctor told her that the headaches were probably related to depression and referred Luz to the women's group, "to make some friends and be able to desahogarme with other women." She remembers how good it felt to get out of the house in Bayview–Hunter's Point and learn to navigate the city by public transit to get to meetings in the Mission District. Although her husband expressed his doubts about her participation in the group, she was able to convince him that both she and her son benefited from the companionship and activities.

Issues of losing and gaining their ability to speak up for themselves and regaining a positive sense of themselves as individuals and members of a community after migration were central to many women's stories. These common themes and words were part of a process of developing a shared language of belonging that could relate subjective experiences, collective dialogue, and political engagement. Adela's story wove the issues of voice and citizenship claims with her history of overcoming violence and her own fears and prejudices in San Francisco.

When she was twenty years old, Adela met Manuel, who was born and raised in the United States and was visiting relatives in Mexico City when they met and fell in love. He told her he wanted to get married and return to San Francisco where he had a permanent job, so she agreed to emigrate, but only if he promised that she could go to school to learn English to be able to work herself. In recounting her experience of immigration, Adela highlighted her struggle to regain her self-assurance in the United States. She had been a teenager when she left her small hometown in the highlands of Jalisco for a job and an apartment in Mexico City. She had completed sixth grade and a vocational course in office skills for executive secretaries. Her sister soon joined her, and they shared expenses and an unusually independent urban life for young working-class women. "I was always quite a rebel!" she said with a laugh.

Adela feels that this independent part of her character has always been a source of conflict for her as well as a source of strength. In my experiences with her, this shy but friendly woman rarely had difficulty expressing herself, but she struggled to articulate how she thought her own attitudes fit in with Mexican cultural constructions of womanhood:

> I was very independent. Now I think that maybe that was, or maybe was one of the problems. I never liked, well, and now I look and think that, one has to, that one's life as a woman, no, well, at least in my country, you're born and you have to be under the authority of your parents, obeying your parents. You get married and you're supposed to obey your husband. And I have always been very rebellious about this. "I am going to go to school to learn English and as soon as I can, I want to work." [He would respond,] "Oh, yes, that's perfect. You can do what you want to," oh yeah, you know. According to him, he totally agreed with everything, but when I arrived here, everything was different. Here he only let me go, at the most, one month, and I don't think I had even finished that one month, right after we arrived.

Within three months of marrying Manuel, Adela was pregnant. Her husband refused to let her return to the free ESL (English as a second language) classes at the community college, first due to her pregnancy and later because their son was so young. As soon as her son was eight months old, Adela enrolled again, but her husband lost his job almost immediately and forbade her to return to class. She needed him to care for the baby while she was in school, but it was the fact of her mobility combined with his unemployment that angered him. "What would his friends say? Me on the street and him at home!" On a certain level, she accepted his reasoning, perhaps because of his apparent efforts to undermine her self-confidence during the preceding months. But she also admitted she had her own expectations and concerns about what others might say.[2] Adela said, "You know, it's like one also brings their own prototype from their country, from where you're from, so you say, yes, that's true. They are going to think that I am all mixed up in this or that."

Manuel was not able to keep a steady job and they soon became dependent on public assistance. Since he was home all day, depressed and demoralized about being unemployed, he exerted even more control over Adela's day-to-day activities, drank more, and beat her when he was drunk. Even years later, after the violence had stopped and Adela was participating in more activities outside the home, those of us who called her had to invent stories or pretexts about our calls to protect her from her husband's interventions. Other group members told me to do as they did—to call her at times when I thought her husband was not home, hope that she picked up the phone herself and would tell me when to call back, or compose myself when I heard his voice and pretend that I was the mother of a classmate from her son's preschool calling about a school activity.[3] Rather than passively tolerate her husband's drunken rages and abuse, Adela reclaimed cultural discourses of resistance and the dignity of women even as she was repeatedly forced to postpone her plans to leave her spouse.

When their relationship turned violent during those early days, she reflected on two comments made to her on her wedding day about the apparently contradictory role she was about to assume as wife and mother. Her father had told her to always remember that "the woman is the key to the home," that she would be the key to the happiness and the center of her household. Another wedding guest warned her to always remember that "the woman is whatever the man wants her to be." Now these words, which were "recorded" like a tape in her memory, remind her of a famous phrase, "Hombres necios que acusáis / a la mujer sin razón" (Misguided men, who will chastise / a woman when no blame is due). This is from the opening stanza of one of the most popular poems of the seventeenth-century Mexican intellectual, nun, poet, and mother of Mexican feminism, Sor Juana Inés de la Cruz.[4] Adela quoted the poem in the ubiquitous, colloquial fashion that I have heard Mexican women of diverse class and educational backgrounds use in reference to or defending themselves from male aggression and irrationality. Adela steeled herself against her husband's disrespect with Sor Juana's words and those of her father. She remained with her husband for economic reasons for many years, but never represented herself as a *mujer abnegada*—a self-pitying or long-suffering woman.

In February 1995, after two years of problems with her husband, Adela found herself becoming violent toward her toddler son. She said that this realization is what finally motivated her to make a change in her life, and she began attending parenting workshops at the county hospital. The parenting workshops were of limited duration, and she was referred to the women's peer support group, which was ongoing. She had first learned of these resources from a Latina police officer who responded to a neighbor's call regarding domestic violence in Adela's household. At that point, Adela had been willing to file a police report, but not to charge her husband. Neither did she consider seeking out the community resources on the list the officer gave her. In the retelling, Adela laughed, shaking her head ruefully and explaining that she had been worried that her husband would miss a call for a job while in jail— "¡*Pobrecito!*" (poor thing).

Fear, Power, and Limits on Women's Citizenship

Learning to articulate challenges to different forms of subjection were key tools women used to overcome family members' obstacles to their participation in popular political organizing (Jelin, 1997; Mamdani, 2000; Stephen, 1998). It took a great deal of determination for Adela to participate in the group because her husband so forcefully opposed it. He told her repeatedly that she was just being "brainwashed" by "that bunch of old women, lesbians, dykes."[5] This issue came up in other women's interviews; their husbands, neighbors, or in-laws told them that the women-only group housed in a building full of women's organizations was really about promoting lesbianism through brainwashing. "He told me they were going to wash my 'coconut' [head]!" was the way one woman described her husband's opposition to her participation, a comment that met with laughs of recognition.[6] Such cautionary tales were as much about controlling women as they were about actual homophobia, which in the end is but one of many possible expressions of female sexual autonomy. Sor Juana's poem again is an apt reference; husbands articulated their fears that, given the chance, women would behave the way men do.

Norma Mogrovejo (1998) has described the divisive power of homophobia in the development of the second wave feminist movement in Mexico in the 1970s and 1980s, and this challenge is familiar to U.S. women's organizations as well. Although she dismissed her husband's fears of lesbian influence, Adela herself associated women's political and social solidarity with sexuality and forbidden desire. She spoke of her initial fears of the support other women might provide in sexualized terms, but also in more general language of distrust and the need to guard herself, to protect herself from betrayals. For Adela, sexual autonomy or sexual citizenship was powerful and threatening. She explained this logic:

> [I]f someone cares about you, it's only because they always want to get something from you in return. Because you're always thinking that, right? . . . You put up this invisible barrier when what you want is for them to give you a hug. . . . But then you're left with that you don't want to ask for love like that. The same thing happened at home, in my relationship with my husband. I would say, "oh no, if I go, and I caress him, he's going to think" this, that, and the other, no? Or if I tell a friend "Oh, give me a hug," she's going to say, "She's already gone over to the other side!" There's always that. I don't know, consciously or not, I always put up this barrier. . . . Or also when you want to help someone, simply just giving them some information and they look at you, as if to say, "She must want something" or "She's going to call immigration on me" or I don't know what. This work is pretty hard, but you have to do it and do it now or we're not going to get anywhere. I want to do it because someone did it for me.

Confianza: Solidarity and Trust in Others

Adela connected her ability to trust others with her trust in herself and a sense of her own power. She gained a sense of security knowing that people of goodwill were interested in helping her without judgment or ulterior motives. This reclaimed self-assurance helped her envision herself as having something to offer others. Adela underlined the hope and sense of knowledge and understanding she drew from being part of a community of values in which an ethic of sharing, trust, and mutual respect constituted a counter-discourse to neoliberal norms of competitive, acquisitive political and social relations:

> It was also very important for me to know that there are people who truly give, without any self-interest, that there are people who will help you without criticizing you. That there are people who you can count on one hundred percent.

And since you can trust them and they make you feel good, you take this, at least I do personally, I take this so that someone else can really place their trust in me as well—not one, not two, not three thousand, I feel like I have the ability to be able to understand thousands of people.

Mujeres Unidas y Activas members' shared language both reflected and enabled a multiplicity of subject positions defined with respect to families, nation-states, and identity groups. This process of discursively constituting complex citizen-subjects was neither straightforward nor free of conflict. Group leaders repeatedly articulated a politics of unity despite differences of nationality, religion, marital and motherhood status, age, immigration status, and sexuality. Lesbian members or members without children noted in interviews that they sometimes felt a lack of sympathy or collective support for their own issues, with this eventually driving a few women farther from the center of the group. Other terrains of conflict or division were products of group participation itself, with some members gaining more personally and/or economically in terms of skills development or even being hired by the group as staff. Despite the realities and challenges of forging an inclusive group identity and solidarity, what was remarkable was the extent to which these tensions and intra-group differences were neither ignored nor elided in praxis.

"My Mouth Just Slammed Shut": Cristina Rodríguez

Like Adela, Cristina Rodríguez also spoke about what it was like to transform from an outspoken and self-confident lay catechist prior to immigration into a woman so fearful of her new surroundings that she warned her young son to look straight ahead on the bus, avoid eye contact, and never, ever speak with strangers. At the time of our interview, Cristina was twenty-eight, and her son was approaching preschool age. Like Carolina Jiménez (Chapter 3), Cristina described her marriage as loving and supportive, but she complained about having to struggle for her husband's full respect and for autonomy and freedom of motion and action. She discussed losing her voice after migrating, when her "mouth just slammed shut," and how she regained it through asserting her autonomy in the face of her husband's opposition to her community activities:

[S]omething happened to me when I arrived here, even though there [her hometown] I gave talks and did all sorts of things, when I got here, I just couldn't get myself to speak. I came to the group, but as I came, I left, without saying a word. There was one training that I did, about preventing child and youth violence and it was about running campaigns. And I, no, the thing is, my husband got so mad with me, that he didn't even let me finish the training, much less carry out the campaign. For the same reason, because he didn't want me to be involved in all this. But I felt that I couldn't speak. It was like the change was so hard, from there where I knew everyone and I could talk with anyone, and then I got here and was immersed in this atmosphere that my mouth just slammed shut and I could not talk anymore with anyone. So, the group has helped me so much.

The women in San Francisco described having to overcome many of the same obstacles to their participation in popular organizations that have been reported in other parts of Latin America (Dore, 1997; Jelin, 1997; Stephen, 1997; Young, 1990). Strategies for changing husbands' minds or resisting male control were common topics at Mujeres Unidas y Activas meetings. Along with stories of "the first time I came to a group meeting," stories about "what my husband says about or against the group" were a narrative genre in and of themselves. These stories could be accompanied by laughter and/or tears, and understanding smiles and nods from around the room. Cristina smiled and laughed as she told me about her experiences, as did I, but our laughter neither silenced nor belittled the real pain and frustration Cristina felt about having to argue with her husband about her activities. She reflected on this struggle, on gender roles, and on how she drew strength from her own personal history to continue to act in the world and make her voice heard. In her telling how she responded to her husband, she alternately spoke directly to him and thought aloud, as if to herself, working through her analysis of the cultural processes that seek to silence and isolate women, but do not always succeed.

Themes in these stories of struggle with husbands included different expectations of physical autonomy and freedom of movement, domestic division of labor, and the role of female friendships and community activism. Adela, Marta, and Cristina felt they had been clear about their expectations of personal autonomy before marriage. They had all married men they had known in their hometowns, and it was difficult to reconcile their different ideas about women's freedom of movement and activity outside the house there with their new lives together in the United States. Other women also described the extent to which their husbands acted to maintain their physical and social isolation. In addition to the kinds of direct pressures or protests Marta's and

Cristina's husbands registered against their educational or community activities, some men and in-laws of both sexes were more indirect, suggesting that it was dangerous for the women to be out on the street by themselves, or that moving about freely on the street might draw the attention of assailants or the INS. Many of the women I interviewed lived in neighborhoods with high crime rates and much gang activity; but once they began moving around on their own, they reported learning how to maneuver more safely through the environment and how good it felt to have a sense of competence with respect to bus routes, as well as an expanded geographical familiarity with the city.[7]

While the women balked at the obstacles some family members placed in the way of their activities outside the home, very few challenged the division of labor in the home. They concurred that childrearing, shopping, cooking, and household maintenance were primarily their responsibilities. Their expectations of a good husband and father emphasized both industry and honesty, and also affection and devotion to their wives and their children. The husbands, according to my subjects, seemed to expect clean homes, well-groomed and polite children, and dignified, devoted wives whose community activities were subordinated to those of the hearth. So when Cristina's husband complained about her activities outside of the home, she responded by asserting her demonstrated fulfillment of her social role, indicating his prepared meals and clean clothing, implying that if she were not able to fulfill these basic duties, she would not also be engaged in a high level of community work.

Of the three women, Cristina was the only one who married her husband after living alone in the United States and working to support herself here. Adela lived and worked independently in Mexico before marriage and found a job at a fast food restaurant during the course of my research. Cristina was the only one of the three who had been active in community organizations in her hometown. She spoke of the importance of demonstrations of her and her husband's respect for one another through their independent behavior in public. Were she behaving in a way that disrespected him, she explained, he would have a right to protest her activities, as would she if he were to behave poorly in public. Respectful behavior, in this context, encompasses fidelity to one's spouse and a dignified representation of the household in the community. For Cristina's husband, this meant that he hoped she would spend more time at home, focused on him and his needs. For Cristina, it meant that she was free to speak publicly at rallies and in print and broadcast media (Spanish and English outlets) about her particular immigration situation and the policies she and the group were working to change. Cristina noted that her husband was not the only one to remark on her activities, especially those reflected in the media, and that neighbors and in-laws had also made concerned remarks to her and her husband, which he relayed to her.

Rather than give the impression that immigration, life in the United States, or joining a feminist organization "gave" women what they needed to "liberate" themselves from patriarchal spousal control, I suggest that individuals' understandings of their gender roles as women, mothers, wives, and citizens were in a constant state of change and renegotiation. Siblings, in-laws, neighbors, and, less frequently, children also sometimes acted to limit women's activities. All of this commentary and women's responses to it reflected both the power and the dynamism of gender role enforcement, resistance, and redefinition. Because so many of my subjects were mothers of young children and were not engaged in steady employment outside the home, their comments represent important contributions to the literature on gender role transformations in the household, which frequently involved women's entrance into the paid workforce as well as their immigration experiences.

In their stories, the women referenced both the institutional and the personal violence they confronted as well as the ways they talked back to the institutions and practices that tried to keep them in subordinate positions. Though the term *citizenship* never appears in their narratives other than in reference to formal legal or institutional status, I found their stories and the common vocabulary they developed in terms of *autoestima* and aprendiendo a hablar truly helpful in understanding citizenship as an evolving cultural institution with dynamic sets of ideas and practices that extend far beyond its formal role linking individuals to the state.

Learning to Speak Up with Institutions and Against Violence

Many of the women I interviewed used language of defense, attack, hate, and homeland—the language of warfare—to describe American attitudes toward Latino immigrants. One Salvadoran woman dubbed this *una guerra psicológica* (a psychological war). In doing so, she signaled a link between immigrant experiences in the United States and the impact of so-called low-intensity warfare in 1980s Central America. This serves as a reminder of the violence of American xenophobia that prefigured the post-9/11 war on terror. It is precisely in such conjunctures between politics, intimate realms such as family life, physical health, and mental health, when put in dialogue with the ethnographic research relationship, that we can begin to understand what citizenship, in all its senses, means in everyday life.

Violence, whether rhetorical, institutional, or between intimates, played a central role in many women's stories about learning to speak. One might think that battered immigrant women from proximate nations like Mexico would prefer to return to their hometowns and families than to remain with abusers. Considering the role of the state and transnational politics in family life and women's status, however, the picture is more complex.

As noted earlier, some women feared homeward migration more than remaining with their spouses, feeling that they would be unable to support their children in their home country and would lack access to legal protection from their husbands. In urban working-class Mexico City (as in the United States), domestic violence is "generally a proscribed activity" but continues to be commonly practiced and experienced (Guttman, 1996). Women reported their sense that, in their home countries, institutional avenues for support and intervention to end violence are even less extensive than the meager services available in the United States for Spanish-speaking women. Their perception about this subject may also be understood in terms of their migration to the United States at a time when domestic violence began to be addressed in both nations in popular women's organizing and by the state. The consciousness raising and support have primarily developed in urban areas, and the women I spoke with who most feared their husbands' power over them were from smaller rural communities. Given that "[e]conomic dependence of women upon their abusive partners is one of the primary reasons they remain in violent relationships" (Jang, Marín, and Pendleton, 1997, 137), greater economic opportunity and more extensive public assistance in the form of cash, subsidized housing, and medical insurance are important reasons why battered women seek to remain in the United States after leaving an abusive partner.

At one point, I heard a cautionary tale circulating among group members about a woman whose abusive husband turned her in to the INS after she left him. On some level, I ascribed this vague story to the sort of folklore that begins "someone told me about a woman who . . ." or "I heard about this woman who . . ." Then I met Mariana Quiñones who, it turned out, was the subject of this local folklore.

Mariana Quiñones emphasized the importance of the process of learning to speak in the face of her husband's, her family's, and the state's efforts to define her social position. When I first interviewed Mariana, she was in her early thirties and a single mother of four children. She had immigrated to San Francisco from Central Mexico in 1994 to rejoin her husband, with whom she had a long and violent history but also shared three children. After several lonely months in their first apartment, they moved to a different building where she was befriended by a neighbor named Tomasa Hernández. Mariana began attending MUA meetings with Tomasa, as well as free ESL classes at the neighborhood adult school, all without her husband's knowledge. One night when Mariana's husband was very drunk, he became violent. Tomasa heard the noise from her apartment and called the police. The police officer, who was Spanish speaking and Latina, convinced Mariana to file a police report, request a temporary restraining order, and let her husband be incarcerated for a week. While he was in jail, Mariana changed the locks on the apartment.

Her husband was so enraged by her actions that he called the INS and provided names, photos, and home and work addresses of Mariana, her sister, and her mother. All were promptly detained and held separately. Another detainee told Mariana to keep quiet and seek help from a nonprofit legal agency. Mariana followed this advice, received legal representation, and ultimately was granted legal residency under the terms of the Violence Against Women Act. However, her mother and sister told their stories without legal representation and were instead given "orders of voluntary departure."

Having failed to get her deported, Mariana's husband proceeded to sue her for custody of their children. This time, she represented herself in family court, and after many court dates and unannounced police and social worker visits to her home, she managed to win sole custody of the children. As with the INS, Mariana's strategy in family court was to remain calm, collected, and confident and to refuse to speak unless she was provided with an interpreter. She told me that her natal family had always ridiculed her for being "a big talker," but it was her willingness to speak to anyone and everyone that got her the resources she needed in times of crisis.

The Violence Against Women Act and Undocumented Immigrant Women

The Violence Against Women Act of 1994 (VAWA) was the product of the first comprehensive legislative attempt to address domestic violence as a national problem. It also included a provision that altered the immigration code. VAWA allowed a victim of domestic violence to petition for permanent residency independently of her spouse (or parent, in the case of a child) if the abusive person is a citizen or a legal resident who uses the victim's undocumented status as a means of controlling her.[8]

I accompanied Mariana Quiñones to the central police station and to INS offices as part of her quest for legal residency under VAWA. Mariana's pro bono lawyer relied on her to do the leg work for her case herself, including trying to unearth the original police reports from an incident several years earlier. That was when Tomasa, who was her neighbor at the time, called the police to intervene during one violent episode, and the police had filed a report. The officer at the central police station found the text, but said that the photos of Mariana's beaten face, which her lawyer had thought would be helpful in her claim, had long since been destroyed or lost. Fortunately for her, Mariana explained with a hint of irony, her husband had forced her to marry him legally in Mexico, so she could establish that part of her claim with official documentation.[9] Her irony stemmed from the fact that the marriage occurred after her husband had kidnapped her off a rural road, removed her to his home state, and raped her and got her pregnant. After keeping her at his home in another state for over a year, he then convinced her father to approve the marriage. Her father's permission was necessary under Mexican law, because she was only fifteen years old at the time.

That the U.S. government responded to the growing movement by survivors of gender-based violence and feminist activists is in many ways an important step in addressing issues of women's citizenship in the United States. At the same time, the specific legal standards for immigrant women's claims under VAWA privileges an applicant who has proof of legal marriage, evidence of her husband's status as a citizen or lawful permanent resident, and official documentation of physical abuse by the husband. A woman who had already filed for divorce from her abusive spouse was unable to apply under VAWA, though once her application was filed she could then divorce him without affecting her chances for residency. As was common in Mexico and Central America among lower-income people, many of the women in MUA never legally married their common-law husbands. For battered undocumented women in abusive relationships with undocumented men, there is no remedy under VAWA; such women often fear the impact on the family economy of calling the police and risking exposure of their legal status to the state.

Mariana was particularly well-organized and careful, yet even for her the process was difficult. She was expected to provide not only documentation of the abuse, but also receipts from rent and utilities and/or pay stubs as proof of continuous residence in the United States and evidence of her husband's legal residency status. Mariana was able to produce all of these, dating back many years. Since she spoke no English, she had to bring her twelve-year-old son to meetings with the police to translate for her, which she regretted since they were discussing his father. The child was not only responsible for interpreting for her but also for helping her negotiate her way through public institutions and bureaucratic procedures. Both were relieved when I was available to accompany and interpret for Mariana, though the first time I did so he came along, perhaps to ensure that I was indeed being helpful.

Mariana resourcefulness was clear in the extent of her personal networks and her capacity to access services she deemed beneficial for her family. Whereas many parents prefer to keep their children in nearby schools, she had her children bused from the inner Mission District to Chinatown for a public afterschool program she preferred to those in her neighborhood. She also was the only person I interviewed to report participation in a religiously based organization (her Catholic church's choir). She began working as a housekeeper at an airport hotel after telling her parish's lay social worker that she was looking for a job and being referred for the part-time position that allows her to be home for her children in the mid-afternoon. In short, Mariana was positioned to engage her legal options to a degree that another survivor of violence with fewer emotional resources and personal skills might not be.

Learning to Speak Up in Ethnography

Vernacular notions such as *autoestima* and the related concept of aprendiendo a hablar were discursive resources on which women drew to sustain themselves in collective political struggle as well as in their personal lives. The women's testimonials about the importance of *autoestima* and aprendiendo a hablar reflected senses of identity located intersubjectively in relationship to family, community, labor, and the state, and posed challenges to neoliberal norms of personhood and citizenship. To understand women's citizenship, it is necessary to appreciate the struggles they were waging to maintain some sort of sovereignty over their values and sense of self, and the kinds of resources they drew on in these efforts.

This is one example of how women developed a language of citizenship, rights, and entitlement that they improvised and elaborated on in their individual interviews. They insisted on the importance of gaining voice in the family and household, and the particular importance of issues of language, culture, economics, and gender in their daily lives. They did not emphasize personal transformations in consciousness over and above group political action but rather struggled for voice simultaneously in intimate and public, individual and collective contexts.

In talking about learning to speak and developing *un buen autoestima*, the women debated the intricacies of welfare and immigration reform and the Violence Against Women Act. They debated the ways that practices they saw as North American, for instance in consumer habits or childrearing practices, held both power and danger. They critiqued what they learned about the history of U.S. immigration and poverty policies in the mini-civics classes offered in MUA's leadership training workshops. Women like Cristina, too afraid to speak at their first MUA meetings, later gave testimonies to the English- and Spanish-language media on how the elimination of prenatal care for the undocumented, or the limits placed on welfare and public housing for immigrant victims of domestic violence, would impact their families, and also what it meant for the moral standing of the country.

Concepts like *autoestima* and learning to speak offer a point of entry into the issues of subjectivity and intimate relationships that are implicated in public political life. Men and children clearly fit into this picture as well. Men's positions and preoccupations are as critical as any to a fuller understanding of citizenship as it is experienced or absent day to day in many different communities. Yet Cristina's choice of the "gilded cage" image to represent her dilemma signals that although these women were sensitive to the gendered experience of citizenship, they did not separate their experiences from broader systems of power and inequality that also subordinate men, including immigrant Latinos.

By sharing personal experiences and collective struggle on behalf of one another and the broader community of immigrants, Adela and Cristina explained how they gained the strength to speak up for themselves to their husbands and in-laws, and also to their employers, doctors, teachers, and social workers. Earlier scholarship on Latino cultural citizenship identified the process of articulating a positive group identity and claiming rights as constituting cultural citizenship, and subsequent work in anthropology focused on the role of state power in the subjectification of immigrants.[10] These women's stories link my theoretical concerns with voice and citizenship claims with my experience of collaborative research with Mujeres Unidas y Activas.

In the process of analyzing interview transcripts and field notes, I noticed the importance of points of contact between different social and cultural domains of belonging and entitlement, from the individual to the family to the local community, and the relationship to transnational forces. In these conjunctures individual women came to be understood and to understand themselves as immigrants, wives, mothers, workers, and bearers of rights. The capacity to reframe the cultural common sense of what is taken to be natural or normal, about citizenship in this case, seems to be one of the principal strengths of our discipline and the ethnographic method.

Cristina, Tomasa, and Mariana linked their aspirations to improvements in their own and their children's lives to their hopes for the larger communities to which they belonged. Their perspective of connection to others and their growing sense of their right to belong allowed them to remain optimistic about their own futures and to continue making claims for both equal status and equal services. The intimate and psychological experiences that the women emphasized in their life and immigration stories are more than just a part of their preparation for claiming legal-juridical rights. Rather than being exceptional or marginal, the women's experiences and analyses demand consideration in any analysis of the functioning of U.S. political and social life. This does not mean adopting a view from the margins of citizenship, but rather a reorientation of assumptions about who and what is central to citizenship practice and identity today.

Through the sharing of personal experiences and collective struggle on behalf of one another and the broader community of immigrants, women in MUA gained the strength to speak up for themselves both in and outside of the home, to their husbands and to their children's teachers. Together they identified forces undermining their (and their loved ones') *autoestima* as personal and psychological, and also as economic, linguistic, cultural, and political, ranging from violence in the family to the psychological war they described against immigrants in California today. These transformative processes were neither inevitable nor inexorable, as Esperanza Navarro's unresolved problems exemplify, despite her extended participation in the group (see Chapter 4). Theirs are not simple progress stories of life after migrating to the United States, but rather are complex narratives of diverse, complicated, and often contradictory experiences. Considered collectively, however, the stories suggest important avenues toward understanding subjectivity and transformation in the lives of economically, socially, and politically marginalized women.

The social analyses of women of MUA enrich citizenship theory by extending the domain of citizenship struggles to embrace transnational migrant women's experiences of solidarity, support, conflict, violence, and personal transformation. Interpreted through vernacularized terms like *autoestima* and *aprender a hablar*, the obstacles that immigration, class, culture, and language presented to the women in MUA were transformed into evidence of the strength that women drew from their individual histories and collective identities to claim a space for themselves both in U.S. society and in their own households. As Tomasa eloquently demonstrated, they needed a sense of *autoestima* to assert themselves in their homes and among their peers in order to be able to learn to speak and make sustained public claims for their position and rights in the broader society. Attention to such expressions of citizenship involves recognizing the liberatory potential of citizenship, its exclusionary history, and problematic potential uses in service to antidemocratic political projects as well.

6

Convivencia, Necesidades y Problemas
Vernaculars of Belonging and Coalition

ON AN UNUSUALLY FOGLESS SATURDAY morning in the late spring of 1996, I drove my minivan around a busy block in San Francisco's Chinatown, trying and failing to find a coveted on-street parking spot. At 9 A.M., the neighborhood was already bustling with families arriving from outer city districts and suburbs to do their weekly grocery shopping or visit elderly relatives. After two trips around the block, I double-parked in front of the enormous concrete cube of a 1970s-era public housing complex and dropped off the seven women and small children who were my passengers. As they closed the car doors, I heard their Spanish conversations join the high-volume English and Cantonese exchanges on the sidewalk.

We were late after our crosstown trip from the Mission District, and the women quickly entered the housing complex. Heading to the community meeting room, they left their children in an older multipurpose room where child care was provided. More than a dozen other women were sitting around a U-shaped table with headphones on, trying to help volunteer interpreters figure out how to broadcast Cantonese and Spanish translations to the appropriate participants and waiting for the meeting to begin.

The staff members of the sponsoring community organizations welcomed everyone and asked the late arrivals to introduce themselves to the group. Thus began a summerlong workshop series on women's leadership developed jointly by Mujeres Unidas y Activas and the Chinese Progressive Association (CPA).

The main goal of the training workshops was to develop the leadership skills of and facilitate exchange between Chinese and Latina women across significant divides, including language, immigration status, and educational backgrounds. Before the start of the summer workshops, in the spirit of coalition-building for direct joint political action around issues of shared concern, the participants had spent time considering themes such as domestic and youth violence, education, and housing. They had agreed that they were most interested in understanding and organizing around pending federal immigration and welfare reform legislation.

Each week's session covered a particular topic or issue related to the facts of the immigration and welfare reform legislation and community organizing. One week the activities and discussion focused on getting to know one another, with each woman designing, drawing, and presenting a graphic representation of herself, her nationality, her family, and her immigration experience. Local school district officials and service agency staff people were invited to speak about their work. Labor organizers and community educators led sessions on the basics of grassroots organizing, and how welfare and immigration reform legislation worked its way through local, state, and federal levels of government. One week a community agency's psychologist led a discussion on self-esteem and what it meant for the participants to have, develop, or project a positive sense of themselves. In another session, a community educator offered a full-day workshop covering American ethnic, immigration, and racial history from conquest, annexation of Mexico, slavery, and nineteenth- and twentieth-century immigration waves, to the African American civil rights movement.

These sessions stood out in the women's later reflections on their experiences in the workshops. They were central to the stories women told about how they came to see themselves as part of a greater national citizenship story about the role of immigration, race, and the struggle for rights in the United States. The workshops themselves revealed an important approach to defining political leadership as well: organization staff members facilitated and influenced preliminary discussions among workshop members, but rank-and-file participants from both community groups were charged with defining and addressing major issues of shared concern around which they would like to educate themselves in order to organize collectively to educate other immigrant women and families. The structure of the MUA/CPA workshops and the projects they generated emphasized the education and mobilization of other immigrants for longer-term and larger-scale political change. While lobbying for an after-school program or stop sign may provide a more achievable victory, the building of women's capacities as social analysts and the development of their relationships with one another through *convivencia* ensured what have proved to be much more robust, sustainable organizations long-term (Zlolniski, 2006; García Bedolla, 2005).

This chapter focuses on how the Latina participants shared time and experiences (*conviviendo*) with a group of women they considered profoundly different from themselves. In the course of their conversations, the women came to identify these commonalities in terms of needs (*necesidades*) and problems (*problemas*) they had in common as immigrant women, mothers, and workers. The ideal of meeting citizens' needs resonated deeply with the women's stories about making demands on individuals and institutions on behalf of themselves, their children, and "everyone else" (*los demás*). MUA members' reformulation of citizenship was forged transnationally, drawing on the needs-based agendas and programs of nongovernmental, community-based, and women's organizations in Mexico and Central America (Díaz-Barriga, 1996; Guttman, 1997).

Concepts of basic needs and rights and the interrelated responsibilities of states and citizens are implicit in an emerging pan-American language of citizenship that the women used to describe their expectations, frustrations, and strategies as they sought to claim their rightful place in U.S. society. In such processes, we find new models for what it means to belong and be entitled politically, socially, and culturally in the United States. This resonates with Taylor's call for a "liberatory . . . internationalist and anti-nationalist" concept of citizenship in which the "right to satisfy need becomes dynamic, political and comes into a confrontation with power." Instead of an abstract notion of universal citizenship rights, Taylor argues for the "right to satisfy need," with the limits and definitions of *need* always changing and confronting power (1994, 143). Collectivities such as those formed by the immigrant Latina and Chinese women described here, who demanded not only recognition of their differences, but also the legitimacy of their needs and rights claims, offer important ways of thinking about political and social values in a changing polity.

I was fortunate to be able to observe the first training in the summer of 1996 and one meeting in a subsequent training program in 1999 by participating as the Spanish-English side of a trilingual team of simultaneous interpreters. Since most of the twenty participants were monolingual Cantonese or Spanish speakers (with one notable exception, discussed below), everyone wore headphones, and a Cantonese-speaking volunteer and I worked together to interpret simultaneously for presenters and participants. With the exceptions of myself, one Chinese American male staff member, and a U.S.-born Latina staff member from the agency sponsoring the grant, all the organizers, participants, and guest speakers were Chinese or Latin American immigrant women. For many of the Latina participants, who had an average of less than six years of formal schooling, it was both exciting and challenging to sit for six hours a day in a classroom-like setting in which presentations were given orally, using whiteboards and sheets of butcher paper, and participants were given pencils and notebooks to take notes. The initial plan was to alternate weekly meetings—one week in the Latino Mission District and the next in Chinatown—but the housing project's meeting space proved congenial, and the group met only twice in the Mission District that summer.

In the months following the summer workshops, I drove and interpreted for delegations of participants during visits to local officials and service providers, including members of the county board of supervisors and the head of the county human services office. The women began these meetings by telling the officials about what they had learned about one another in the leadership training, focusing especially on their common needs and problems. Participants from both groups expressed their concerns about the content of the new federal welfare and immigration reform policies and about how the policies would affect immigrants in San Francisco. They emphasized why it was important to divert other local or state monies to cover federal cuts that would disproportionately affect already vulnerable immigrant families, immigrant elders, and battered women. During these visits, both MUA and CPA members provided the officials with concrete stories from their communities. They offered personal testimonials about how public services help immigrant families, including U.S.-born children, and rationales for how such support strengthens the whole local community. They spoke of what they as Chinese and Latina immigrant parents, workers, and community members needed from the state in terms of instrumental public support, and also dignified and humane treatment.

While several Mujeres Unidas y Activas members joked that they felt quite comfortable in the Human Services building, having spent so much time in waiting rooms there over the years, they also stated how remarkable it was to be received with respect at the chief administrator's and various supervisors' offices in City Hall. Officials were limited in terms of what they could promise these delegations in terms of protecting services, but they were attentive, respectful, and engaged with the political actors before them. The elected officials and service providers were themselves African American, Asian, and Latina women, with the exception of one gay white male official. Some were first- and second-generation immigrants who could speak Spanish or Cantonese. The question of public resources and services was urgent, material, and far more than symbolic. However, the demands for instrumental supports were bound up with interrelated issues of dignity and respect underlying group members' formulation of the rights due them as community members.

Caridad Ríos was a forty-year-old native of Lake Chapala in Jalisco, Mexico, who had lived in the United States for more than twenty years at the time of the leadership training. She had worked as a unionized hotel room cleaner and in the garment industry in San Francisco during most of these years and had three children whom she was raising alone. Reflecting on her experiences after the final workshop of the summer, Caridad said she had been impressed by how much the two groups of women had in common. She volunteered that, prior to this experience, she had had little contact with Chinese people and had ridiculed their language when she heard it. After the workshops, she instead focused on what they had in common: "One knows that, well, we have almost the same needs and worries. They also have children, work a lot, and want the best for their children, like us. They are mothers with families like us. They are also hardworking and honest people, just like us."[1]

Caridad's emphasis on the women's shared necesidades was a significant and common theme. These needs included quality education, health care, and housing for their children and themselves, as well as equality of opportunity for their economic survival and a political voice for themselves, their families, and other community members. The discourse of necesidades, instrumental support, and public services also reflected Latin American popular discourses about citizenship and human dignity (Díaz-Barriga, 1996, 2000). In Latin America, urban popular movements that demand of the state such basic social and infrastructural services as pavement, water, and electricity are perhaps the most common and powerful form of grassroots expressions of citizenship, and women play prominent roles.[2] Neither Caridad nor any of the other women I interviewed reported participating in such urban movements in their countries of origin. However, they apparently agreed that there is a significant relationship between self-respect, having one's dignity recognized by others both privately and publicly, and state accountability for providing basic human services. This insertion of expectations of state-funded housing, health care, and education into North American discussions about individual rights and individual obligations was a powerful political move. It was especially significant at a moment when the U.S. government was exponentially accelerating the devolution of welfare provisions not just for immigrants, but for all citizens.

When I interviewed Marta Cordero in September, she was excited about the workshops that she had just completed and was animated and enthusiastic about her experiences in the project. At first I thought that her discussion of shared needs and problems glossed over all differences in a sentimental assertion of sameness: "I had never had anything to do with them before. They are really emotional, just like us. They have many problems. Although ours are such different cultures and such different countries, we are the same in our feelings and way of thinking. Like us, they suffer a lot from racism in this country." Marta's direct reference to racism, however, was a signal that hers was no romantic, idealized view. Instead she rooted her sense of solidarity and identification with her Chinese co-participants not only in the life experiences they shared and discussed in the workshop, but also in a sense of shared history that developed from learning more about immigration, race, and citizenship in the United States. Marta spoke with particular emotion about the session devoted to immigration history, in which a community organizer gave a down-to-earth summary of U.S. conquest and expansion, slavery, and immigration. This was the first time most of the Latina participants had heard a version of the U.S. national story in which they could locate themselves and their experiences. When I asked Marta if she had been particularly impressed by anything during the summer, she replied that yes, some information had really taken her aback:

> For example, the workshop that they gave on immigration . . . it was the one that I liked the most. Because I learned things that I never imagined could exist. For example, . . . these people that they brought from Africa . . . the slaves . . . it seemed so inhuman to me, so unjust. In that moment, I got to thinking that today we are suffering from so much discrimination but we don't think about how back then they lived in such inhumane conditions, so unjustly were they treated. . . . I began to reflect on why people are so, so bad that they treat other humans like animals.

Before this workshop, Marta had never before heard of African slavery or the nineteenth-century xenophobia against European and Asian immigrants. It was the first time she had considered how she might write herself into the national citizenship story. Rather than eliding differences in the experiences of Chinese, Mexicans, and Africans in the United States, Marta identified (but did not generalize) her own experiences of discrimination with those of other people of color, especially African Americans. In doing so, Marta and her colleagues discussed, developed, and practiced the "politics of difference" Iris Marion Young argues is necessary for "equal respect and genuinely equal opportunity for every person to develop and exercise her or his capacities and participate in public life" (Young, 1990, 191, quoted in García Bedolla 2005).

Intersections of Difference and Solidarity

In the course of the training workshops, participants spoke of shared concerns as immigrant mothers, with their self-introductions usually consisting of their names, nationalities, number of children, and length of residence in the United States. Even though so much of their coalitional identity was expressed in terms of their needs as mothers, one participant who was not herself a parent managed to avoid marginalization, in part because she was the only person in the room fluent in both Spanish and Cantonese. An outgoing and personable woman in her sixties, Wei-Ying "Alicia" Chu was born in Panama and lived there sixteen years before moving to China with her family.[3] None of the participants seemed surprised by her life story, and Mujeres Unidas y Activas members made special efforts to speak with her and invite her to their group activities and meetings. In many ways, Alicia embodied the slippery nature of ethnic identity as a coalitional mobilizing tool and an analytical category. In the face of a project that emphasized speaking across the Chinese-Latino divide, thus often reinscribing difference at the same time it sought to emphasize commonalties, she reminded everyone of the flexibility and the social constructedness of ethnic, racial, and national boundaries. Her ability to be both a senior leader of the Chinese women and an ambassador between the two groups of women was not impeded by her lack of status as a mother, which otherwise seemed a principal source of commonalities between the other participants.

In his study of ethnicity and race in the diverse London suburb of Southall, Gerd Baumann (1996) found that, despite dominant discourses portraying culture as both static and neatly circumscribed, the people he interviewed posited multiple identities and communities for themselves and others based on such factors as nationality, religion, local or neighborhood identities, race, and changing identities over time. Iris Marion Young asserts that the daily lived reality of diverse urban life reframes the definition of citizenship, leading away from an insistence on a homogeneous assimilating polity to an emphasis on social differentiation without exclusion (1990, 237).

In the U.S. context, a "politics of difference" is both a racializing and a racialized process. When I heard the women of Mujeres Unidas y Activas using the term *Latina* in group discussions and interviews, I wondered at first to what extent this represented the necessity of adopting one of the racialized big five ethnic categories (white, black, Latino, Asian, Native American). Despite official efforts to normalize the term *Hispanic* in the 1980s, *Latino* has much more popular currency in California. However, I expected to find among immigrants a stronger emphasis on distinctive national identities such as *mexicanas, guatemaltecas,* and *salvadoreñas.* Yet after analyzing the contexts in which they used the term with respect to themselves, others, and a broader immigrant community, it seemed clear that *Latina* was important among many positional identities that the women called on in different contexts.

Latina was a consciously coalitional term that neither diminished nor replaced women's other personal identifiers, such as national identity, immigrant status, domestic arrangements, religion, and social class. When speaking of themselves personally and of their own cultural identity, they most often referred to their nationality of origin, but when referring to issues of collective concern, the terms *latinos, latinoamericanos,* and even more commonly *la comunidad inmigrante*—the immigrant community—were most salient. The specific choices of how and when to deploy such labels are important not only because they reveal the multifaceted and contextualized nature of identity, but because these dynamics also indicate how personal and public, private and political frames of reference are themselves overlapping and mutually constitutive of identity. Patricia Zavella (1996) identified similar dynamics regarding the "complexity of identification" among California Chicanas,[4] while in polyglot Queens, New York, Ricourt and Danta found that *convivencia* in daily life as well as politics was crucial for women to come to identify as Latinas, though they never abandoned their pride of nationality (2003). The diversity and specificity of experiences that the social identity "Latinas" seeks to embrace brings us back to the broader issues of race, ethnicity, and family that frame contemporary discussions of culture, community, and politics in the United States.

Multicultural Understanding and Notions of Citizenship

Modern Western notions of citizenship have sought either to homogenize certain social groups or to exclude them from full citizenship. Young argues that the assimilationist, exclusionary vision of citizenship associated with modern political theorists is rooted not only in racial and class hierarchies but also in gendered notions of citizenship. As do the women of Mujeres Unidas y Activas, Young's discourse of citizenship questions the distinction between the public and private spheres, the masculinity of citizenship as opposed to femininity of home and family:

> European and American republicans found little contradiction in promoting a universality of citizenship that excluded some groups, because the idea that citizenship is the same for all translated in practice to the requirement that all citizens be the same. . . . These early American republicans were also quite explicit about the need for the homogeneity of citizens, fearing that group differences would tend to undermine commitment to the general interests. This meant that the presence of blacks and Indians, and later Mexicans and Chinese, in the territories of the republic posed a threat that only assimilation, extermination, or dehumanization could thwart. . . . [R]epublican exclusions were not accidental, nor were they inconsistent with the ideal of universal citizenship as understood by these theorists. They were a direct consequence of a dichotomy between public and private that defined the public as a realm of generality in which all particularities are left behind, and defined the private as the particular, the realm of affectivity, affiliation, need, and the body. (1995, 180–81)

Latino/a cultural citizenship scholars put forward a notion of cultural citizenship that recognizes that all members of a society seek to claim their rights without being either marginalized or forced to assimilate to hegemonic norms (Flores and Benmayor, 1997). The rights of distinct groups to assert themselves as such is not threatening to the unity of the polity but rather is constitutive of a society that truly struggles to balance diversity, group rights, and broader social solidarity. Whereas most citizenship theory, including discussions of cultural citizenship, refer to people with formal citizenship rights in their country of residence, my interest lies in decentering citizenship studies by examining the theory and practice of citizenship of noncitizen immigrant women in the United States. This research suggests that while legal citizenship is neither undesirable nor irrelevant to discussions of politics and life in a transnational context, defining citizenship exclusively in terms of formal legal-juridical status obscures the multiplicity of ways in which immigrants seek to claim their rights and exercise their obligations as cultural citizens of the United States.

The sense of the whole will change as the borders between ethnic and national histories are crossed and in certain respects dissolved. When one moves beyond [Arthur] Schlesinger's notion of our history and their history and sees instead interconnected histories that interact and mutually shape one another, subordinated histories and dissident traditions become a pathway, not to separatism and fundamentalism, but to a renewed vision of national histories. The inclusion of excluded and marginalized histories offers a vision of the social whole. (R. Rosaldo, 1996, 1041)

Working together in the workshops taught the women about immigration history, legislation, and one another's families and life stories. Many cited this new knowledge and experience as prompting them to strengthen their claims for social belonging and membership in the United States. They based these claims on the notion that marginalization, organization, and activism for inclusion are experiences shared by many current U.S. citizens or their ancestors. Mujeres Unidas y Activas members cited the struggle for citizenship rights itself as the basis of claims for their rightful place in U.S. society. They spoke of the importance of learning about U.S. immigration history as well as getting to know women they had previously deemed totally different from themselves in reformulating their sense of their position and rights.

Esperanza Solórzano reported that the popular history education about immigration, race, and ethnicity in the United States was one of the "best things" about the entire leadership training experience. This was particularly significant for Esperanza because among the MUA members in this training, she was the most willing to verbalize her profound ambivalence about, if not distrust and fear of, both African Americans and American-born Latinos. Like Marta, she was moved personally and politically by the history of African American slavery in particular, as explained by the workshop's popular educator and organizer:

I learned about history. What disturbs me a lot and was always something I wondered about, was the history of black folks, of the laws that enslaved them, taking away even their names, that their children were not citizens. It was one of the classes which affected me the most and I had my hand in the air the whole time with more questions, until Clara Ruz said to go read some book, I don't remember which . . . she even gave us the name of the book. The whole history's there. Because we were so enthusiastic learning about this subject that we kept getting more and more excited asking questions of Maricarmen.

Sometimes the language of necesidades referred not to instrumental needs, but to emotional bonds and relationships stressed by migration. Caridad Ríos had legalized her status under the 1986 IRCA amnesty provisions. After five years of residency, she was eligible for naturalization; she even attended informational sessions on naturalization sponsored by a nonprofit legal services group. Caridad reported having wanted to naturalize, and she had the list of questions in English and Spanish to study, but she feared both the content of the test and the language requirement. Although she remained fearful of the legal process of naturalization, she felt quite settled in the United States. At first she justified her plan to remain permanently in terms of her children's necesidades, their need for their mother's physical proximity:

> I don't believe I'll ever return to my country, because of them. Because how could I leave them? For better or worse they need their mother here, even if they're grown. . . . [I'll leave] only if Clinton runs me out of the country! . . . I have now gotten used to living here. I'd like to go [to Mexico] for a week, at the most, two, because I'm such a clown [fool] now that I get sick to my stomach!

The summer leadership training workshops helped her articulate a legitimate place for herself in the United States. Caridad offered an expansive and inclusive, if somewhat primordialist, notion of American citizenship that contrasted with the exclusivity of classic formulations of who legally belongs in this country:

> This country is made up of immigrants. From the earliest times, immigrants came. . . . Since the very first people arrived, across the Bering Straits from Asia, starting in Alaska, they were immigrants. This country belongs to the whole world. . . . I have worked, now I am receiving food stamps but who cares? I have worked, I have contributed here. . . . Well, during the training, like I told you, everything was very good, because through drawings, talks, writing, cartoons and everything, they made us understand a lot of things that we didn't know . . . the rights that we all have, as human beings, as immigrants, as hardworking people, everything. I did not know a lot of that.

As Caridad's words make clear, this process of claiming a legitimate place for oneself, one's children, and community in an inhospitable nation-state can lead to conflicting or contradictory discursive strategies to define one's own status. Even though Caridad at first based her own desire to remain in the United States on her children's need for their mother, it is clear that she herself did not imagine returning to live permanently in Mexico. She was more than sheepish about this, calling herself a "clown" for embodying the outsider subject-position in her hometown, symbolized by her physical inability to stomach life in Mexico anymore. Although she was now qualified to naturalize, she still referred to her own sense of insecurity with respect to the state, embodied by then-President Clinton, that might try to run her out of the country. Caridad claimed her rightful place in the United States by linking her own decades of contributions as a worker to the history of immigration and the invaluable contributions of other immigrants over time.

Problemas: Productive Encounters with Difference

The women's narratives specifically linked personal changes in their sense of self to the transformation of their ideas about their political identities, roles, and rights in the United States. Intimate needs and problems were not only fodder for solidarity and identification with other women in the leadership training workshops, but the quest for solutions to such problems motivated these women to political engagement as well. Adela Aguirre remembered a moment, after the training had been under way for several weeks, when she finally felt personally engaged in the project and interested in the workshop. The workshop dealt with the concept of self-esteem, what the women thought it meant and how it related to how they felt about themselves, individually and as immigrant women. Although Adela had heard the concept discussed in meetings with the Latina women's group, she cited the power of this experience as what she learned about the Chinese women in this discussion:

> The first time that I really got interested, I think was in the third session [of the workshop], when it was about self-esteem . . . that I began to notice, that I said that yes, they also feel bad, they also have problems. They also go through what I'm going through, so, Adela, what are you complaining about? Yes. That was when I began to get more interested in everything. It was when I began to pay more attention to them. Because I said, I have to learn from them. I have to learn a lot from all my *compañeras*, but even more from them [the Chinese women]. First of all, because they are another, they are another nationality, they have other customs, they have another language. And maybe the nicest thing they made me learn was just that, that I realized that there are people, of whatever origin or whatever nationality that will help you, will motivate you. And you know whose example I really learned from? From Lily—she's the one

in the wheelchair, right? I said, "She's here. Why, if she's here, doing things for her people, and I'm perfectly fine—Can't I do something for mine? Can't I also do something for myself?" So she helped me a lot. That was really motivating for me. . . . I learned a lot from everyone.

Adela formulated self-esteem issues as collective ones that could be shared among women of very different backgrounds and whose solutions lay not in individual life changes but in collective action for social transformation. Adela did not assert that she had to "get herself together" before she could help her community, but rather that both processes needed to occur together in mutually supportive ways. Iris Marion Young (1990) asserts that the daily experience of diverse urban life reframes the very definition of citizenship, leading away from an insistence on a homogeneous, assimilating polity to a "politics of difference" that emphasizes social differentiation without exclusion. In part through such engagement with difference in structured and sustained multiethnic and multilingual encounters, the women came to see themselves as occupying legitimate, significant social roles in the United States as immigrants, mothers, workers, and political agents. The most powerful discursive shift in their own sense of belonging came with increased personal identification with U.S. immigration and ethnic history and with the legacy of the African American struggle in particular. Women credited the history lessons and also what they had learned in the course of life in the United States and in fellowship with one another in their weekly Mujeres Unidas y Activas meetings.

Adela seemed to consider life in San Francisco as well as the workshops to be productive sites for encountering and working through issues of difference. She spoke of how, with the right mindset, just living in the United States provided her with multiple opportunities to "open your mind" to concerns, histories, and people who were different from herself. As an example, she cited her feelings when she watched a television program about Martin Luther King, Jr., and the March on Washington. "If they could do it, why can't we?" she asked herself at the time, without resentment or anger, but rather with surprise at her own identification with African Americans and a civil rights movement she had never before heard about.

This shift in mindset, however, entailed a whole new kind of resistance at the household level for Adela. She described a constant struggle to overcome the influence of her U.S.-born Mexican American husband's racism on her and her son, while also trying to understand how he could have those attitudes despite having grown up in the diverse Bay Area rather than in "a little town in Mexico." "I believe that most of all it was from him that I learned what the word 'racism' means. . . . [In the United States] you are more open-minded, you have more opportunities for everything, and you can learn about more things. So you can't have that mentality. You can't."

Adela repeatedly interrogated the contradictory nature of U.S. pluralism and democracy. According to her thinking, the chance to interact with diverse peoples is one of many opportunities (including educational and economic opportunities) that should preclude the derogatory attitudes her husband espoused. Even though she insists that "you can't" think these things, she knows that her husband has "that mentality." Adela shared stories of her own experiences of poor treatment by white Americans simply because she was Latina, and by some middle-class Latino service providers because she was poor and an immigrant. In other words, Adela was not all that surprised at her husband's prejudices because his attitudes are more normal than exceptional in the United States.

Adela struggled with both the promise of equality and the reality of racism and discrimination that characterize the U.S. national experience. Like Marta, she gently and indirectly addressed my own subjectivity with respect to middle-class, nonimmigrant American racism. Marta did this by abstract references to third-person "others," and Adela, through the example of her husband. In general, I am sure that my own identity softened the language that women used in interviews to describe their experiences and critiques of American racism, though they still found these indirect third-person strategies to make their points while trying to avoid putting me in a defensive position.

Adela's narratives of what she called her husband's *racismo* were intertwined with stories of his abusive attitude toward her. This politicized her personal resistance to him, signaling that "private" arguments between husband and wife can also be part of women's process of claiming cultural citizenship. Adela explained that, without provocation, he would launch into a litany of stereotypes or generalizations about other groups, always beginning with her as a point of departure. Since he considered her to be from Mexico City, he would begin by targeting her, saying, "*Chilangos* are like this" and then expand with comments such as "Los salvadoreños son así" (Salvadorans are like this).[5] Adela did not dwell on the particularities of his comments, but on their overgeneralizing and dehumanizing nature. Resisting his prejudices with the strength garnered from information and experience thus became part of her resistance to his emotional abuse.

She reported being surprised and impressed by how many people in Mujeres Unidas y Activas were from different countries, including Central and South Americans. "Since we all spoke Spanish, I thought we were all from Mexico!" she said, laughing a little. "I felt so good to be spending time with people from so many different places." Participating in the Mujeres Unidas y Activas women's group gave her a position of strength from which to not only resist her husband's prejudices, but also argue back at him with authority. Now, she said, when her husband started insulting Salvadorans or Nicaraguans, "I tell him that the women in the group [from other countries] speak better Spanish than he does." She felt that sharing information and personal experiences with diverse women provided her with strength to resist her husband's hateful comments about her and others:

> But then I said, how strange that one says, why does this only happen to me? And why me? And one makes themselves the sufferer, and one makes oneself out to be the martyr, and one says, "Oh, God, only me, only to me, only to me," and "This and that only happens to me" and "Why does this only happen to me?" But that's not the truth. One always, like me in the group, I saw that, regardless of nationality, we are women and we all have the same problems. As much as in marriage as in society as sometimes spiritually as well. That's the truth."

Adela's stories of coming to identify with other Latinas and people of color in the United States were, of course, complex and multilayered, shaped by her national identity, political views, and domestic life. In addition to addressing gender solidarity and common experiences as women, she discussed the importance of recognizing the cultural differences that were invisible to her until she got to know other immigrant women better. Adela assumed no global or even ethnic sisterhood or solidarity, as she indicated in her discussions of class and cultural diversity among Latinas and between Latinas and other immigrant women. However, her ability to appreciate differences without either trivializing or reifying them positioned her to respond positively to the chance to participate in the leadership training project with Chinese women.

Most of the women I interviewed subsequent to these workshops either asserted directly or alluded to strong prejudices about Chinese people that they held prior to participating in the leadership training. Adela reflected a deep ambivalence about some of her views of Asian people, at one point seeming to ascribe them to a third party, and another time speculating about which attitudes she may have brought with her from Mexico rather than learned in the United States. This ambivalence may have been part of coming to terms with the "model minority myth"—attitudes that may seem complementary on the surface but signal underlying distrust of or hostility toward Asian Americans—or it may have reflected a familiarity with historic prejudices against Asians in Mexico that led to violent attacks on immigrants and a subsequent large-scale Chinese exodus from Mexico in the early twentieth century.

The following passage from her interview conveys the struggle Adela faced trying to articulate her ideas on this topic. The fact that this otherwise eloquent woman's speech became disjointed reflects the genuine difficulty she had articulating her conflicting feelings about Chinese people. She traced the logic and genealogy of her prejudices as she sought to reject them after convivencia, or sharing experiences, with Chinese women. She also linked these views to her own adjustment to the idea of national and other differences among Latinas, as well as between differently racialized immigrant communities:

Another one of the things which really surprised me, because I tell you that in the beginning when I saw people here from Guatemala, from El Salvador, from Honduras, from Nicaragua, I said "Oh! How can this be possible, no?" Imagine how nice it was for me to know that I could work with Asian people, I never could have imagined that. I had never really had much of an impression, neither good nor bad, of them. For me they were simply another group, another class of people, that's about it, just with other customs, another language. . . . But even on this I say, how can it be possible that I had the idea that, there's always someone saying that, "No, if you pay attention, [you'll see that] the Chinese are really united." They, if something happens to one of them, they are all there, and I had not ever seen that until now. I had never seen evidence, that it was true that they are so united, but I had observed living in Mexico was that they are so intelligent and that's why they do so well in all the businesses, and I always said that they were rich. Think of that! Or at least, if not rich, that they lacked nothing. And wouldn't you know, what a surprise to find out that that's not true. It is like with our races, there are people who struggle, who get ahead, who are united. But that's not to say that they all are. . . . That was one thing that I really liked a lot.

Like Adela, Isabel Monreal also spoke of the unique opportunity the training provided to speak across divides of race and language. Although she lived in a public housing project that she described as 75 percent African American and 25 percent Latino, she had not previously had such a chance to spend time with and communicate with non-Latinos. When I asked what she liked best about the workshop experience, she returned to the notion of convivencia:

> Number one, the experience of spending time with two different races, because in this country we Latinos are always separate, the Chinese are separate, the Black people are separate, and all the ethnic groups are separated, divided and what I liked is that for the first time we are, we took a training with different races, with different languages, even though it was really difficult because of the translations—but it still turned out nicely . . . because we know that Latinas just like any other race have the same problems, the same discrimination in this country and that is something that helps us, makes it possible to unite. And when the Chinese have a protest, we Latinos can go support it and when the African Americans protest, we can unite with them and say "we are supporting them" and not because they are a different color or race that they must be protesting for another thing and that's what I learned the most from this group. That we all have the same problems in this country.

Isabel's strong identification with Chinese and African Americans seemed remarkable in a woman who lived in a predominantly African American housing project and who reported being afraid to speak to any of her black and Latino neighbors. Isabel explained that the hostile atmosphere in the public housing development undermined friendships among neighbors in general, but that did not affect her ability to politically identify with African American civil rights struggles and the racism she knew to be directed against all people of color in the United States, and that also affected relations between communities of color like Latinos and blacks. "I pretty much don't start friendships because I don't know them and am afraid, because I don't know how they might be. Because they are always tarred by the fact that people says that blacks are really bad-hearted, and that's really not true, there are many good people too, but because of this same fear, I try not to make friends there [in public housing]."

Isabel regarded her African American neighbors with a mixture of fear and solidarity. She knew that Latinos and blacks are both "tarred" by negative stereotypes. At the same time, there was crime in the housing projects, hers was the only lesbian family and the only non-African American family she knew there, she did not speak English, and she did feel anxiety. She desired convivencia, the opportunity to spend time with and get to know other people of color in particular, but there seemed to be many obstacles to real convivencia with others in her daily experience of urban American life.

Challenges to *Convivencia*

These women's stories reflect how, even in the most diverse American cities, racial and ethnic groups can live alongside one another yet find very little opportunity to interact in meaningful ways or get to know one another well. What is striking is these women's evident interest in bridging the parallel social worlds, and how few opportunities to do so they found in day-to-day life. They repeatedly used the term *convivencia* to describe both their unique opportunity to get to know the Chinese women and their issues and concerns, and the real barriers to forging deeper personal and political connections that remained after the workshops concluded. Language stood in for the multiple barriers to sustained communication and personal connection that the women faced in their work together. As Adela Aguirre explained it, her enthusiasm about the workshops was diminished to a certain extent by the fact that the dialogue was mediated entirely through third parties:

> Yes, that was a really big problem, the languages, because I would have really liked to have been able to talk personally with a Chinese woman and tell her what I feel and how I would have expressed myself with her and it was something that I couldn't do because it's so different with translation, but that was something I wish it could change. . . . What I would like to improve is to give us the chance to spend more time together.

The fact that Alicia Chu's capacity to move socially between the two groups did not actually lead to sustained relationships with the Mujeres Unidas y Activas members revealed some of the internal contradictions of a project that promoted equality without sameness and without addressing thornier obstacles to more egalitarian social relations. Racism and prejudice against immigrants were discussed only in the U.S. context. It would have taken far longer to achieve the mutual trust necessary to consider other attitudes that might have originated in Asia or Latin America. Convivencia was a positive ideal, but also a profoundly difficult one to achieve outside the structured setting of the leadership training. Even in the workshops, where interpretation was readily available, women rarely tried to engage members of the other group in conversation during breaks or lunch. In fact, as Mujeres Unidas y Activas members pointed out, it was difficult to make real connections through an interpreter (particularly a nonprofessional volunteer interpreter).

The women were able to develop new tools for understanding social divisions and potentials for solidarity outside the protected realm of the workshops. However, the moments of stress and disagreement among at least the Latina participants reflect some of the very real global institutional challenges to extending ideas of belonging and citizenship from the community meeting space out into mainstream U.S. political and social life.

In the United States, the term *coalition-building* evokes images of understanding across boundaries of political interest, class, race, language, gender, ability-disability, and/or sexuality. These categories are among the most salient in defining categories of citizenship identity around which political subjectivity and collective agency emerge in contemporary liberal democratic politics (Hall and Held, 1989; R. Rosaldo, 1994). While the formulation of a Chinese-Latina women's leadership training project itself reinscribed U.S. racial boundaries, the women also discussed their own diversity along national lines, immigrant generation, level of education, family structure, physical disability, and sexual preference. While the constant trilingual translation continually marked certain kinds of difference, the content of the discussions and the women's own analysis of their structural location led them to focus on the commonalities of their needs and experiences across ethnic and racial lines.

The experience of working together as Latinas, rather than in groups defined by Latin American nationality, contributed to the women's analyses of their position and rights in the United States. Yet the shared identity they referred to was not a homogenized vision of a uniform community, politics, or experience. Their sense of place and rights was defined out of a new idea of historic relationships to non-Latinas and people of color, with their divergent experiences of struggle against racial, sexual, and national oppression. The workshops structured a multilingual and multiracial "contact zone" in which the women could develop analyses of "how differences and hierarchies are produced in and through contact across such lines" (Pratt, 1993, 88). These women offer a striking comparison to popular American notions of immigrants' coming to feel a part of the United States over time through increasing identification with the state, dominant cultural practices, and social groups. Instead, the women reported a greater sense of belonging in this society as they learned that their experiences of exclusion related them to more insurgent versions of U.S. citizenship. The emergent discourses of Latina immigrant citizenship in women's stories of comparison and contrast with the Chinese women are products of the specific process of dialogue and exchange they experienced with this particular group. In this urban landscape, whether they ever manage more sustained convivencia with one another or not, they remain related through the public health care and education systems and other public institutions, and through a postindustrial service and manufacturing economy dependent on immigrant workers. They also refused to privilege home or family concerns over social or national ones in their understanding of what constituted interests they shared with other immigrant women.

Mujeres Unidas y Activas members articulated their claims for belonging and entitlement in the United States relative not only to codified rights and political institutions, but also in more expansive and processual terms that encompassed emotion, personal relationships, racial oppression, and social movements. In the workshops and their subsequent reflections, the women shared stories of the intersections between their struggles to gain voice outside the domestic sphere and their struggles to gain influence and control over their personal lives. Their choice of narratives indicated that they acted to claim their rights and define their own subjectivity, sometimes alternately and other times simultaneously on individual, familial, community, and national levels.

Herein lies the power of the new models of citizenship suggested in these encounters. As low-income, sometimes undocumented, often non-English-speaking women of color, MUA and CPA members occupied multiple positions and offered diverse perspectives that have been excluded from normative definitions of U.S. citizenship. Yet in discussing, defining, and asserting their common necesidades and problemas as mothers, immigrants, and women in ways that are politically and personally empowering for them, the participants I interviewed revealed the resilient artifice of the public-private dichotomy embedded in Western ideas of citizenship. Taken as vernacular expressions of citizenship, problemas, necesidades, and a more problematized understanding of convivencia constituted bases for coalitions among new citizen-subjects and link the discourses of both Latin American and North American popular movements, especially African American and Asian American liberation traditions. Grassroots social analysts like Adela, Esperanza, and their compañeras suggest that not only is a new, more multifaceted and inclusive citizenship theoretically possible, but that the processes of building on and changing the terms of belonging and entitlement in the United States are already well under way.

7 Remaking Citizenship

Immigrants, Personhood, and Human Rights

> *Cultural citizenship is a process by which rights are claimed and expanded. . . . So-called new citizens—people of color, recent immigrants, women, gays, and lesbians—are not only "imagining" America; they are creating it anew.*
>
> —R. Rosaldo, 1994

THIS BOOK PRESENTS ONE VERSION of a particular story of how a group of immigrant women worked together in a contentious time to write themselves into American history as neither victims nor heroes, but rather as mothers, workers, Latinas, and human beings bearing rights regardless of their gender, class, nationality, or location. In many ways, it is also the story of how this writer, a fifth-generation San Franciscan descended from Irish and German immigrants, found herself learning about the dynamism of American citizenship from women who faced problems common to previous groups of immigrants, as well as legal and political obstacles that her ancestors could never have imagined as newcomers. These women's stories tied them not only to immigrants who came before them, but also to communities around the country where women and men face similar struggles embedded in their own widely diverse local and personal histories. Their work together enacts citizenship as process and practice, collective experience and product of individual personal as well as political transformation. While women came to understand themselves as rights-bearing political subjects through local-level activism and close affective bonds with their compañeras, their experiences of local community life were embedded in their own migration and the global political and economic forces that sought to define them mainly as aliens and laborers, no matter how many years they resided in San Francisco. Their examples are significant in order to understand how marginalized or disempowered citizen-subjects may not only dissent from exclusionary ideologies, but offer resources and models for more inclusive, dynamic, and liberatory political practice.

For all my pride in the "only in San Francisco" ways of my home town, part of what I have learned through this research is that San Francisco is neither truly exceptional nor simply exemplary. Rather it is one important site among many in which we can come to understand the always-contested and shifting terrain of American citizenship. Like San Francisco, other U.S. metropolitan centers are increasingly multicultural, multilingual, postindustrial, and too expensive for low- and middle-income families. As a result, American suburbs and exurbs are increasingly racially and linguistically diverse. Los Angeles, New York, and Miami may vie for the title of "the capital of Latin America," but immigration from Asia, Africa, and Europe is also remaking language, culture, and geography from Anchorage to Omaha and from New Orleans to New Bedford.

I wrote parts of this book while living in the four-hundred-year-old Yankee town of Cambridge, Massachusetts, where local public schools provided information and services in English, Spanish, Haitian Creole, Portuguese, Korean, Mandarin, and Eritrean. The New England cities and towns that were among the original thirteen colonies were reborn at the turn of the twenty-first century when Central Americans, Brazilians, Cambodians, Vietnamese, Russians, Armenians, Cape Verdeans, Ethiopians, Mexicans, and Colombians began taking their place alongside Irish and Italians. This creative metropolitan dynamic, including the conservative, nativist forces that resist it, has been a defining force in U.S. urban life since immigration rates began to rise markedly in the mid-nineteenth century.

Non-English-speaking working-class immigrant women will continue to play increasingly important roles in local community and political life in American cities. Recognizing this requires a reformulation of the image of the Latino immigrant from a surreptitious border crosser or disposable laborer to a politically and culturally active community member and an exemplar of a new American polity. As U.S.-born Latina/os struggle collectively for full citizenship rights, they create a space in which whole new public political actors and subjectivities can emerge, including those largely excluded from legal residency and enfranchisement, such as many migrant Latina/os.

There are several senses in which personhood and citizenship are conflated in the United States. From a legal standpoint, individuals' relationship to the social contract embodied in law grants them a juridical existence in addition to their physical and social existences (Coutin and Chock, 1995). Who is a full person in the eyes of the state as well as in the eyes of her neighbors?

Who really belongs? Who is entitled to rights, services, and benefits? Within modernist theories of the nation-state, juridical citizenship and territorial residence have been presumed to be equivalent; that is, aside from temporary excursions, the geographical location of a nation's citizenry is expected to co-incide with that nation's territorial boundaries, and vice versa (Gupta and Ferguson, 1992).

These notions of legal personhood do not take into account the possibility that individuals who are juridically nonexistent from the perspective of the nation-state might enter that nation's territory for more than a temporary so-journ. When such individuals do arrive, the presumed equivalence of physical existence and legal identity produces contradictory assessments of their per-sonhood. If physical presence within a nation's boundaries gives individuals a claim to legal identity, then the individuals may be juridical persons. If, on the other hand, personhood derives from membership in a polity, they are not legal persons, and the discrepancy between their physical presence and their legal nonexistence can be overcome by expelling them (Coutin and Chock, 1995, 123–24).

National belonging, international human rights, and the responsibilities of states are intertwined in discussions of citizenship, and they point to broader discursive traditions against which the women I interviewed articulated a col-lective vision and also drew other programs and politics. In San Francisco, Central American solidarity and church-based refugee assistance organiza-tions working with Southeast Asian and Latin American communities formed the institutional foundation in the 1980s in which a women immigrants' rights group like Mujeres Unidas y Activas could develop in the 1990s. The early leadership of the group that became MUA comprised a Central Ameri-can woman and a South American woman with high levels of left-wing opposition political experience and with postsecondary education in their countries of origin. Later leaders as well as rank-and-file members did not ar-rive in the United States with such training and experience in political mili-tancy, but they nonetheless arrived from different and often more populist and participatory political traditions. Just as women's groups in the 1980s began asserting that "women's rights are human rights,"[1] in California in the 1990s, immigrant organizations took up the refrain "immigrant rights are human rights" in their efforts to claim a strategic legal and moral position from which to assert their rights and seek new allies (Brown, 2004; Merry, 2006b, 2006c).

MUA's activism rooted itself firmly in at least three activist traditions: human rights, civil rights, and women's rights. It joined previous generations of U.S. and Latin American women's rights groups that grew out of struggles for political, social, and economic rights, including community organizing to meet basic needs. Each of these political traditions has relied not only on a discourse of rights but also on the importance of telling individual and collective stories of oppression and survival to mobilize peers and allies toward shared goals. Most of the women I observed and talked with immigrated to the United States after the 1970s, when the Latin American human rights and women's movements were organizing women and communities around issues of health, reproduction, economic development, social justice, and violence, and where the language of human rights has been applied to these demands as well.

The norms and language of human rights discourse date back at least to the founding of the United Nations (UN) in San Francisco in 1945, and were codified in the Universal Declaration of Human Rights in 1948. Nongovernmental institutions both contributed to and were shaped by liberal post–World War II and cold war internationalism, anticolonial movements for national liberation, and third world peoples' civil rights movements in the United States. In particular, Latin American states and U.S. nongovernmental institutions were responsible for the central role played by human rights ideals and standards in the founding and development of the UN (Merry, 2006b, 85–86). By the 1970s, the basic concepts of human rights were popularized, and institutions developed to the extent that international human rights networks were able to effectively publicize and mobilize across borders and pressure states, both north and south.

The deployment of dramatic personal testimony to mobilize political support is basic to most contemporary human rights pratices. With the proliferation of transnational networks comes an emphasis on the reporting and sharing of facts alongside personal experiences. Individuals' stories bring the facts to life. Pairing such testimonies with empirical data is politically potent. But the trouble with the rights framework, as opposed to previous discrimination or development modes of orienting international women's politics, lies in part in this reliance on the power of individual narratives to describe what might otherwise be analyzed structurally or institutionally as injustice and inequality among nations, races, and social classes (Merry, 2006b, 184). Although deployment of *testimonios* by Mujeres Unidas y Activas might have fallen into this pattern of depoliticizing oppression by individualizing suffer-ing, the collective context in which women shared their stories and promoted analyses of racial, class, and cultural inequality, as well as women's oppres-sion, encouraged rather than defused political activism. These stories as well as the context in which they are told are central to new forms of politics and citizenship at the end of the twentieth century and the late modern period (Plummer, 1995).

The common concepts that women referred to in discussing their sense of their rights and social position made up their vernacular of belonging and entitlement and defined their ideas of cultural citizenship (R. Rosaldo, 1994). These citizenship stories spoke simultaneously to intimate, community, and political relationships and claimed culture and language as sources of pride and distinction but not as motives for disengagement or alienation from broader U.S. social life. The interaction of these issues and dynamics in individual lives and collective organizing activities were critical for understanding the multi-layered, multidimensional notion of cultural citizenship arising from analy-ses of the women's experiences. The combined effects of economic and political globalization, devolution of industrial welfare states, and postcolonial civil rights, human rights, and feminist movements all signal the need for more dy-namic and practice-oriented approaches to understanding citizenship (Bru-baker, 1989; Taylor, 1994; Turner, 1990, 1993; Somers, 1993). From this perspec-tive, MUA members' citizenship processes should be of interest to nonimmi-grant citizens and other marginalized social groups, including those most often excluded from citizenship studies, such as children, the disabled, and the poor (Massey, 2004), as a model of inclusive citizenship that seeks to expand rights without reinscribing new forms of exclusion (Lister, 1997).

From Local Organization to National Leader

Mujeres Unidas y Activas has undergone important changes in its first twenty years of history. In 1998, the group expanded geographically, opening an Oakland office to serve the increasing numbers of Latina immigrants in the deindustrialized East Bay suburbs. Not only were immigrants arriving directly to the East Bay from Mexico and Central America, but many MUA members and staff had themselves moved across the Bay Bridge in search of more affordable housing. When its founding sponsor organization, the North-ern California Coalition for Immigrant and Refugee Rights and Services, closed its doors in 2001, MUA entered a difficult period now sometimes referred to as the "crisis," during which the group struggled to survive and the staff worked without pay until another fiscal sponsor was found. By mid-2002, MUA had formed a strategic planning committee made up of staff, members, and outside consultants to evaluate and plan for development into an independent nonprofit organization. The group that was firmly centered in San Francisco's Mission District in the 1990s and had been dependent on a multicultural coalition of service providers became an independent regional organization, a model and a resource to emerging Latina immigrant groups around the country.[2]

The coalition infrastructure had provided accounting, fundraising, and grant writing and provided the Mujeres Unidas y Activas staff with up-to-date information on current lobbying campaigns, legislative issues, and general political orientation to U.S. governmental systems and structures. During the mid-1990s, the only computer in the MUA office belonged to the home health and domestic work economic development project initiated by the group Manos Cariñosas (Caring Hands). For the first few years following the founding of the Manos Cariñosas project in 1994, the only non-Latina staff person was in charge of this project and, in turn, of the computer. MUA members and staff wanted to learn more about computers and the Internet, but felt unable to do so on their own. Given the chronic stress on resources in the nonprofit sector, it is understandable that the sponsoring coalition was loath to duplicate services available elsewhere (such as computer classes) and provide the materials and support that doing so would entail without additional resources to support the services. However, the impact was that for its first ten years MUA remained dependent on the mainly non-Latino coalition staff for most of its fundraising, grant writing, legal and political news, written communications, and even word processing and database management.

The relationship was mutually beneficial in that Mujeres Unidas y Activas provided the coalition with a grassroots base of support, as well as a source of mass mobilization and working-class Latina political analysis that the coalition's leadership valued. The benefits for MUA included institutionalized relationships with non-Latino and nonimmigrant organizations and their associated political experience and resources. In addition, staff members were able to focus on political education and organizing to a much greater extent than if they had to do their own fundraising, accounting, and administrative tasks. With the closing of the coalition, however, MUA had to make large jumps to independence quite a bit sooner than expected.

MUA members identified women's needs for economic independence and labor rights as critical issues the organization needed to address. Since 1994, the Manos Cariñosas / Caring Hands Workers Association project of MUA has offered job training, employment referrals, and peer support for women to help them understand their rights as workers and develop new job skills. Women integrated their concerns as workers into their collective work and citizenship claims, specifically their issues as informal service workers and domestic workers excluded from most labor protections.[3] As the Manos Cariñosas project grew and developed, MUA began collaborating with the predominantly Latina Women's Collective of the San Francisco Day Laborers program and People Organizing to Demand Environmental and Economic Rights (PODER) to support diverse women workers with job development, peer support, legal advocacy, and training in skills such as negotiations with employers. At the U.S. Social Forum in Atlanta, Georgia, in the summer of 2007, women from these San Francisco groups participated in the formation of the National Alliance of Domestic Workers. Building in part on its work on state overtime pay legislation for domestic workers in California coalitions with Filipina domestic workers and others, MUA helped organize the first National Domestic Workers Congress in June 2008 in New York City (Buckley and Correal, 2008), now serves as the fiscal sponsor for the national group, and has helped represent the National Alliance at international congresses in Venezuela and South Africa.

MUA and Immigrant Activism Post-2001

Before September 11, 2001, MUA members' concerns for the rights of immigrant youth centered on guaranteeing immigrant children equity in health care, education, and social services and protecting the integrity of families in the face of hostile immigration policies. After the terrorist attacks on the World Trade Center and the Pentagon, immigrant youth became increasingly vulnerable to both militarization and the reconfiguration of immigrants as not just foreigners, but also as potential threats to security. The intersection of two pieces of federal legislation passed in 2001—the No Child Left Behind Act and the Patriot Act—enabled new federal incursions into local political life. Provisions of the Patriot Act made records and documents at all levels of government accessible to any federal agency involved in homeland security, including immigration bureaucrats. In the months leading up to the U.S. invasion of Iraq, the MUA women debated the implications of such federal acts at the local level and testified at school board meetings to oppose the release of names and contact information for public school students to military recruiters.[4] The San Francisco school board agreed to prohibit the practice.[5]

These events condensed many of the ironies and contradictions of contemporary immigrant life in the United States. Women at this Mujeres Unidas y Activas meeting included babysitters, housekeepers, hotel room cleaners, restaurant workers, garment workers, wives, and stay-at-home mothers of young children. Many worked for low wages in difficult conditions. Their labor facilitated the work of their employers, whose children and elders the immigrant women cared for, and directly contributed to the tourist- and service-based economy of San Francisco. Many were undocumented, receiving no benefits in return for payroll taxes withheld, were without the protections provided by organized labor or legal immigrant status, and were doubly disenfranchised because they were unable to vote in the United States, where they resided, or in their home countries because of the lack of absentee voting rights and procedures.

Yet the children and youth of their community, whether citizens, legal residents, or undocumented immigrants, were all subject to the threat posed by a warring state in search of its enemies. Immigrant youth in the most precarious positions were particularly vulnerable to recruitment, since fighting for the U.S. military in wartime is a historically important avenue to citizenship. In March 2003, José Antonio Gutierrez was one of the first U.S. soldiers (some sources name him as the first) to die during the invasion of Iraq. He was an orphan and Guatemalan refugee who first crossed the border into the United States illegally at age fourteen, and who was not granted U.S. citizenship until after his death.[6] Subjects of the psychological war against immigrants by parts of the United States, immigrant parents of all legal statuses faced the real possibility that their children might now serve in that same state as soldiers—or, as one woman put it at that MUA meeting, "carne de cañon" (cannon fodder).

Belonging and Citizenship in a Sanctuary City

The particular vulnerability of immigrant youth due to their marginal citizenship status again became a matter of public debate in San Francisco in 2008. The ensuing debates over local responsibility to these young people, especially the undocumented and unaccompanied among them, reveal the contradictions of a notion of immigrant citizenship that configures only the economically contributing, law-abiding, and nonreproducing immigrant adult as worthy of social acceptance (Coutin and Chock, 1995). In the United States today, unaccompanied children continue to face detention, sometimes with adults, and deportation without the right to state-funded legal representation or even basic guarantees of the proper review of their claims for asylum or residency. Legal advocates and academic experts cite bias against children's asylum claims by a system that refuses to recognize the differences between experiences of violent persecution by minors and adults, as well as youths' incapacity to articulate their claims in effective legal narratives, and the levels to which migrant young people may be manipulated and abused by traffickers, gang members, or even family members (Bhabha and Schmidt, 2008).

San Francisco prides itself on being a progressive and welcoming city (De León, 1992). It cites the 1989 City and County of Refuge ordinance as an example of its largesse.[7] However, current debates over San Francisco's identity as a sanctuary city reveal the fragility and tensions underlying local ideals of multicultural acceptance and solidarity with migrants. The Sanctuary Ordinance was the result of lobbying by local Central American refugees and their allies during the 1980s. They succeeded in obtaining passage of the original ordinance and subsequent administrative rules prohibiting local governmental cooperation with federal immigration officials based on the argument that undocumented people needing health care or protection from police were avoiding city agencies, putting public health and safety at risk.

Citing the 1989 ordinance (and some might also argue, continuing his efforts to raise his national political profile after championing same-sex marriage), San Francisco Mayor Gavin Newsom took a strong public stand against human trafficking in 2006. He focused on protecting young Asian women and girls who were being brought from overseas to work in the local sex industry. While the mayor's high-profile public statements on behalf of trafficked Asian women and girls led to little concrete progress, the emphasis on compassion and non-prosecution of migrants provided a notable example of how sanctuary was usually discussed by liberal and nonimmigrant San Franciscans.

In 2007 and 2008, news of Immigration and Customs Enforcement (ICE) raids and deportations around the country were in the news, striking fear into immigrant communities. Alarmed by the chilling effect this might have on the reporting of crimes, including domestic violence, child abuse, and labor violations, the mayor's office announced a public awareness campaign of San

Francisco's sanctuary policy on April 2, 2008. The renewed effort was unveiled at a City Hall press conference, and for months afterward, the brightly colored, multilingual posters, bus stop advertisements, and radio and TV public service announcements raised the visibility of San Francisco as a sanctuary city.[8] One month after the mayor's press conference, and the day after the 2008 May Day immigrant rights rally, ICE agents raided eleven outlets of the El Balazo Bay Area chain of taquerias, detaining sixty-three undocumented workers, including unaccompanied minors, and precipitating local mobilization in support of the workers and in opposition to the mass raids (Knight, 2008; Camayd-Freixas, 2008).

The tensions in San Francisco's progressivism and the fragility of liberal solidarity with immigrant neighbors was about to explode in the context of mass raids and deportations of thousands of Latin American workers around the country. Just as the tenor of the local immigrant rights movement in the mid-1990s was shaped by statewide anti-immigrant politics and national anti-poor-people policies, local debates about San Francisco's commitment to its immigrant population's rights occur today in a stark national political context. Often it is difficult to get news about these events; they are shrouded in secrecy, and the immigration court system is far more opaque than the true judiciary system. In one of many coordinated invasions of workplaces with large undocumented workforces around the country, a court interpreter broke ranks and many professional codes to publicize the details of a May 12, 2008, raid by 900 ICE agents at the largest U.S. kosher meatpacking plant in Postville, Iowa, a town of fewer than 2,300 residents. With 697 arrest warrants in hand, agents missed the late-shift workers but managed to arrest 390 mainly Guatemalan and Mexican men and women. The women were held in the county jail, but the men were removed to what one court interpreter described to a U.S. congressional subcommittee as "a concentration camp" set up at a cattle fairground outside the town limits (Camayd-Freixas, 2008, 6). Reporters and photographers were barred from the camp. In the following days, the detainees, most of them indigenous Mayans with limited Spanish and no literacy skills, were paraded through the immigration court's "judicial assembly line" in hand and foot shackles (Camayd-Freixas, 2008, 9). Even though they were accused without any precedent with the crimes of felony identity theft, "[i]n every instance, detainees who cried did so for their children, never for themselves," reported the court interpreter (Camayd-Freixas, 2008, 9). The town's economy and its public education ground to a halt, as migrants fled the

MUA member and her grandchild protesting immigrant raids at San Francisco ICE offices, August 22, 2008

March to ICE offices to protest immigration raids, August 22, 2008

area and families took sanctuary in the local Catholic church. Like the El Balazo workers in San Francisco, whose case the interpreter referred to in his statement, the detainees who managed to obtain conditional releases (usually because their spouses remained detained and there was no one to care for their children) were still wearing GPS ankle bracelets many months after their arrest. Media reports discussed the profound impact of such raids on local communities from Georgia to Iowa, where significant portions of neighborhoods and workplaces simply disappeared after *redadas* (literally, roundups), either into the hands of ICE or deep underground to escape detention. The disruption to family life and individuals was perhaps even more profound, with detained parents losing custody of their children, sometimes forever. In Missouri, one raid on a poultry processing plant in 2007 led to the detention of 136 workers, including one single mother who said the state authorized the adoption of her child to an American family against her express wishes (Thompson, 2009).

Susan Coutin describes the shift in attitudes toward immigrants "from restriction to inclusion to suspicion" as immigrant rights advocates responded

March to ICE offices to protest immigration raids, August 22, 2008

to exclusionary immigration laws with arguments claiming de facto citizenship status based on their residence and the extent of their social and economic contributions (2007, 201). Despite their successes in reminding elected officials that one does not need to be a citizen to be a constituent, they still remained vulnerable to extreme state surveillance and criminalizing, par-

Rallying outside ICE offices in San Francisco to protest immigration raids, August 22, 2008

ticularly after further restrictive legislation and the increase in ICE raids beginning in 2006. One local manifestation of the shift from inclusion to suspicion, and many Americans' profound distrust and fear of Latin American migrants and young men of color in particular, is the debate today in San Francisco over the meaning of sanctuary and the rights of undocumented youth to the same treatment as other minor San Franciscans charged with crimes.

In the summer of 2008, the *San Francisco Chronicle* wrote a series of articles exposing local juvenile justice officials for following the strictures of the City of Refuge ordinance and subsequent administrative rules by not notifying ICE officials about undocumented minors in their custody. Juvenile probation officers, public defenders, and administrative officials were seen as responsible for endangering the local population by treating undocumented minors like other youth offenders, placing them in group homes or rehabilitative programs, supporting them in legal efforts to legalize their status, and in some cases returning them directly to their countries of origin. However, after several violent crimes, including a triple murder, were attributed to undocumented men who had been in the juvenile justice system as minors, and a youth probation officer was detained in the process of putting two Honduran minors on a flight home, the sanctuary policy came under attack by the families of murder victims, the U.S. Attorney's Office, and members of the general public.

The mayor reversed the protections of Sanctuary Ordinance for any accused minors, while claiming to maintain his support for the other provisions of it because "we must always keep in mind that the underlying purpose of the sanctuary-city policy, going back nearly 30 years and encompassing five San Francisco mayors, is to protect public safety" (Newsom, 2008). While public defenders and juvenile probation officers emphasized that many of the youths were themselves victims of trafficking, abandonment, or abuse and could not return safely to their home countries, there are no provisions in place to safeguard the rights of youth who are turned over to ICE, nor is there a way to track them or the dispositions of their cases once they disappear into federal custody. The mayor's office began intervening even more aggressively in juvenile justice administration after the city's Immigrant Rights Commission reiterated its support for the Sanctuary Ordinance,[9] and the Juvenile Court and probation officers decided to treat one abandoned undocumented minor in custody as needing services rather than criminal prosecution (Van Derbeken, 2008a). The mayor's office asked the juvenile court to hold that boy for two days prior to placing him in foster care, during which time ICE officials removed him from the Youth Guidance Center and began deportation proceedings against him (Van Derbeken, 2008b).

Mujeres Unidas y Activas and other community groups mobilized in defense of San Francisco's identity as a City of Refuge and refigured sanctuary as a question of justice in the context of global forces that simultaneously dismember family units, precipitate migration, promote the exploitation of children, and prevent the legalization of many migrants. The official emphasis on the Sanctuary Ordinance as a humanitarian response to immigrants as victims, as well as an administrative measure in service to law enforcement, made sanctuary vulnerable to precisely the scenario that unfolded in San Francisco in 2008. When the right of undocumented people to live in San Francisco without fearing their local officials and agencies is based on humanitarian protection of certain types of victims or, even more perversely, as strictly a way to improve policing of these communities, it will be rescinded as soon as immigrants move outside their prescribed roles. Given that contemporary geopolitics configure undocumented migrants as inherent threats to security, the claiming of rights and recognition by immigrants may appear to be a Sisyphean endeavor. In this context, what does it mean to recognize the discourses and practices of immigrant women activists as resources for new ways of thinking about and doing citizenship?

Citizenship Acts, Subjectivity, and Rights

The new articulations and renewed practices of citizenship I observed in San Francisco in the 1990s, and continue to notice today, entailed a form of empowerment that worked individually and collectively, at home and in the public spheres of the economy, social services, and politics. By inserting intimate and subjective realms of experience into the politics of immigrant activism, these women offered a model that both incorporated and moved beyond the constraints of liberal democratic rights discourse about citizenship. By speaking in terms of needs, respect, and a redefined version of self-esteem that countered the hyper-individualism of "rights talk," they also modeled new discourses that foregrounded issues of gender, race, class, and culture as equally important political as well as identity issues. This is not the narrow identity politics of the post–cold war period of resurgent economic liberalism (Hobson, Berggren, and Fraser, 1997) but rather an example of how the struggle for cultural recognition need not eclipse political activism for economic justice and class solidarity. Such citizenship is built through individual and collective action to address immediate needs and also entails a vision of a more secure cultural and economic future for individuals, their families, and their neighbors. Efforts that focus on issues of gender, language, and cultural identity that are implicated in class identities and economic issues are models for the vision and programs of a new politics integrating race, class, culture, and gender. Such efforts assume, however, very different things about the relationships between individuals, families, communities, and larger political groupings and institutions than do the dominant notions and institutions of U.S. citizenship.

The popularization of liberal democratic notions of rights in the post–World War II period has contributed to a narrowing of our language of political rights to a hyper-individualized concept of self-fulfillment without any sense of relationship or responsibility to community or national welfare—what legal scholar Mary Ann Glendon (1991) calls the superficial and simplistic "rights talk" of the sound bite in the United States in the 1990s. She suggests that women and immigrants, among other social entities, offer alternative discourses on rights and responsibilities in the home and the community that reinforce the importance of the collective, of social relatedness, and that individual and social fulfillment are intimately linked. The themes of rights, responsibilities, trust, and mutual support that arose in my interviews and during MUA meetings were exemplary of just the type of counter-rights discourse that Glendon advocates. Cultural geographer Doreen Massey (2004) suggests that cosmopolitan local communities and urban areas like London (and San Francisco) demand a reconfiguration of nation-state-centric formulations of rights and obligations into more complex, transnational, and multilayered "geographies of responsibility."

Local Citizenship in Global Context

Local immigrant rights advocates in the United States entered the new century from a not altogether different position than they occupied in the previous decade, but the broader political context had shifted. The shifts were transnational in scope and seemed sudden and violent. However, like the forces driving individual women to immigrate, the political and economic context was a product of decades-old developments.[10]

Since I began this research in 1996, the last of the Central American guerrilla wars came to a formal end, while state-sponsored terror against youth in El Salvador and Guatemala made corpses of young people derided as "gangbangers" deported from the United States. The Nicaraguan and Central American Relief Act (NACARA) provided an important avenue for amnesty for many Nicaraguans, Guatemalans, and Salvadorans who had been living without documents in the United States. International narcotics trafficking gave transnational military institutions a new focus and criminalized low-income and ethnic minority young men, while "narco-terrorism" led to military operations in Colombia at a scale that had not been seen since the wars in Southeast Asia. A new insurgency in southern Mexico that began in Chiapas claimed cultural and political rights for indigenous Mexicans long silenced by internal colonial conditions, official nationalist ideologies, and institutionalized racism.

In large part as a response to early-twenty-first-century anti-immigrant politics, Latino voter registration and turnout climbed steadily after 1996, while overall U.S. voter turnout declined. Latino Californians helped elect President Clinton in 1996 and oust Governor Wilson in 1998, and they carried new Latino state legislators into office in each election. While Latinos may compose less than 10 percent of registered voters nationally, the Latino vote can swing elections in the four states richest in electoral college votes— California, Florida, Texas, and New York—and may thereby come to determine presidential elections (Davis, 2000). The extent to which both Democratic and Republican parties and candidates in the subsequent presidential elections spoke to Latino organizations, hosted mariachis at rallies and conventions, and spoke broken Spanish in stump speeches represents a notable, albeit cynical, turnabout from the hostile rhetoric that my informants described.[11]

However, the national impact of California's anti-immigrant discourse has been great, fueling copycat movements to end bilingual education and affirmative action and restrict access to driver's licenses and public higher education in other states (Bacon, 2008). In the first seven months of 2000, the bodies of seventy-nine people who died trying to cross the border into Arizona were located in the desert (Sheridan, 2000). U.S. politicians and border vigilantes, such as the paramilitary Neighborhood Ranch Watch, called for increasing militarization of the border (Martínez, 2000). In 2005 Minutemen vigilantes remilitarized the U.S.-Mexico border, backed by increased popular sentiment that incursions even of workers from Mexico constituted potential security threats.

These events also had a significant impact on electoral politics in Mexico. New democratic state and nongovernmental institutions allowed for the expression of popular discontent embodied in Vicente Fox's slick North American campaign organization and slogan "¡Ya! ¡Basta con el PRI!" that overturned seventy-one years of one-party rule in Mexico. For the first time in Mexican electoral history, presidential candidates explicitly focused on women, who made up 52 percent of the electorate, as key voters (Thompson, 2000). As candidate Francisco Labastida said to a rally of party women during the 2000 presidential campaign, "You have the power. . . . You will decide the next president of Mexico!" (Sheridan, 2000, A1).[12] For the first time, all three parties also acknowledged the legitimate political role of Mexican citizens who lived in the United States in Mexican politics.[13] In June 2005 the Mexican legislature passed historic measures allowing Mexicans in the United States to vote by mail in the 2006 national elections.

In the United States, where just a few years earlier candidates from both parties decried the immigration problem, so-called Hispanic voters were dubbed the "soccer moms" of the 2000 national elections, replacing affluent suburban white women as the targeted voters of both parties. Then-candidate George W. Bush, from the party of most ardent immigration reform advocates, made a point of speaking to Latino organizations, using Spanish phrases in his speeches, and making frequent references to his Mexican American sister-in-law and her children. More substantively, he promised to address Latino complaints about long application backlogs at the INS and immigration reforms (such as section 245i discussed in Chapter 2) that attempted to separate petitioners for residency from their immediate family members (Janofsky, 2000; Sarkar, 2000). While the events and aftermath of September 11, 2001, led the Bush administration and the national leadership of both political parties to step away from the question of how to regularize the status of undocumented workers, that question was back on domestic and diplomatic agendas by 2005.

The stories of the members of MUA are exceptional and exemplary at the same time. Extreme or dramatic as some might seem, others are familiar to many other immigrants. Many immigrants of diverse national backgrounds confront inequalities manifested in everyday social interactions, in economic life, and in state surveillance. Women and men of varying immigration statuses and duration of residency live, work, pay taxes, raise children, and serve in the military, all without publicly recognized equal rights. As long as U.S. immigration policy prevents the naturalization of so many migrants, depending on their nationality, social class, and original immigration status, there will be large classes of immigrants for whom acquiring naturalized citizenship is a decades-long process. Collective actions such as May Day marches along with more personal and everyday acts may be understood as strategic direct challenges, based on more universal claims to human rights, to the state's monopoly on authority over citizenship. Recognition of systematic state injustices against certain populations calls into question the state's legitimacy in moral as well as political terms. In 2006 advocates for humane immigration politics and policies linked their struggle to previous national and international struggles against state-sponsored injustice. So it was in 2006 that immigrant rights Web sites invoked the admonition of Martin Luther King, Jr.: "Never forget that everything Hitler did in Germany was legal."

Public recognition of the emerging electoral power of Latina/os at the turn of the twentieth century both fed anti-immigrant xenophobia and bolstered the confidence of activists about the legitimacy of their claims. The sense of humor and creativity that I often witnessed in group meetings and social events also emerged in the public realm during this period, whether in the form of humorous popular theater skits or of political manifestations drawing on cultural resources. This alludes to another level in which the cultural gets deployed in citizenship as process and practice, and how small collectivities like Mujeres Unidas y Activas make their challenge to citizenship norms visible and audible outside the immigrant community in which they spend most of their time. For example, domestic workers from all over the Bay Area marched and demonstrated on behalf of a housekeeper who was suing her former employers for years of back wages in front of a mansion in the leafy suburb of Atherton, one of the wealthiest Zip codes in the nation. The march was led by members of MUA, including one former rank-and-file leader who has since become a full-time paid organizer for the Women's Collective of the San Francisco Day Laborer's Program. The alliance between Mujeres Unidas y Activas, the Women's Collective, PODER/POWER (People Organizing for Workers and Economic Rights), and Filipina, African American, and Caribbean women across the country played a central role in the formation of a national alliance and movement for domestic workers' rights. At the first National Domestic Workers Congress in New York City in June 2008, immigrants from Mexico, Central America, the Caribbean, India, and the Philippines representing more than ten U.S. cities shared their work and organizing experiences in more than five simultaneously translated languages, much like MUA's leadership trainings with CPA in San Francisco, though on a much larger scale. Together they represented their concerns in demonstrations on the streets and effective media work, as well as in lobbying state legislatures for specific labor reforms and protections (Buckley and Correal, 2008).

While some of the women I interviewed and observed in 1996 no longer participate in weekly MUA meetings, many contribute to political and social life in San Francisco in other arenas, such as community groups, schools, churches, and labor rights groups. Other women who no longer come to meetings laughingly describe themselves as "remote-control" members willing to be called on for mobilizations or special events in times of crisis, such as the heated debate in spring 2006 about specific national immigration reform proposals that local immigrant rights groups opposed.

One such special event took place in early 2007 as part of MUA's efforts to hold elected officials accountable to immigrants as local residents, regardless of formal nationality or status. Women from MUA, the Day Laborer's Program, and some independent media reporters gathered in the landscaped public gardens in front of Diane Feinstein's Pacific Heights mansion at 7 A.M. on the senator's birthday. The uninvited guests had decided to honor her with the Mexican birthday morning serenade "Las Mañanitas." The serenade tradition involves arriving unannounced in the middle of the night or early in the morning to sing on the street, awaking those inside, who listen discreetly until the singing is done and then invite the singers in for coffee and pan dulce (sweet bread). Senator Feinstein never emerged from her house that morning, but those present kept singing the song over and over again. The senator's husband, businessman and University of California regent Richard Blum, eventually came out to tell the crowd that the senator was still in bed and would not be joining them. The demonstrators asked that he listen to their remarks about the bill in order to share them with his wife, which he did, bringing the demonstration to a relatively quiet resolution.

These are a few examples of the many ways women used creative protest and mobilized their cultural traditions and identities in support of their struggles for social justice and political recognition. If we admit that citizenship is a cultural field including but not limited to legal institutions and forms, these acts constitute an important new infusion into American citizenship, not a threat to it.

Remaking Citizenship

One of the results of converging neoliberal political and economic policies has been the emergence of discourses of globalization, transnationalism, and post-nationalism in both academic and policy settings. Global economic institutions argue that liberty in the new millennium requires fewer barriers to the free flow of capital, if not workers, and the development of regional free trade zones is the result. Local actors in turn invoke international political norms to bolster claims on their own states. For example, beginning in the 1990s, immigrant rights advocates, like women's rights advocates before them, began using human rights language to pressure the liberal states in which they resided. Globalization may have spawned a language of world citizenship, and people's lives may be lived across and between national boundaries, but political, legal, and civil citizenship continues to exist in relation to nation-states. Today's discussions and debates of academics about whether citizenship is flexible, cultural, post-national, transnational, local, global, and so on do not diminish the power of the liberal definitions of citizenship in civic life and political discourse.

Both academic and political discussions of citizenship need to include those who are legally excluded from the category of citizen. There are moral as well as intellectual rationales for recognizing immigrant, noncitizen, and other marginalized people's claims to political representation and cultural equality both within and outside of traditional liberal democratic arenas. Either citizenship and nationality laws need to be revamped to acknowledge the permanence and legitimacy of all long-term residents of a nation-state, or local communities need to continue forcing the issue by instituting local forms of enfranchisement, such as the increasingly common practice of allowing all residents of a municipality to vote in specific elections affecting them, such as school board elections.

Cultural studies of citizenship and critical feminist studies of citizenship provide two main foundations for such new theory, first by asserting the agency of those traditionally excluded from the definition of full citizenship and the legitimacy of new claims for equity and enfranchisement, and second by forcing the particularly dicey issues of colonialism, race, gender, immigration, language, and sexuality into discussions normally governed by seemingly transparent legal categories and definitions. Perhaps the contradictions between the emancipatory expectations promoted by liberal democratic ideology and the historically stratified and exclusionary ways nation-states have codified citizenship law are inherent and unavoidable, but this is not the level at which vernacular debates over political power and participation occurred in my fieldwork experiences. A politically engaged ethnography of traditionally excluded and marginalized citizens and their experiences of belonging, entitlement, institutional discipline, and personal agency will help ground such social theory in the real lives and analyses of those most often silenced by both political and academic debates.

Studies of immigration, cultural citizenship, motherhood, and domestic, social, and economic violence need to consider the issues and what they mean for analyses of politics, gender, and subjectivity. *Autoestima* is about both intimate and collective processes of coming to value oneself and the contributions of one's community in the broader society. When the women referred to the importance of *información*, they spoke of the power of knowledge, particularly of legal processes and state services, and how difficult it is for working-class and poor people in this country to access the good information that they need to advocate for themselves, their children, and their community. *Apoyo* is the dynamic peer support that friends, sisters, neighbors, and children provide women as they create a new life and sense of self in the United States. Apoyo consists to a great degree in supporting one another's *autoestima* and helping provide the buena información that is so difficult to gain access to without high levels of education, English skills, or social networks that include diverse professionals. *Acción*, which the women usually used to refer to public, collective acts to claim or assert their rights, was both a means to specific instrumental goals and also a way of reinforcing the *autoestima* of the participants, while at the same time providing información and apoyo to other immigrants who might be observing and to influential advocates working on their behalf.

The organization emphasized the importance of understanding and participating in electoral processes and public institutions, going so far as to turn general meetings into civics lessons. Participants asked animated questions about charts of the three branches of government, the relationships between governmental institutions, and the processes by which bills are enacted into laws. In 1996, MUA members participated in a citywide coalitional effort with other immigrant groups to register immigrant voters and get them out to vote. This door-to-door campaign had women canvassing large neighborhoods and keeping track of those they registered. Staff members later cited the higher-than-average voter turnout among those they registered and the impact of this on the city's overwhelming veto of statewide anti-immigrant ballot measures, which San Franciscans rejected in higher numbers than any county in the state. The collective political action of groups such as MUA entailed a transformation in the lives of their members and participants, but also in the broader community and political terrain of the United States.

These women did not pass through specific preordained steps or phases en route to a sense of entitlement as citizens, but they did identify variations of a transformational process that included seeking out and finding trustworthy peer support (apoyo, *confianza*, información), developing a sense of self-worth leading them to assert claims for autonomy and respect in their homes and community (*autoestima*), and collectively reaching out to others to identify, demand, and obtain redress for shared concerns (*acción política, ayudar a los demás*). The stories of how the women came to be active in collective processes of demanding rights resonated with themes of the importance of emotional and instrumental support, economic opportunity, and the influence that *conviviendo*—passing time with people from different national and cultural backgrounds—had on their participation in the public political sphere.

When the women I interviewed spoke from their multiply marginalized positions about life, culture, politics, and society in the United States, they claimed their right to speak and the legitimacy of their experiences, perspectives, and their very presence in this society. They did so in a way that reminded listeners of the hierarchies of power and privilege infusing their experiences in the United States. They also walked a fine line between claiming the liberal rights promised by the U.S. state and critiquing the basis for the legitimacy of certain rights over oneself, property, and person. Liberal rights–based discourse reinscribes as well as obscures the many historical, political, and economic reasons for people's social context and personal experiences (Razack, 1998). In the case of immigrant women who experience domestic violence, such laws also reinforce the northern chauvinism that views immigrant Latinas as long-suffering victims of backward practices in their cultures of origin.

As long-term residents often fail to learn English, naturalize, cease remittances to their families, or acquire any of the other cultural capital associated with settlement, they also question social science models of the dichotomy between settlers and sojourners. Many who arrive with the intention of working in the United States only temporarily raise their children here and find themselves wanting to, but never actually, returning to their home country permanently. In some cases, husbands wished to return home, but the women resisted returning to small towns or communities that they believed (correctly or not) to be hostile to independent women, single mothers, and women who would not tolerate domestic violence. Although most cited economic need as driving their initial immigration, few mentioned economics as a reason to not return to Mexico. Instead they insisted that their children and/or they themselves had changed too much to return home again.

In the aftermath of September 11, 2001, it is tempting to see organized harassment of immigrants and border vigilance as new by-products of the war on terror. On March 1, 2003, the Immigration and Naturalization Service was dissolved and merged into the newly formed Department of Homeland Security.[14] Yet immigrants experienced low-intensity terrorism in the pre-9/11 years as well. Reviewing their active redefinition of citizenship in the context of the late 1990s and the continuities, rather than divergences, between the pre- and post-9/11 periods leads to my conclusion that these women's analyses and activism have broader implications for understanding U.S. citizenship for immigrants and nonimmigrants as well.

What the women shared in their stories constituted new visions of citizenship, multiculturalism, and feminism for our times. Operating in a context of extreme antagonism to immigrants, poor people, and low-income women and children in particular, as well as perceived late-twentieth-century social and economic gains by people of color in the United States, these women deployed what might be called "a critical multiculturalism."[15] Their political analysis includes the role of race, class, and language in women's experiences of their social role and political agency, not only the ways in which institutions define their positions and status. Our understanding of gender and citizenship must overcome the persistent division between domestic and public cultural domains that both enforce a second-class citizenship status for women and obscure the ways in which domestic realms are political arenas in which women, men, and children struggle over power, rights, social benefits, and how to balance these issues in intimate family relationships.

The immigrant activists I spoke and spent time with were not unified in their perspectives or beliefs, but through the telling of stories and the sharing of analyses, information, and activism, a more inclusive vision of what it means to belong in the United States emerges. Citizenship in this sense is both a deeply personal and cultural and a legal-political category. Although they were displaced from their countries of origin and thereby lost political rights as citizens of those nations, they continued to exercise citizenship through community organizing and personal demands for entitlement in the United States, where they had no formal citizenship or voting rights. Speaking Spanish and insisting on their own and their children's right to do so, they listened to one another's tales of struggle, violence, and hardship and collectively told a story of survival and determination that had little to do with the Horatio Alger rags-to-riches myths of previous generations.[16]

They embraced a vision of an America in which every person would have the right to work legally and in safe conditions for a just wage, regardless of birthplace. They aspired to comfortable, affordable housing better than the cramped rental units most shared with other households, and they insisted that homelessness and poor housing were unacceptable in such a rich nation. The women spoke of their goals for the future in terms of their own economic independence and their children's education, and they occasionally dreamed of returning to their home country either temporarily or to stay. Coming from precarious but not the most dire conditions in Mexico and Central America, they spoke of the false promise of petty consumerism and the importance of maintaining the values with which they were raised to avoid the moral and personal traps commercialism offers.

In these ways, MUA members both articulated and challenged liberal discourses of rights and entitlement by asserting female working-class perspectives on social justice growing out of their transnational experiences of motherhood, work, and community life. By unlinking political rights from legal status, they asserted human rights standards and norms in the face of exclusionary ideology and policy in the United States. Basing political claims around their agendas as nonwhite immigrant mothers and wives referenced their legitimacy under the problematic but still influential ideology of the mother-citizen. At the same time, their internal practice and organizational functioning called into question the division of the world into gendered domestic and public realms. While rooting themselves politically and historically in Latin American popular movements and U.S. women's and civil rights movements, and by institutionally affiliating with a pan-ethnic, pan-racial immigration coalition, they also rejected the increasing tendency in California and elsewhere to pit Latina/o immigrants and other communities of color against one another for political and economic purposes. By embracing a Latina/o identity in addition to their nationality of origin, without wholly giving up the hope of returning home some day, they manifested the multiplicity of identity and the bankruptcy of assimilationist understandings of immigration and culture change. While my sample was predominantly Mexican and Central American, the collective experience of political struggle as Latinas and the shared day-to-day experiences of living with new friends and neighbors from throughout Latin America encouraged a coalitional, inclusive view of Latina/o identity and the diversity internal to the community that outsiders perceive as uniformly Mexican, poor, and rural in origin.

After a MUA meeting in the fall of 2002 in which women discussed how to organize against military recruitment of local youth through inner-city public high schools, I was asked to talk about this book project to the group. Patricia García, a rank-and-file leader in the Oakland group, listened intently but made no comments until we were in a smaller group afterwards. When I asked her for her opinion, she replied, "I am not sure why you are so concerned about our citizenship and what we are doing here. I think you should be worried about your own citizenship. Look at all the rights and protections that are being taken away from you. What will it mean to be a citizen anymore in this country?" Patricia's analysis was prescient, not only because of the increasing concern in the United States over state surveillance of the citizenry, but also because by 2009, hundreds of U.S. citizens were being wrongly detained by ICE, imprisoned for months, and in some cases, even deported to other countries. As the number of detainees in ICE custody tripled in this decade, to over 33,000 per year, such cases became more common. The fact that immigration violations are a civil matter means that immigration detainees lack the same rights to due process and legal representation granted suspects in criminal cases, making it very difficult for them, whether or not they are citizens, to assert their rights (Hendricks, 2009).

Patricia's comment about the issues of security, sovereignty, equality, and liberty facing the United States poses a complex challenge to both citizenship theory and political practice. How can we understand the implications of the similarities as well as differences between the mid-1990s post-welfare- and post-immigration-reform context and the post-9/11 period? The key struggles MUA confronted in the 1990s included defending immigrant rights and social citizenship in the form of welfare and other state benefits. Though uniquely positioned as low-income parents and immigrants at the intersection of welfare and immigration reform, immigrant families were far outnumbered by non-immigrants who faced severe cuts in their social citizenship benefits. After 2001, immigrant-rights advocates found themselves continuing their advocacy work, but they were newly joined by an ever-widening group of immigrants and other citizens who opposing the negative effects of federal educational policy, threats to Social Security, and unprecedented restrictions of civil liberties. What is striking is the continuity between Patricia's analysis in 2002 and earlier articulations of other women's visions of citizenship rights and entitlements on one hand, and the ongoing relevance of this vision for U.S.-born citizens as well as immigrant women on the other hand. While the past twenty-five years have been marked by an increasing privatization of citizenship (Berlant, 1997), they have also offered diverse and dynamic examples of new forms of citizenship, political, and social identities that can emerge when the state is no longer the primary arbiter of national belonging. This is not the same as asserting a post-national world in which states no longer matter. The condition and concerns of stateless and undocumented people the world over show just how relevant nation-states continue to be for most people. However, the words and actions of Patricia and her compañeras highlight the stake that citizens and noncitizens alike have in remaking our ideas and ideals of citizenship based on transnational notions of women's rights, workers' rights, and human rights.

Reference Matter

Appendix

WHILE OUR RESEARCH questions guide our choice of methods, fieldwork itself often leads us in unforeseen directions. Fieldwork required me to be willing and able to shift my focus and methods when the data demanded it. Collaborative research like mine is increasingly the norm in cultural anthropology (Marcus, 2008), raising new and different ethical concerns than those commonly confronted in traditional ethnographic relationships. How we conduct ourselves in the field is one among many ethical concerns facing ethnographers, including how what we write might affect our subjects (directly and indirectly) and the shared authorship we acknowledge (or obscure) in the articulation of our research findings.[1]

Whereas earlier "native anthropologists" were subject to intense scrutiny for blurring the lines of authority between author and ethnographic subject, contemporary anthropologists see these tensions as part of the ethnographic method. If we acknowledge that people's ideas and what they say and do are more than just the raw material on which the social scientist builds theories (Ebron, 2007; R. Rosaldo, 1989), how do we write in a way that respects their analyses and also contributes something of our own to the ethnographic conversation? Malkki (2007) writes that ethnography, method, and theory are related reciprocally and improvisationally, requiring attention to the dynamics of how our focus in the field changes during the writing process. In my case, the research reflected the multi-sitedness of citizenship and involved struggles with my subjects over the terms of my research. Ultimately, my research process embodied this dialogue between methods and theory.

Ethnography is, at best, an artfully humanistic endeavor that may have more to teach us precisely because it requires us to be careful readers and critical thinkers capable of challenging numbers, word choices, and interpretations. I include the following information for readers interested in further background on my own position and relationship to my subjects, as well as details about this study's sample in the aggregate.

Ethnography, Identity, and Misunderstandings

After giving birth to my first child in 1995 in a San Francisco hospital, with my husband present and parents nearby, I looked around the clean, quiet, private room, unable to shake the images of very different birth experiences that forty women had described to me during a year of fieldwork in Mexico I had carried out while pregnant in 1994, before even deciding to apply to anthropology doctoral programs. That day in the hospital, I had my first embodied understanding of the power and pain underlying women's stories of giving birth, whether in humble homes, private clinics, or free public hospitals. Looking back on interviews I conducted before and during my pregnancy, I realized how well my research subjects had perceived my own limits of understanding. Lila Abu-Lughod (1995) writes compellingly about similar sentiments after becoming pregnant after many years of fieldwork among Bedouin women.

On the several occasions when I became ill during interviews, women smiled, showed me to the toilet or outhouse, and then launched into elaborate narratives of their own and their kins' and neighbors' similar experiences and remedies. Through this process, I first understood the physical side of knowledge and the extent to which mind–body binarism marginalizes women's ways of knowing from what are usually considered to be legitimate academic pursuits. This is neither to say that physical experience constitutes a privileged form of knowledge of birth and motherhood, nor that motherhood is an essential aspect of womanhood, only that it is a means of learning, knowing, and sharing knowledge with others that is marginalized in traditionally masculine intellectual life.

Returning to Mexico for a short visit, I brought my four-month-old daughter to a meeting of volunteer health promoters in southeastern Mexico City. These women had shared their stories with me and introduced me to their friends and neighbors the previous year. At the meeting in the spare room of a state public health clinic, I found myself jokingly chiding those present for having not warned me about how difficult birth would be. One woman in her forties said pointedly, but not without humor, "Well, we couldn't scare you like that! What good would that have done?" Then the women told me how they individually and collectively try to shield younger women who have not given birth from the intensity of the experience so as not to negatively influence their future experiences. These previous personal and research experiences oriented this research project as well as my interest in identity, gender, and immigration in the United States.

In light of these experiences, I faced the question of what women in San Francisco may have kept from me, either to protect themselves and their privacy or to protect me from the power of life experiences they believed, as did the Mexican health promoters, that I could not handle. Despite my relative (to them) dominant social and economic position, my research was conducted in complex relations of power and knowledge in which I was not always the more privileged party. Withholding or concealing information from an anthropologist is a common form of resistance to the ethnographic gaze, yet I was also surprised by the extent to which the women exerted themselves to make me understand their stories and in turn hoped that I could share them with others. As do most fieldworkers, I have struggled with what to reveal and what to obscure, what knowledge I have accrued that should be shared, and what kinds of knowledge might be harmful or helpful to the individuals or community with whom I worked. The politics of how we come to know what we do and if, when, and how to share it infuse my experiences conducting research with an activist women's organization committed to asserting the citizenship rights of immigrant women.

My own social identity likely influenced women's discussions of motherhood, the relative paucity of information I gathered about sexuality, and the heteronormative slant of many of our conversations. This was not as apparent to me during interviews as it was in writing this book. During the early days of my fieldwork, many MUA members and staff knew that my mother was suffering from cancer and that I was her primary caregiver. When she died that year, several members attended her funeral on very short notice to show their support for me. I had one small child who often attended meetings and events with me. I was pregnant and had my second child during the fieldwork period. This made me part of a cohort of five women in the group who gave birth within two months of one another. MUA threw us a collective baby shower, and I continued to see several of the women regularly, not only at group meetings, but also at the public schools and religious education classes our children attended together. Many women also knew my husband from community events, or from the general hospital at which he was one of very few Mexican pediatric residents. I am left with the impression that all this is likely responsible, at least in part, for what I perceive now in my primary data to be the emphasis on women's narratives about their experiences and identities as mothers, daughters, women married to Latino men, and, less frequently, Catholics.

The staff members of Mujeres Unidas y Activas and the regional Coalition for Immigrant and Refugee Rights and Services came up with projects for me such as evaluative interviews of participants in group *entrenamientos* (training workshops). These interviews not only provided data, but also structured my accountability to the group's needs and priorities into my primary research and allowed me to include the women's comments on my preliminary findings in my conclusions. Staff members also included me in the collective process of writing an oral history of the group for an organizing manual they hoped to distribute to other incipient immigrant Latina organizations. As part of this project, group members met and together came up with an interview questionnaire and a list of past and present members and community allies to interview for the project. I was not only provided a questionnaire on issues they were concerned with but also a list of people with varying relationships to the group to interview. They also gave me my first taste of being the object of ethnographic inquiry when Socorro Méndez interviewed me as a subject for the project. Staff members introduced me to members and others as "una amiga del grupo," clearly distinct from "una compañera" or "una miembra del grupo," as they referred to one another. Just as I would decide that everyone had agreed on my identity as a white, middle-class student-researcher and solidarity volunteer, someone would make a comment or remark that made me realize that none of our positions were at all transparent.

One of the most striking examples of this was during my interview with Socorro Méndez, a forty-one-year-old Salvadoran mother of two who had left her own teenage daughters in El Salvador with her mother when she migrated in search of a way to support them and their education. Socorro was motherly in her demeanor with me and concerned about my own mother's terminal illness, going so far as to recommend her herbalist and parish priest as a spiritual counselor. When I asked if her priest spoke English and she said he preferred Spanish, I said that would make things difficult for my English-speaking mother. She looked confused and asked how my mother could not speak Spanish. Wasn't she Latina? I later wondered at my own naiveté about how my subjects might be constructing my own subjectivity and answering their own questions about my interest in their lives. Could I think that I was the only one capable of creatively (mis)interpreting another woman's subjectivity? Or did I have illusions about my security in my own identity and how I was projecting it in an all-Latina context? Judith Butler offers words of warning about the false innocence of politically inspired social criticism and the ways in which it may reify the relationships and subject positions of the critic and the object of study: "Surely there is a caution offered here, that in the very struggle toward enfranchisement and democratization, we might adopt the very models of domination by which we were oppressed, not realizing that one way that domination works is through the regulation and production of the subject" (1992, 14).

Methods and Sampling Issues

I removed this description to an appendix and avoided more precise enumeration for several reasons. With respect to providing more details about the organization or its members, I wanted to be sure to protect the identities of the women I spoke with and respect the confidentiality rules of MUA. I was also concerned that too precise a statistical portrait, no matter how representative it might appear to be of broader trends in California's immigrant female population, may lead to a false, overly scientific impression about this project. Of the thirty women with whom I worked most closely in this research, twenty-three were from Mexico, six were from Central America, and one was from South America. Ten were in their twenties, nine in their thirties, and eleven in their forties at the time of our interviews. The majority had immigrated since 1990, two as recently as just a few months earlier. The older women had, by and large, immigrated to California in the 1980s as young women. Those who were eligible but had not yet applied for naturalization said that their principal reason for not doing so was their anxiety about the language requirement and the naturalization exam. According to Portes and Rumbaut, Mexicans and Canadians have the lowest naturalization rates among eligible immigrants. They conclude that "resistance to naturalization varies inversely with the reversibility of migration and with average socioeducational backgrounds of individual flow" (Portes and Rumbaut, 1996, 121, 130).

The organization had a very strong ethic of neither asking nor revealing individuals' immigration status, but women were cautiously open with one another and with me about their situations. One Guatemalan, two Mexican, and one Salvadoran subject received their legal residency during the period of my research. One Mexican and one South American woman applied for political asylum during this period based on their documented experiences of political and gender-based discrimination in their countries of origin. Two women were married to U.S. citizens but were themselves undocumented because their husbands had never helped them legalize their status. Three were lawful permanent residents, all having legalized through marriage to men who had received legal residency under the 1986 IRCA amnesty program. The balance—more than two-thirds of my principal subjects—entered the United States illegally on foot, crossing the border in Texas, Arizona, or California with the aid of *coyotes* and often with small children in tow, usually to reunite with their husbands. Women who arrived before marriage tended to be younger and in search of employment opportunities. These women subsequently married (legally or by common law) immigrant Latin American men; one of them blended families with a female partner she met in San Francisco.

Mujeres Unidas y Activas members also shared a commitment to a group policy that precluded much discussion of religion and religious issues, emphasizing instead the group's religious diversity and efforts to maintain tolerance and mutual respect. Most women identified as Roman Catholic, yet several were currently or had at some past time been members of evangelical or Pentecostal Christian churches. Others did not attend church services except on holidays or for ritual occasions. The group had an annual Christmas party and smaller, more informal celebrations for Easter and the Day of the Dead. These parties were nondenominational, if not almost secular, and emphasized the sharing of the differing Latin American holiday traditions. Perhaps this aspect of the organizational culture explains in part why the subject of religion played a relatively small role in interviews. One woman was a former nun, another was a former lay church worker, another was active in her church choir, and yet another spoke of returning to Catholicism after several years as an evangelical Christian. Most of the women I interviewed, though, spoke of religion in the context of family and ethnic culture rather than in connection to their community work with MUA. Thus religiosity and spirituality play a relatively small role in my interview materials. It is possible that religion may be more influential than the women intimated because there was a strong commitment in the group to keeping the MUA as free as possible of conflict along religious or national lines. The women also may have wanted to show respect for religious differences they might have had with me as well.

With respect to household structure, the group was also diverse. All but one of my principal subjects had one or more children at the time of our interviews. Three had left children in their home countries with their own mothers when they emigrated, which was a tremendous source of sadness and pain in their interviews. Twenty-three had one or two children, five had three or four children, and two had more than four children. Only two expressed interest in having more children in the future, but another two had unplanned pregnancies subsequent to our interviews. The lone childless woman I interviewed told me later that she had been several weeks pregnant at the time of our interview, though she had told me she was not planning to get pregnant soon. Two of the women lived as a lesbian couple with their three daughters from previous relationships. Another woman returned to the unhappy marriage she had left earlier in my research, after becoming pregnant again by her husband. Another moved herself and her other children in with her new boyfriend after becoming pregnant with his child. Two women had children attending college, one had a son in a juvenile detention facility, and another had sent one of her two sons back to Mexico to live with his grandparents after repeated incarcerations and threats from gang members. Many had lived with extended family upon immigrating, but most no longer did, although most shared their households with unrelated persons. Six were single mothers, five of whom had ended abusive relationships with their children's fathers. Another woman left her husband shortly after my research concluded. A total of twenty women were living with their husbands and children at the time of our contacts, two of whom lived with grandchildren as well.

Three of the married women reported currently living in abusive marriages, while five separated or divorced women said that they had been victims of domestic violence during their marriages. That there were many survivors of domestic violence in my sample may be due to the fact that many women first joined Mujeres Unidas y Activas after being referred by police, health workers, or peers for support as battered women. At the same time, the percentage of women reporting some experience of battering by an intimate partner (eight out of thirty women, or 27 percent) is not much higher than contemporary statistics for all women in the United States. According to a national survey of eight thousand women in the late 1990s, 22.1 percent reported having been physically assaulted by an intimate partner in their lifetime (Tjaden and Thoennes, 1998). In a smaller survey of immigrant women in the San Francisco Bay Area, 20 percent of Filipinas and 34 percent of Latinas reported experiencing some form of domestic violence by their partners, either in their country of origin or after immigrating to the United States (Hogeland and Rosen, 1990; Jang, Lee, and Morello-Frosch, 1990).[2] These numbers may clarify why much of the Mujeres Unidas y Activas group discourse grew out of the centrality of domestic violence to many women's experiences. However, the prevalence of domestic violence throughout North and Central America demonstrates that theories of citizenship must also account for such violence against women as one important example of how different forms of institutional and structural violence shape the way people engage (or not) in civic life.

Notes

Introduction

1. The Big Four refer to Stanford, Crocker, Huntington, and Hopkins. For a detailed discussion of the significance of the Stanford palace for the gentrification of Nob Hill and the development of San Francisco into a city of national importance, see Strazdes (2001).

2. See also Susan Coutin's (2003) account of a similar ceremony and her outstanding analysis of the naturalization process and immigration policies. Lynn Fujiwara (2005) details how the Personal Responsibility and Work Opportunity Reconciliation Act of 1996 forced some immigrant elders to naturalize to continue receiving benefits, while terrifying the families of those too cognitively or physically impaired to complete naturalization.

3. "The groups that are less likely to naturalize in California than in the rest of the nation include recent immigrants, Mexican immigrants, immigrants with noncitizen spouses, and immigrants with fewer than eight years of education. Moreover, California has a disproportionate number of unauthorized immigrants and temporary migrants; most of the recent immigrants may not qualify for naturalization, and others may not plan to remain in this country long enough to naturalize" (H. Johnson et al., 1999, 82).

4. The oath of allegiance begins, "I hereby declare, on oath, that I absolutely and entirely renounce and abjure all allegiance and fidelity to any foreign prince, potentate, state, or sovereignty, of whom or which I have heretofore been a subject or citizen; that I will bear true faith and allegiance to the same" (U.S. Code of Federal Regulations, Aliens and Nationality, 8 CFR Part 337 Sec. 337.1).

5. The law provided that immigrant recipients of Social Security Income (SSI) or food stamps would lose these benefits as of August 1997 unless they had naturalized as citizens, had obtained refugee or asylum status, had been granted withholding of

deportation, were veterans or on active duty military, or had worked in the United States for ten years or more (CIR 1997).

6. Unpublished document from the Greater Boston Legal Services and the Harvard Law School Immigration Project, 2000.

7. The Enlightenment notion of the free and right-bearing individual allowed for the development of what Marshall calls "civil rights," individual rights such as the right to individual liberty, the right to hold property, the right to participate in the market and contracts, and the right to justice through the judicial system. In the nineteenth century, citizenship rights expanded to include "political rights," such as the right to vote in a representational democracy. In the twentieth century, "social rights" promised a certain level of economic security and social development through the elaboration of the welfare state.

8. The current composition of the mesa directiva is six rank-and-file MUA members and three *aliadas* (allies and nonmembers like myself). All board meetings, notes, reports, and documents are produced entirely in Spanish, and all four elected officers of the board are rank-and-file MUA members, who are also responsible for chairing and recording the meetings.

9. Mary Louise Pratt used the phrase "resources for hope" in an oral presentation at Symposium on Gender, Cultural Citizenship and Transnationalism, New York University, October 11, 2002.

10. In 1990, 96,649 (or 13.3 percent) of the population of the City and County of San Francisco was Hispanic (all races). Other local Latino populations included 1,772 Cubans, 154 Dominicans, 330 Costa Ricans, 591 Hondurans, 438 Panamanians, and 5,549 South Americans, about half of them from Peru.

11. Milton Marks served as a registered Republican state senator from 1967 to 1988, but later switched parties to gain election to the state assembly in 1992 as a Democrat. Quentin Kopp was elected to the Board of Supervisors in 1970 while a registered Republican, but later switched to an Independent affiliation to win a seat in the state senate in 1986.

12. According to U.S. Census estimates, San Franciscans had a median household income of $57,833 (2.3 persons per household) compared to the national median of $43,564 (2.6 persons per household). Fourteen percent of the employed population of the city worked in construction, manufacturing, transportation, utilities, or warehousing. After the city and county government, the second largest employer in San Francisco is the University of California, with its health and biological sciences graduate programs, affiliated hospitals, and new Mission Bay research and biotechnology campus.

13. "Lower income people and communities have been burdened with increasing economic hardship from the interrelated effect of the national redistribution of wealth during the 1980s and the recession in the early 1990s. . . . With the average price for a

home at nearly triple the national average, fewer than 9% of households can afford to purchase a home in San Francisco" (Reed and Krebs-Dean, 1996, 5–6).

14. The May 4, 1998, *San Francisco Chronicle* found a growing gap between the representation of blacks/Latinos and whites/Asians among Bay Area high-tech employees (Davis, 2000, 102).

15. Like San Francisco's Bayview–Hunter's Point, East Palo Alto, East Oakland, Long Beach, and South-Central Los Angeles also developed as black working-class family neighborhoods and cities near military and other heavy industrial plants in California.

16. San Francisco's black population in the southern and eastern neighborhoods of San Francisco was concentrated in the Oceanview, Ingleside, Excelsior, and Visitation Valley neighborhoods, as well as Bayview and Hunter's Point. Between 1990 and 1997, the African American population of Bayview–Hunter's Point declined from 64 percent to 59.7 percent, while the Latino population of the Ingleside-Excelsior area increased from 28.8 percent to 30.9 percent and the Asian population of Visitation Valley increased from 42.6 to 49.4 percent, continuing trends begun in the 1970s as Asian and Latino families moved from Chinatown and the inner Mission to more affordable, outlying, and historically African American areas (*San Francisco Examiner*, April 26, 1998, A-15).

17. Throughout this book, I use the term *Latina* (rather than Latin American) because the women referred to themselves collectively as *latinas* and individually in terms of their own nationalities (*mexicana, salvadoreña, guatemalteca*).

Chapter 1

1. The media reported from 30,000 to 100,000 participants in San Francisco, with much larger crowds in Los Angeles, New York, and Chicago.

2. I thank Robin Balliger for sharing this particular exchange, as well as for reminding me of the radical political practice embedded in what the media covered exclusively as a march of working-class family people.

3. The legislative target of the mass mobilization, House Resolution 4437, sponsored by Wisconsin congressman F. James Sensenbrenner, Jr., included dozens of proposals to change immigration laws ranging from making unlawful presence in the United States a felony, to mandating prison sentences for service providers working with the undocumented and authorizing the construction of a seven-hundred-mile long wall between the United States and Mexico.

4. See the Appendix for more details on sample demographics.

5. In this section and throughout the text, I try to be as specific as possible about the organization's structure and members' descriptions, while also trying to preserve as much organizational and individual anonymity as possible through a combination of pseudonyms and incomplete descriptions.

6. Immigration Reform and Control Act, P.L. 99-603, 100 Stat. 3359, November 6, 1986.

7. Throughout this book, I use the term *refugee* rather than *asylee* because it was the vernacular designation people in San Francisco used (both in English and in Spanish) to indicate a person who could not return to their country of origin for fear of persecution for political or social-identity reasons. In the eyes of U.S. law, a refugee is someone who obtains permission to immigrate to the United States as a refugee while still residing in their country of origin. An asylee is someone who requests asylum at their port of entry, or after already having entered the United States.

8. In response to lobbying by immigrant rights and domestic violence advocacy groups, VAWA allows battered women married to permanent legal residents (with proof of battery such as medical and police reports) to petition for residency independently of their husbands. Since some batterers also exploit their wives' undocumented status as part of their abuse, this has been an important provision for many women seeking legal status.

9. For a detailed ethnography of processes of racialization among Mexican immigrants in the United States, see De Genova (2005).

10. Translation of this and subsequent quotations from the original Spanish by the author from interview with Carolina Jiménez, February 11, 1998.

Chapter 2

1. Conversation, August 13, 1997, San Francisco.

2. Aid to Families with Dependent Children was replaced by Temporary Aid to Needy Families (TANF) under the 1996 welfare reform legislation.

3. Juan Andrade, press release from United States Hispanic Leadership Institute, Washington, D.C., October 1, 1998, quoted in Davis, (2000).

4. William Blackstone, Commentaries 442 (1783), laid the foundation of the coverture doctrine, stating: "By marriage, the husband and wife are one person in the law: that is, the very being or legal existence of the woman is suspended during the marriage, or at least is incorporated and consolidated into that of the husband: under whose wing, protection, and cover, she performs every thing; and is therefore called . . . a feme-covert, . . . is said to be covertbaron, or under the protection and influence of her husband, her baron, or lord; and her condition during her marriage is called her coverture" (Lilienthal, 1996, note 311).

5. Also known as the Cable Act, P.L. 67-346, Ch. 411, 42 Stat. 1021 (1922), in Lilienthal (1996, note 311).

6. "Act of Mar. 3, 1891, ch. 551, 26 Stat. 1084, 1084; see, e.g., *Nishimura Ekiu v. United States*, 142 U.S. 651 (1892) (upholding exclusion of Japanese woman as a public charge)" (Lilienthal, 1996, note 43).

7. Violence Against Women Act of 1994, P.L. 103-322, 108 Stat. 1796.

8. Cf. U.S. Department of State Visa Bulletin (http://travel.state.gov/visa/frvi/bulletin/bulletin_4428.html).

9. Illegal Immigration Reform and Immigrant Responsibility Act of 1996, P.L. No. 104-208, 100 Stat. 3009-546, signed September 30, 1996.

10. "The 1996 law gave low-level INS officers at the border and at international airports the power to expel noncitizens because they lack entry documents or use fraudulent documents. [INA §235(b)(1)(a)(i)] This new form of deportation, called summary (or expedited) removal, has the same extremely serious consequences for a noncitizen as being deported after a full-fledge immigration hearing. [INA §212(a)(9)(A)]" (Pendleton, 1999, 15).

11. 8 CFR §245(i). I would like to acknowledge the attorney and legal anthropologist Professor Arzoo Osanloo for her patient explication of these issues. When Congress allowed section 245(i) to expire, women like Cristina who had entered the United States without inspection lost the right to remain in the United States while awaiting the approval of their petition for residency as an immediate relative of a lawful permanent resident or citizen. The 1996 legislation expected such persons to return to their home country and wait for their petitions to be approved, a process that could take several years for Mexican spouses of permanent residents.

12. Translation of this and subsequent quotations from original Spanish by author. Interview with Cristina Rodríguez, February 18, 1998.

13. Also known as "unlawful presence" bars; INA §212(a)(9)(B).

14. The ongoing impact of these policies on families was recognized by nongovernmental social services agencies, such as Catholic Charities, which continue to oppose policies that force "Solomonic choices" between commitments to parents, spouses, and children and obedience to U.S. law. Such agencies report that the 1996 immigration law changes are also responsible for: (1) backlogs in visa applications for immediate family members of up to five years, (2) the inability of more than 30 percent of immigrant families to meet the newly increased financial support requirements for sponsoring a relative for a visa, (3) the inhumane detention and incarceration of undocumented children without a parent or guardian in the United States, and (4) the separation of families by mandatory detention and deportation provisions for even past minor legal offenses (Zapor, 2000, 6).

15. On November 8, 1995, Proposition 187 passed 59 to 41 percent statewide, with 59 percent of white voters supporting the initiative, and 78 percent of Latino, 54 percent of Asian, and 56 percent of African American voters opposing it.

16. Sections 5 through 7 of Proposition 187 (Cervantes, Khokha, and Murray, 1995; K. Johnson, 1995).

17. On November 20, 1995, U.S. district court judge Marian Pfaelzer ruled the initiative to be an unconstitutional infringement on the federal government's jurisdiction over immigration law (García 1995, 131, note 85).

18. Linda B. Hayes, "Letter to the Editor: California's Prop. 187," *New York Times*, October 15, 1994, A18; cited in Sandino-Glasser, (1998, 74–75, note 21). Hayes was the Proposition 187 campaign media director. For more press citations with explicit references to the imminent reconquest, see Neumann (1995). Inda (2002) has analyzed the particular significance of Mexican immigrant women and their reproductive health in the xenophobic discourse of this period.

19. Several thousand health workers, teachers, and other service providers statewide signed the San Francisco–based Immigrant Rights Action Pledge, promising to defy efforts to make them de facto agents of the INS, even if they were threatened with arrest or other disciplinary actions by their employers.

20. The most widely publicized cases were that of an elderly Chinese woman in San Francisco and that of a Mexican boy in Los Angeles. Both died after they or their families failed to seek medical attention for fear of deportation (K. Johnson, 1995, 1559, note 234).

21. Mike Davis calls Proposition 227 "an ingenious repackaging of English Only as a rescue plan to bring immigrant children into the mainstream. With only sixty days to develop a new curriculum, schools were ordered to transfer immigrant kids into 'structured English immersion' for a maximum of a year, then—regardless of proficiency—into regular English-only classrooms" (Davis, 2000, 122).

22. Interview with Cristina Rodríguez, February 18, 1998.

23. Arzoo Osanloo, professor of law and society at the University of Washington, points out the irony that this was true "even though just prior to the Declaration of Independence, new settlers were just that. Criminal convicts and debtors were often given a choice in sentencing, either prison in England, or banishment to the colonies, of which they often chose the latter." Personal communication, August 8, 2000.

24. In 1875, federal immigration legislation barred convicts, prostitutes, and Chinese contract laborers. In 1882, Congress barred anyone likely to become a public charge, and in 1891, Congress defined "All idiots, insane persons, paupers or persons likely to become a public charge, persons suffering from a loathsome or a dangerous contagious disease, persons who have been convicted of a felony or other infamous crime or misdemeanor involving moral turpitude, [and] polygamists" as undesirable and excludable (K. Johnson, 1995). In 1903, epileptics, professional beggars, and anarchists were added to the list of excluded immigrants.

25. "There can be no doubt but that the presence of numbers among us of a degraded and distinct people must exercise a deleterious influence upon the superior race, and, to a certain extent, repel desirable immigration. It will afford me great pleasure to concur with the Legislature in any constitutional action, having for its object the repression of the immigration of the Asiatic races" (Stanford, 1862). For more on the political context and impact of Stanford's speech and the role of Dennis Kearney

and organized labor in fueling anti-Chinese legislation and violence, see Daniels (1989), and Takaki, (1990).

26. Asylum applicants receive temporary permission to reside and work in the United States while their applications are considered. If asylum is granted, such refugees wait one year and then are able to apply for lawful permanent resident (LPR) status.

27. Daniel's transgender identity and the gender dynamics between Daniel and Isabel, even more than Isabel's sexuality or the blending of their families, posed a challenge to the couple's comfort and integration in the group. As Daniel progressed toward surgery, members criticized the way he treated Isabel as "too macho," especially since she was a survivor of domestic violence.

28. "And the sentence that condemns or acquits is not simply a judgment of guilt, a legal decision that lays down punishment; it bears within it an assessment of normality and a technical prescription for a possible normalization. Today the judge—magistrate or juror—certainly does more than 'judge'" (Foucault, 1979, 20–21).

Chapter 3

1. Rhacel Parreñas (2001, 2005) has documented this phenomenon and its tremendous impact on migrant women, children, and extended family in and from the Philippines.

2. See Personal Responsibility and Work Opportunity Reconciliation Act of 1996, P. L. 104-193, 110 Stat. 2105, codified as amended in scattered sections of 8 U.S.C. An as-yet untracked outcome of the change in welfare policy was the privatization of social services through private and for-profit work training programs and provisions forcing clients to work for a certain number of hours to continue receiving benefits—in effect, government subsidies of employers through the provision of free or low-cost laborers.

3. An example is "the 2,500-bed Youth Services International, started five years ago by the founder of the quick oil-change franchise Jiffy Lube, who grew up in an orphanage. . . . This booming market is another example of how the welfare overhaul has opened up opportunities in the business of poverty. Corporations as large as Lockheed Martin and Electronic Data Systems are bidding to privatize an array of state welfare services" (Bernstein, 1997, A-4).

4. Despite Governor Pete Wilson's efforts during the time of my fieldwork to eliminate prenatal care coverage for undocumented women, counties like San Francisco continued to fund such care regardless of immigrant status, and eventually the state legislature agreed to continue reimbursing counties for such services.

5. Cf. C. Chang, (1997), for analysis of the disproportionate impact of welfare reform on Asian and Latin American immigrants, the history of exclusion of the poor

from immigration, and the deployment of bars on re-entry for immigrants who have received public assistance.

6. Anabel's story is told in Chapter 2.

7. Tomasa Hernández and Caridad Ríos were from the same small town, but they did not know one another before migrating, and met in Nosotros in the 1990s. Both were single mothers who had left battering husbands after many years of partnership, but Caridad looked a bit askance at Tomasa's occasionally illicit efforts to earn money fencing stolen clothing, for example.

8. "Public charge is a term used by the INS to deny lawful permanent residency to person who, they believe, will not be able to support themselves or will have to depend on public benefits in the future. . . . Many battered immigrant women don't even apply for benefits because they fear these consequences" (Goldfarb, 1999, 9). Specific INS officials handling a case are able to make discretionary determinations on this point. "Even receiving public assistance may cause a problem in showing good moral character" (Jang, Marín, and Pendleton, 1997, 77).

9. Until the Bay Area housing market hit historic highs after 1998, small homes outside the city and in southeastern San Francisco were still affordable for working-class people. These women and their families benefited from government-financed programs to promote first-time home ownership. By the close of the decade, most Bay Area communities had been engulfed by a real estate frenzy that saw home values doubling in a matter of a few years.

10. See Oliva Espín (1997) for an in-depth discussion from a psychological perspective on the impact of dislocation on immigrant Latinas, as well as the importance of life narratives to self-healing and a productive clinical relationship.

11. "La ciudad me pareció muy fea, no me gustó."

12. Marta is Cristina Rodríguez's sister. Of the women I interviewed, Carolina was the only non-sibling who knew someone from the same town before immigrating.

13. For instance, despite the fact that it is illegal in California for notaries public to represent themselves as attorneys or to give legal advice, group members, staff members, and community nonprofit legal services attorneys reported personal experiences with notaries who had submitted legal paperwork for clients, including immigration petitions, with disastrous results. In Latin America, a notario is usually an attorney, which is why it is illegal in California for notaries public to advertise using the translation of their Spanish title. Notaries were not the only group cited for taking advantage of immigrants. I also personally witnessed at least two cases of incompetent representation by private immigration attorneys before the INS, one of which had an unfortunate outcome for the immigrant clients.

14. "As industrial capitalism changed the conditions of motherhood, so women began to redefine motherhood in ways that would influence the entire culture. They

'used' motherhood simultaneously to increase their own status, to promote greater social expenditure on children, and to loosen their dependence on men, just as capitalists 'used' motherhood as a form of unpaid labor" (Gordon, 1990, 188–89).

15. This and subsequent quotations translated from the original Spanish by another from interview with Cristina Rodríguez, February 18, 1998.

16. As did most women with whom I discussed this issue, Cristina made clear both her strong personal opposition to abortion and her conviction that a woman's decisions about her body and her unborn children were private and hers alone to make. Thus when she asserted the rights of the unborn child in this discussion, she was not posing a competition of rights between mother and fetus.

17. That institutional forces track Latino children into specific sectors of the economy is amply demonstrated by increasing Latino high school dropout rates around the country and national data supporting the contention that Latino students are the most educationally segregated minority in the country and the most affected by increasing racial segregation in American public education (Shepard, 2000).

Chapter 4

1. "Si yo lo pude lograr, Usted también puede."

2. I refer here to the notion of self-esteem deployed in everyday discourse and popular culture in the United States. Recent feminist and cross-cultural psychology indicates increased critiques of such traditional categories and concepts as self-esteem (Espín, 1997). That the colloquial force of the concept remains powerful is born out by its frequent use without definition, qualification, or deconstruction in even progressive social psychology, social work, and sociological literature (Gutierrez and Lewis, 1999).

3. Anthony Giddens (1992) asserts that although the struggle for public political democracy has been a predominantly male project, the future of democracy depends to a great extent on the ongoing efforts of women to democratize the private spheres of life and intimate personal relationships. This analysis may be particularly apt for a bourgeois, metropolitan female subject, but the women interviewed did not discuss *autoestima*, intimacy, and democracy in these terms. Evidence of the influence and resonance of these ideas, at least with global metropolitans, can be found in the February 2002 issue of the Mexico City literary magazine *Nexos* entitled "La Rebelión de la Intimidad," which translates portions of Giddens and generates a diverse discussion of the relationship between gender, intimacy, and democracy in Mexico (www.nexos .com.mx).

4. This and subsequent quotations translated from the original Spanish by the author.

5. "Fue lo máximo que yo he hecho en mi vida, porque después de este entrenamiento me siento *útil* [her emphasis]. Me siento que puedo hacer algo por nosotros

por los latinos, que estoy haciendo algo positivo. No siento ese nervio cuando empiezo a hablar. También en mi familia me siento, como madre, me siento útil."

6. "Era un miedo con el que yo vivía, era una tristeza, un. . . . por todo lo que pasó a la mujer, este, que está sufriendo violencia doméstica, no tenía gustos para nada, para nada. Yo me sentía bien fea. . . . es que el papá de los niños me decía 'si es que túestás bien fea, ¿quién te va a andar queriendo a tí?'. . . . me humillaba de lo peor. De lo más peor. 'Si tú estás más fea que una de las que anden en la calle que cobran diez dólares!'"

7. U.S. Department of Justice statistics bear out Tomasa's observations about patterns and issues in domestic violence, as well as the definitions of domestic violence deployed by the organization and its members. The DOJ researchers found consensus among service-providing agencies that "battering is a constellation of physical, sexual, and psychological abuses that may include physical violence, intimidation, threats, emotional abuse, isolation, sexual abuse, manipulation, the using of children, economic coercion, and the assertion of male privilege such as making all major family decisions, or expecting the woman to perform all household duties" (Healey, Smith, and O'Sullivan, 1998). Of these behaviors, only actual physical and/or sexual assault is illegal; prior to the 1994 Violence Against Women Act, there was no recognition of the special forms of threats and intimidation batterers use to control immigrant or undocumented partners.

8. Note the difference in approach of the politicized staff and members of this organization of primarily undocumented Latinas to the interventionist "feminist" social workers serving officially recognized Cambodian refugees, as described by Ong (2003).

9. Under the Mexican penal code, domestic violence is an illegal offense, and women have the right to file formal complaints and press charges against batterers. At the same time, government corruption on every level diminishes citizens' sense of trust or faith in the system's ability to intervene effectively. In my research in Mexico, I met and heard of several women who had filed police reports about their husbands' violence who noted that filing reports was much more common in the 1990s than previously.

10. Others have pointed out the gendered differential in male and female attitudes about return to the country of origin, with men generally more likely than women to report a desire to return. Mujeres Unidas y Activas members' dreams of returning home reflect the conflicted feelings that many migrants sustain throughout their lives in the United States (Goldring, 2001).

11. Provisions of the IIRIRA §501 [new 8 USC §1641(c)] defined battered immigrant women as "qualified aliens" eligible for federally funded services, but some states failed to incorporate this into their state welfare plans (Jang, Marín, and Pendleton, 1997, 141).

12. In invoking "multilayered citizenship," I distinguish my use of the term somewhat from Nira Yuval-Davis's notion of the multilayered citizen whose allegiances are

layered among ethnic, local, national, and transnational levels. Instead I emphasize the interrelatedness of the various social levels Yuval-Davis separates for the purpose of analytical clarity, and add other layers of the individual, subjective, and familial realms (Yuval-Davis, 1999).

13. "Since discourse is by definition shared, experience is collective as well as individual. Experience is a subject's history. Language is the site of history's enactment. Historical explanation cannot, therefore, separate the two" (Scott, 1992).

14. None of the women I met or interviewed in the course of this research refused to legalize or naturalize if they met the formal requirements. However, the women I interviewed who were eligible for naturalization but had not naturalized overwhelmingly explained this in terms of formal obstacles in the U.S. side of the process. This was true for women with relatively little formal education in Mexico and almost no English literacy skills, who were sure that they would be unable to pass the naturalization exam and/or the interview portion of the application process. Another set of obstacles arose with the reorganization of federal immigration administration after September 11, 2001, and in 2007, increases of almost 70 percent in the fees for naturalization applications, along with a doubling of the backlog / waiting time for processing of applications from 18 months to 3 years (Chishti and Bergeron, 2008).

Chapter 5

1. Translated from the original Spanish by author from interview with Adela on September 18, 1996.

2. "El qué dirán."

3. Though I only spoke with him a couple of times over the course of several years, her husband eventually saw through my ruse. Even though I thought I was being convincing, Adela would tell me later, always with a disarming laugh, that her husband had said that "that woman, your friend, the gringa, called again." He even seemed to know me if I hung up before speaking to him. My stomach would always knot up when I heard his voice and I got the smallest taste of Adela's quotidian stress and worried that my calls would contribute further to it.

4. In 1691, at the age of forty-three, Sor Juana was officially silenced by the Catholic Church hierarchy and ordered never to write again. In quoting this particular poem, Adela reminded me and herself that even though a powerful woman like Sor Juana could be silenced in her time, her words outlasted those of her detractors.

Sátira filosófica	*[A Philosophical Satire*
Hombres necios que acusáis	Misguided men, who will chastise
a la mujer sin razón,	a woman when no blame is due,
sin ver que sois la ocasión	oblivious that it is you
de lo mismo que culpáis:	who prompted what you criticize;

si con ansia sin igual	if your passions are so strong
solicitáis su desdén,	that you elicit their disdain,
¿por qué queréis que obren bien	how can you wish that they refrain
si las incitáis al mal?	when you incite them to their wrong?]

Translation from Sor Juana Inés de la Cruz, *Poems, Protest, and a Dream: Selected Writings*, translated by Margaret Sayers Peden (New York: Penguin, 1997), p. 149.

5. "¿A eso vas? ¡A que te laven el cerebro! Bola de viejas, lesbianas, marimachas." (Is that why you go there? So they can brainwash you? Bunch of old women, lesbians, dykes!) *Marimachas* may be translated as tomboys, she-men, or dykes.

6. "Me dijo que me iban a hacer un cocowash."

7. Very few of the women I interviewed drove or had access to cars, and many had never been to the other end of the city, either to the beach or Golden Gate Park, until they went on excursions with friends from the women's group.

8. "Domestic violence is not confined to physical battery; it includes psychological and emotional harm. Example of extreme cruelty include social isolation, threats, economic abuse, and other behaviors intended to control and exercise power over the applicant." VAWA also allows children in abusive parent-child relationships to self-petition (8 CFR §204) or for a parent to petition on a child's behalf (Pendleton, 1999, 9, 13). Estimates based on studies at battered women's shelters suggest that almost 70 percent of children in homes with spousal violence were themselves subjected to physical abuse or neglect, while almost 50 percent were physically or sexually abused. Advocates also point out the lasting psychological damage to children of witnessing abuse between parents (Jang, Marín, and Pendleton, 1997, 8).

9. VAWA requires the self-petitioner to be legally married to the abusive person and at least some of the abuse to have occurred in the United States. Other remedies, such as "suspension/cancellation of removal," have more flexible interpretations of what constitutes a "good faith marriage" (Pendleton, 1999, 18).

10. This work preceded Ong's more Foucauldian view of cultural citizenship as a process of subjectification, of transnational subjects making and being made into national citizens in relationship to the neoliberal state and its institutions, programs, and services (Ong, 1995, 1996).

Chapter 6

Portions of this chapter appeared earlier in my article "Necesidades y problemas: Immigrant Latina Vernaculars of Belonging, Coalition, and Citizenship in San Francisco, California," *Latino Studies* 2:1 (2004): 186–209.

1. This and subsequent quotations translated from the original Spanish by the author from interview with Caridad on September 20, 1996.

2. See also Andreas, (1985), Alvarez, (1990), Massolo, (1991), and Jelin, (1997).

3. Lok C. D. Siu (2005) describes how the Panamanian Constitution of 1940 revoked Chinese immigrants' citizenship rights and prohibited noncitizens from owning small retail businesses. These explicitly anti-Chinese laws prompted a large Chinese exodus from Panama. According to Siu, families with more resources tended to return to China, and others moved to the American Canal Zone, which operated outside of Panamanian law. Alicia did not contextualize her own family's return to China to the group in this fashion, but acknowledged to me in an understated way that it was a "difficult" time for Chinese people in Panama.

4. "When referring to ourselves within a white context, we often prefer more generic terms, like *Las Mujeres* or the combination *Chicana/Latina*, in opposition to *Hispanic*, which is often seen as inappropriate because of its conservative political connotations. When speaking among ourselves, we highlight and celebrate all of the nuances of identity—we are *Chicanas, Mexicanas, Mexican Americans, Spanish Americans, Tejanas, Hispanas, Mestizas, Indias,* or *Latinas*—and the terms of identification vary according to the context. This complexity of identification reflects the conundrum many Chicanas experience: on the one hand, together we are seen by others as a single social category, often Hispanic women. Yet the term *Hispanic,* imposed by the census bureau, is seen as inappropriate by many women who prefer to identify themselves in oppositional political terms" (Zavella, 1991, 74).

5. Chilango is the slightly pejorative Mexican nickname for people from Mexico City.

Chapter 7

1. This slogan constituted the theme of the 1995 United Nations Beijing Conference on Women, revealing the lag time between popular discourses and institutional appropriation thereof.

2. Since 1999, MUA has provided technical assistance to immigrant women's groups in Texas, Iowa, Washington, Alaska, Alabama, and Kentucky.

3. http://www.mujeresunidas.net/english/caring.html.

4. Section 9528 of the federal No Child Left Behind Act of 2001 allowed the military access to records of public school students.

5. Resolution 212-10A15, Student/Parent Privacy, introduced on December 10, 2002, United Nations' Human Rights Day, by Commissioners Eric Mar, Mark Sanchez, Eddie Chin, Emilio B. Cruz, Dan Kelly, Sarah Lipson, and Jill Wynns. Adopted by the San Francisco Board of Education on January 14, 2003.

6. José was placed in foster care and graduated from high school in Los Angeles; he dreamed of college before enlisting as a "green-card soldier." His story was told in a 2006 Swiss documentary entitled *The Short Life of José Antonio Gutierrez.* As a result of the publicity generated by such postmortem naturalizations and pressure from increasingly desperate military recruiters, President George W. Bush approved a

fast-track process in 2003 that allowed active military members to naturalize without paying the $320 application fee, meeting the minimum residency requirement, or being physically present in the United States for immigration interviews and hearings. There are at least twenty-seven thousand members of the armed forces without U.S. citizenship (Wong, 2005).

7. Ordinance No. 375-89, Appl 10/24/89, also known as the Sanctuary Ordinance, implemented as Chapter 12H of the local administrative code (http://www.bayswan.org/sftraffick/SFcityrefuge.html) and followed in 1999 by Board of Supervisors Resolution No. 515-99 declaring the city an "I.N.S. Raid-Free Zone."

8. " 'The City's public awareness campaign is a reminder that City employees will not report individuals or their immigration status to federal immigration agents,' said Mayor Newsom. 'San Francisco residents should feel safe when they visit a public health clinic, enroll their children in school, report a crime to the Police Department or seek out other City services' " (Office of the Mayor, 2008).

9. Immigrant Rights Commission, Resolution 003-2008, May 12, 2008, http://www.sfgov.org/site/immigrant_page.asp?id=81303.

10. The Mexican national development plan in the 1970s was tied to foreign debt based on oil production, so that when oil prices dropped in 1981, capital fled the country, the peso was devalued 50 percent, and inflation reached 150 percent (Stephen 1997, 114). Structural adjustment programs aimed at shoring up available cash to meet the foreign debt payments led to shrinking government expenditures on social programs and services for the poor, especially for women and children. Although both rural and urban workers were affected drastically, the process accelerated existing urbanization as subsistence farmers left the countryside in search of employment. By 1990, 71.3 percent of the Mexico population lived in cities (cited in Stephen, 1997, 124).

11. In 2004, Antonio Villaraigosa was elected the first Latino mayor of Los Angeles in 133 years, while at the national level Robert Menendez of New Jersey chaired the Democratic Caucus, making him the highest-ranking Latino in the history of the Congress. Mexican American Governor Bill Richardson of New Mexico has made two consecutive shortlists for Democratic vice presidential candidates. In addition to being promoted to attorney general of the United States by President George W. Bush, Alberto Gonzalez was widely discussed as possible choice for elevation to the Supreme Court.

12. The PRI also sponsored bizarre women-oriented events such as a performance by ten male strippers sporting PRI boxer shorts that spelled out "Vota PRI" on their backsides (Quiñones, 2000, A1).

13. "The Mexican government estimates that as many as 1.5 million Mexicans living in the United States have valid voter credentials and could cast ballots either in their hometowns or at the special polling stations that are designed for all Mexicans in transit" (Iliff and Corchada, 2000).

14. U.S. Citizenship and Immigration Services (USCIS), U.S. Customs and Border Protection (CBP), U.S. Immigration and Customs Enforcement (ICE).

15. "[A] critical multicultural approach interprets issues of national identity both dialectically and dialogically to propose, not only a synthesis of national expression, but the persistence and validation of ethnic and cultural difference" (García, 1995, 153).

16. For a historicized treatment of the relationship between immigration and the development of this national myth, see Steinberg, (1989).

Appendix

1. This collaborative relationship explains in part my resistance to requests from some readers to evaluate or critique aspects of MUA's programs or practice.

2. Thanks to Professor Seline Szkupinski-Quiroga for directing me to these statistics.

References

Abu-Lughod, Lila. 1995. A tale of two pregnancies. In *Women writing culture*, edited by Ruth Behard and Deborah Gordon, 339–49. Berkeley: University of California Press.

Alvarez, Sonia. 1990. *Engendering democracy in Brazil: Women's movements in transitional politics*. Princeton, N.J.: Princeton University Press.

Andreas, Carol. 1985. *Why women rebel: The rise of popular feminism in Peru*. Westport, Conn.: Lawrence Hill and Company.

Anzaldúa, Gloria. 1990. La conciencia de la mestiza: Towards a new consciousness. In *Making face, making soul/Haciendo caras: Creative and critical perspectives by women of color*, edited by Gloria Anzaldúa, 377–89. San Francisco: Aunt Lute Foundation.

Asen, Robert. 2004. A discourse theory of citizenship. *Quarterly Journal of Speech* 90(2): 189–211.

Bacon, David. 2008. *Illegal people: How globalization causes migration and criminalizes people*. Boston: Beacon Press.

Barbalet, J. M. 1988. *Citizenship: Rights, struggle and class inequality*. Minneapolis: University of Minnesota Press.

Bassin, Donna, Margaret Honney, and Meryle Mahere Kaplan. 1994. *Representations of motherhood*. New Haven, Conn.: Yale University Press.

Baumann, Gerd. 1996. *Contesting culture: Discourses of identity in multi-ethnic London*. Cambridge, U.K.: Cambridge University Press.

Bell, David, and Jon Binnie. 2000. *The sexual citizen: Queer politics and beyond*. Cambridge, U.K.: Polity Press.

Benmayor, Rina, Ana Juarbe, Celia Alarez, and Blanca Vasquez. 1988. Stories to live by: Continuity and change in three generations of Puerto Rican women. *Oral History Review* 16 (Fall): 1–46.

Benmayor, Rina, Rosa M. Torruellas, and Ana L. Juarbe. 1992. *Responses to poverty among Puerto Rican women: Identity, community, and cultural citizenship.* New York: Centro de Estudios Puertorriqueños, Hunter College.

Berlant, Lauren. 1997. *The queen of America goes to Washington City: Essays on sex and citizenship.* Durham, N.C.: Duke University Press.

Bernstein, Nina. 1997. Deletion of word in welfare bill opens foster care to big business. *New York Times* May 4, http://www.nytimes.com/1997/05/04/us/deletion -of-word-in-welfare-bill-opens-foster-care-to-big-business.html?pagewanted= all.

Beverly, John. 2004. *Testimonio: On the politics of truth.* Minneapolis: University of Minnesota Press.

Bhabha, Jacqueline. 1998. "Get back to where you once belonged": Identity, citizenship, and exclusion in Europe. *Human Rights Quarterly* 20: 592–627.

Bhabha, Jacqueline, and Susan Schmidt. 2008. Seeking asylum alone: Unaccompanied and separated children and refugee protection in the U.S. *Journal of the History of Childhood and Youth* 1(1): 127–37.

Bloemraad, Irene. 2006. *Becoming a citizen: Incorporating immigrants and refugees in the United States and Canada.* Berkeley: University of California Press.

Boehm, Deborah A. 2008. "Now I am a man and a woman!": Gendered moves and migrations in a transnational Mexican community. *Latin American Perspectives* 35(1): 16–30.

Boswell, Richard A. 1995. Restrictions on non-citizens' access to public benefits: Flawed premise, unnecessary response. *UCLA Law Review* 42(August): 1475.

Bredbenner, Candice Lewis. 1998. A nationality of her own: Women, marriage, and the law of citizenship. Berkeley: University of California Press.

Brodkin, Karen. 2007. *Making democracy matter: Identity and activism in Los Angeles.* New Brunswick, N.J.: Rutgers University Press.

Brown, Wendy. 2004. "The most we can hope for . . .": Human rights and the politics of fatalism. *South Atlantic Quarterly* 2(3): 451–63.

Brubaker, William Rogers. 1989. *Immigration and the politics of citizenship in Europe and the United States.* Lanham, Md.: University Press of America.

Buckley, Cara, and Annie Correal. 2008. Domestic workers organize to end an 'atmosphere of violence' on the job. *New York Times,* June 9, http://www.nytimes.com/ 2008/06/09/nyregion/09domestic.html?scp=1&sq=domestic%20workers%20or ganize&st=cse.

Butler, Judith. 1992. Contingent foundations: Feminism and the question of "postmodernism." In *Feminists theorize the political,* edited by Judith Butler and Joan W. Scott, 3–21. New York: Routledge.

Calvo, Janet M. 1991. Spouse-based immigration laws: The legacies of coverture. *San Diego Law Review* 28(3): 593–644.

Camayd-Freixas, Erik. 2008. Statement of Dr. Erik Camayd-Freixas, federally certi-
fied interpreter at the U.S. District Court for the Northern District of Iowa. In
*Subcommittee on Immigration, citizenship, refugees, border security and interna-
tional law*, 20. U.S. House of Representatives. Washington, D.C. (judiciary.house
.gov/hearings/pdf/Camayd-Freixas080724.pdf).

Castañeda, Alejandro. 2004. Roads to citizenship: Mexican migrants in the United
States. *Latino Studies* 2(1): 70–98.

Cervantes, Nancy, Sasha Khokha, and Bobbie Murray. 1995. Hate unleashed: Los Angeles in the aftermath of Proposition 187. *Chicano-Latino Law Review* 17 (Fall): 1–23.

Cerwonka, Allaine, and Liisa H. Malkki. 2007. *Improvising theory: Process and temporality in ethnographic fieldwork*. Chicago: University of Chicago Press.

Chang, Connie. 1997. Immigrants under the new welfare law: A call for uniformity,
a call for justice. *UCLA Law Review* 45(October): 205–80.

Chang, Grace. 2000. *Disposable domestics: Immigrant women workers in the global
economy*. Cambridge, Mass.: South End Press.

Chavez, Leo. 2001. *Covering immigration: Popular images and the politics of the nation*. Berkeley: University of California Press.

———. 2007. A glass half empty: Latina reproduction and public discourse. In *Women
and migration in the U.S.-Mexico borderlands*, edited by Denise A. Segura and
Patricia Zavella, 67–91. Durham, N.C.: Duke University Press.

Chishti, Muzzafar, and Claire Bergeron. 2008. USCIS: Backlog in naturalization applications will take nearly three years to clear. *Migration Information Source*,
February 15, http://www.migrationinformation.org/USfocus/display.cfm?id=673.

Clarke, John. 2005. New Labour's citizens: Activated, empowered, responsibilized,
abandoned? *Critical Social Policy Ltd.* 25(4): 447–63.

Clarke, Paul A. 1996. *Deep citizenship*. East Haven, Conn.: Pluto Press.

Coalition for Immigrant Rights (CIR). 1997. *Newsletter* 5(1), May.

Coll, Kathleen. 2004. Necesidades y problemas: Immigrant Latina vernaculars of
belonging, coalition, and citizenship in San Francisco, California. *Latino Studies*
2(1): 186–209.

———. 2005. "Yo no estoy perdida": Immigrant women (re)locating citizenship. In
Passing lines: Sexuality and immigration, edited by Keja Valens, Bill Johnson
González, and Brad Epps, 389–410. Cambridge, Mass.: Harvard University Press
and David Rockefeller Center Series on Latin American Studies.

Collier, Jane. 2000. Victorian visions. In *Gender Matters: Rereading Michelle Z. Rosaldo*, edited by Bill Maurer and Alejandro Lugo, 145–159. Ann Arbor: University
of Michigan Press.

Collier, Jane, and Sylvia J. Yanagisako. 1979. Introduction to *Gender and kinship:
Essays toward a unified analysis*, edited by Jane Collier and Sylvia J. Yanagisako,
14–52. Stanford, Calif.: Stanford University Press.

———. 1987. Introduction to *Gender and kinship: Essays toward a unified analysis*, edited by Jane Collier and Sylvia J. Yanagisako, 1–13. Stanford, Calif.: Stanford University Press.

Coombe, Rosemary. 2007. The work of rights at the limits of governmentality. *Anthropologica* 48(2): 284–89.

Cornelius, Wayne. 1990. Impacts of the 1986 U.S. immigration law on emigration from rural Mexican sending communities. In *Undocumented migration to the United States: IRCA and the experience of the 1990s*, edited by Frank D. Bean, Barry Edmonston, and Jeffrey S. Passel, 227–46. Santa Monica, Calif.: RAND Corporation and the Urban Institute.

Coutin, Susan Bibler. 2000. *Legalizing moves: Salvadoran immigrants' struggle for U.S. residency*. Ann Arbor: University of Michigan Press.

———. 2003. Cultural logics of belonging and movement in transnationalism, naturalization, and U.S. immigration politics. *American Ethnologist* 30 (4): 508–26.

———. 2007. *Nations of emigrants: Shifting boundaries of citizenship in El Salvador and the United States*. Ithaca, N.Y.: Cornell University Press.

Coutin, Susan Bibler, and Phyllis Pease Chock. 1995. "Your friend the illegal": Definition and paradox in newspaper accounts of U.S. immigration reform. *Identities* 2(1–2): 123–48.

Cruikshank, Barbara. 1999. *The will to empower: Democratic citizens and other subjects*. Ithaca, N.Y.: Cornell University Press.

Cruz, Sor Juana Inés de la. 1997. *Poems, protest, and a dream: Selected writings*, translated by Margaret Sayers Peden, 149. New York: Penguin.

Dagnino, Evelina. 1994. On becoming a citizen: The story of Dona Marlene. In *Migration and identity*, vol. 3, edited by Rina Benmayor and Andor Skotnes, 69–84. Oxford, U.K.: Oxford University Press.

———. 2003. Citizenship in Latin America: An introduction. *Latin American Perspectives* 30(2): 3–17.

———. 2007. "We all have rights, but . . .": Contesting concepts of citizenship in Brazil. In *Inclusive citizenship: Meanings and expressions*, edited by N. Kabeer, 149–63. London: Zed Books.

Daniels, Roger. 1989. *Asian America: Chinese and Japanese in the United States since 1850*. Seattle: University of Washington Press.

Dávila, Arlene. 2001. *Latinos, Inc.: The making and marketing of a people*. Berkeley: University of California Press.

———. 2004. *Barrio Dreams: Puerto Ricans, Latinos, and the Neoliberal City*. Berkeley: University of California Press.

Davis, Mike, 2000. *Magical urbanism: Latinos reinvent the U.S. big city*. London: Verso.

De Genova, Nicholas. 2005. *Working the boundaries: Race, space, and "illegality" in Mexican Chicago*. Durham, N.C.: Duke University Press.

De Genova, Nicholas, and Ana Yolanda Ramos-Zayas. 2003. *Latino crossings: Mexicans, Puerto Ricans, and the politics of race and citizenship.* New York: Routledge.

Dehart, Monica. 2010. *Ethnic entrepreneurs.* Stanford: Stanford University Press.

de la Garza, Rodolfo O., and Louis DeSipio. 1993. Save the baby, change the bathwater after seventeen years of the Voting Rights Act coverage. *Texas Law Review* 71(June): 1479.

Delaney, Carol. 1995. Father state, motherland, and the birth of modern Turkey. In *Naturalizing power: Essays in feminist cultural analysis,* edited by Sylvia Yanagisako and Carol Delaney, 177–200. New York: Routledge.

De León, Richard Edward. 1992. *Left Coast city: Progressive politics in San Francisco, 1975–1991.* Lawrence: University Press of Kansas.

Díaz-Barriga, Miguel. 1996. Necesidad: Notes on the discourses of urban politics in the Ajusco Foothills of Mexico City. *American Ethnologist* 23(2): 291–310.

———. 2000. The domestic/public in Mexico City: Notes on theory, social movements, and the essentializations of everyday life. In *Rereading Michelle Z. Rosaldo,* edited by Bill Maurer and Alejandro Lugo, 116–42. Ann Arbor: University of Michigan Press.

Dore, Elizabeth. 1997. *Gender politics in Latin America: Debates in theory and practice.* New York: Monthly Review Press.

Dummett, Ann, and Andrew Nicol. 1990. *Subjects, citizens, aliens and others: Nationality and immigration law.* London: Weidenfeld and Nicolson.

Ebron, Paulla A. 2007. "Constituting the subject through performative acts." In *Africa after gender?* edited by Catherine M. Cole, Takyiwaa Manuh, and Stephan Miescher, 171–90. Bloomington: Indiana University Press.

Espín, Olivia. 1997. *Latina realities: Essays on healing, migration and sexuality.* Boulder, Colo.: Westview Press.

Flores, William. 2003. New citizens, new rights: Undocumented immigrants and Latino cultural citizenship. *Latin American Perspectives* 30(2): 87–100.

Flores, William, and Rina Benmayor. 1997. *Latino cultural citizenship.* Boston: Beacon.

Foucault, Michel. 1979. *Discipline and punish: The birth of the prison.* New York: Vintage.

Fujiwara, Lynn H. 2005. Immigrant rights are human rights: The reframing of immigrant entitlement and welfare. *Social Problems* 52(1): 79–101.

García, Rubén. 1995. Critical race theory and Proposition 187: The racial politics of immigration law. *Chicano-Latino Law Review* 1: 118–48.

García Bedolla, Lisa. 2005. *Fluid borders: Latino power, identity, and politics in Los Angeles.* Berkeley: University of California Press.

Giddens, Anthony. 1992. *The transformation of intimacy.* Cambridge, U.K.: Polity Press.

Glendon, Mary Ann. 1991. *Rights talk: The impoverishment of political discourse.* New York: Free Press.

Godfrey, Brian. 1988. *Neighborhoods in transition: The making of San Francisco's ethnic and non-conformist communities.* Berkeley: University of California Press.

Goldfarb, Emily. 1999. Caught at the public policy crossroads: The impact of welfare reform on battered immigrant women. In *Report on behalf of the National Network on Behalf of Battered Immigrant Women.* San Francisco: Family Violence Prevention Fund.

Goldring, Luin. 2001. The gender and geography of citizenship in Mexico–U.S. transnational spaces. *Identities* 7(4): 501–37.

Gordon, Linda. 1990. Family violence, feminism, and social control. In *Women, the state, and welfare,* edited by Linda Gordon, 178–98. Madison: University of Wisconsin Press.

Gupta, Akhil, and James Ferguson. 1992. Beyond "culture": Space, identity, and the politics of difference. *Cultural Anthropology* 7(1): 6–23.

Gutierrez, Lorraine M., and Edith A. Lewis. 1999. *Empowering women of color.* New York: Columbia University Press.

Guttman, Matthew. 1996. *The meanings of macho: Being a man in Mexico City.* Berkeley: University of California Press.

———. 1997. The ethnographic (g)ambit: Women and the negotiation of masculinity in Mexico City. *American Ethnologist* 24(4): 833–55.

Hall, Stuart. 1990. Identity and diaspora. In *Identity: Community, culture and difference,* edited by J. Rutherford, 222–37. London: Lawrence and Wishart.

Hall, Stuart, and David Held. 1989. Citizens and citizenship. In *New times: The changing face of politics in the 1990s,* edited by Stuart Hall and Martin Jacque, 172–88. New York: Verso.

Handler, Joel. 1995. *The poverty of welfare reform.* New Haven, Conn.: Yale University Press.

Haney-López, Ian F. 1995. *White by law: The legal construction of race.* New York: New York University Press.

Hansen, Gladys. 1995. *The San Francisco almanac.* San Francisco: Chronicle Books.

Hardy-Fanta, Carol. 1993. *Latina politics, Latino politics: Gender, cultural and political participation in Boston.* Philadelphia: Temple University Press.

Hartman, Chester, with Sarah Carnochan. 2002. *City for sale: The transformation of San Francisco.* Berkeley: University of California Press.

Hayes, Linda B. 1994. California's Prop. 187. *New York Times,* October 15, A18.

Healey, Kelly, and Christine Smith, with Chris O'Sullivan. 1998. *Batterer intervention: Program approaches and criminal justice strategies.* Washington, D.C.: U.S. Department of Justice, Office of Justice Programs, National Institute of Justice.

Hendricks, Tyche. 2009. Suits for wrongful deportation by ICE rise. *San Francisco Chronicle,* July 2, http://www.sfgate.com/cgi-bin/article.cgi?f=/c/a/2009/07/27/MNH618NPM6.DTL.

Herrell, Richard K. 1996. Sin, sickness, crime: Queer desire and the American state. *Identities: Global Studies in Culture and Power* 2(3): 273–300.

Hobson, Barbara, Anne Marie Berggren, and Nancy Fraser. 1997. *Crossing borders: Gender and citizenship in transition.* Stockholm, Sweden: FRN.

Hogeland, Chris, and Karen A. Rosen. 1990. *A needs assessment of undocumented women.* San Francisco: Northern California Coalition for Immigrant Rights.

Holder, Ann S. 2008. What's sex got to do with it? Race, power, citizenship, and "intermediate identities" in the post-emancipation United States. *Journal of African American History* 93(2): 153–73.

Hondagneu-Sotelo, Pierrette. 1994. *Gendered transitions: Mexican experiences of immigration.* Berkeley: University of California Press.

———. 2001. *Doméstica: Immigrant workers cleaning and caring in the shadows of affluence.* Berkeley: University of California Press.

Iliff, Laurence, and Alfredo Corchada. 2000. Mexican emigrants face ballot shortage. *San Francisco Examiner,* July 2.

Immigration and Naturalization Service (INS). 1999. Illegal alien resident population, Summary August 11. http://www.ins.usdoj.gov/graphics/aboutins/statistics/illegalalien/#Table1.

Inda, Jonathan Xavier. 2002. Biopower, reproduction, and the migrant woman's body. In *Decolonial voices: Chicana and Chicano cultural studies in the 21st century,* edited by Arturo J. Aldama and Naomi Quiñonez, 98–112. Bloomington: Indiana University Press.

———. 2005. *Targeting immigrants: Government, technology, and ethics.* Malden, Mass.: Blackwell.

———. 2007. The value of immigrant life. In *Women and migration in the U.S.-Mexico borderlands,* edited by Denise Segura and Patricia Zavella, 134–57. Durham, N.C.: Duke University Press.

Jacobson, Robin Dale. 2008. *The new nativism: Proposition 187 and the debate over immigration.* Minneapolis: University of Minnesota Press.

Jang, Deeana, Debbie Lee, and Rachel Morello-Frosch. 1990. Domestic violence in the immigrant and refugee communities: Asserting the rights of battered women. *Response* 13(4): 1–7.

Jang, Deeana, Leni Marín, and Gail Pendleton. 1997. *Domestic violence in immigrant and refugee communities: Asserting the rights of battered women,* 2nd ed. San Francisco: Family Violence Prevention Fund.

Janofsky, Michael. 2000. Candidates courting Hispanic vote: "Soccer moms" of 2000 elections enjoy their increasing power. *New York Times,* June 25.

Jelin, Elizabeth. 1997. Engendering human rights. In *Gender politics in Latin America: Debates in theory and practice,* edited by E. Dore, 65–83. New York: Monthly Review Press.

Johnson, Hans. 1996. *Undocumented immigration to California, 1980–1993.* San Francisco: Public Policy Institute of California.

Johnson, Hans P., Belinda I. Reyes, Laura Mameesh, and Elisa Barbour. 1999. *Taking the oath: An analysis of naturalization in California and the United States.* San Francisco: Public Policy Institute of California.

Johnson, Kevin R. 1995. Public benefits and immigration: The intersection of immigration status, ethnicity, gender, and class. *UCLA Law Review* 42(August): 1509–75.

Jonas, Susanne, and Suzi Dod Thomas. 1999. *Immigration: A civil rights issue for the Americas.* Wilmington, Del.: Social Justice Press.

Kivisto, Peter. 2001. Theorizing transnational immigration: A critical review of current efforts. *Racial and Ethnic Studies* 24(4): 549–77.

Knight, Heather. 2008. Immigration raids at 11 El Balazo restaurants—63 seized. *San Francisco Chronicle,* May 3, B3.

Kymlicka, Will. 2001. *Politics in the vernacular: Nationalism, multiculturalism and citizenship.* Oxford, U.K.: Oxford University Press.

Kymlicka, Will, and Wayne Norman. 2000. Citizenship in culturally diverse societies: Issues, contexts, concepts. In *Citizenship in diverse societies,* edited by Will Kymlicka and Wayne Norman, 1–41. Oxford, U.K.: Oxford University Press.

Li, Tania Murray. 2005. Beyond the state and failed schemes. *American Anthropologist* 107(3): 383–94.

———. 2007. *The will to improve: Governmentality, development, and the practice of politics.* Durham, N.C.: Duke University Press.

Lilienthal, Ryan. 1996. Note: Old hurdles hamper new options for battered immigrant women. *Brooklyn Law Review* 62(Winter): 1595–1633.

Lister, Ruth. 1997. *Citizenship: Feminist perspectives.* Basingstoke, U.K.: Macmillan.

———. 2007. Inclusive citizenship: Realizing the potential. *Citizenship Studies* 11(1): 49–61.

Lowe, Lisa. 1996. *Immigrant acts: On Asian American cultural politics.* Durham, N.C.: Duke University Press.

Lubhéid, Eithne. 2005. Entry denied: Heteronormativity, responsibility, and neoliberal governance. In *Passing lines: Sexuality and immigration,* edited by Brad Epps, Keja Valens, and Bill Johnson Gonzalez. Cambridge, Mass.: David Rockefeller Center for Latin American Studies / Harvard University.

Mahler, Sarah. 1995. *American dreaming: Immigrant life on the margins.* Princeton, N.J.: Princeton University Press.

Malkki, Liisa H. 2007. Tradition and improvisation in ethnographic fieldwork. In *Improvising theory: Process and temporality in ethnographic fieldwork,* edited by Allaine Cerwonka and Liisa Malkki, 162–87. Chicago: University of Chicago Press.

Mamdani, Mahmood. 2000. *Beyond rights talk and culture talk: Comparative essays on the politics of rights and culture.* Cape Town, South Africa: David Philip.

Marcus, George E. 2008. The end(s) of ethnography: Social/cultural anthropology's signature form of producing knowledge in transition. *Cultural Anthropology* 23(1): 1–14.

Marshall, T. H. 1964. Citizenship and social class. In *Class, citizenship, and social development*. Westport, Conn.: Greenwood Press.

Martínez, Demetria. 2000. Tally of the dead rises on Mexican border. *National Catholic Reporter*, June 30.

Massey, Doreen. 2004. Geographies of responsibility. *Geografiska Annaler* 86(B): 5–18.

Massolo, Alejandra. 1991. *Por amor y coraje: Mujeres en movimientos urbanos en la ciudad de México*. Mexico City: PIEM/UNAM.

McCarthy, Kevin F., and Georges Vernez. 1997. *Immigration in a changing economy: California's experience*. Santa Monica, Calif.: Rand Corporation.

Menjivar, Cecilia, 2000. *Fragmented ties: Salvadoran immigrant networks in America*. Berkeley: University of California Press.

———. 2006. Liminal legality: Salvadoran and Guatemalan immigrants' lives in the United States. *American Journal of Sociology* 111(4): 999–1037.

Merry, Sally Engle. 1995. Gender violence and legally engendered selves. *Identities* 2(1–2): 49–73.

———. 2006a. Anthropology, law and transnational processes. *Annual Review of Anthropology* 35(1): 99–116.

———. 2006b. *Human rights and gender violence: Translating international law into local justice*. Chicago: University of Chicago Press.

———. 2006c. Transnational human rights and local activism: Mapping the middle. *American Anthropologist* 108(1): 38–51.

Mirabal, Nancy Raquel. 2009. Geographies of displacement: Latina/os, oral history and the politics of gentrification in San Francisco's Mission District. *Public Historian* 31(2): 7–31.

Mogrovejo, Norma. 1998. Sexual preference, the ugly duckling of feminist demands: The lesbian movement in Mexico. In *Female desires: Same sex relations and transgender practices across cultures*, edited by Evelyn Blackwood and Saskia Wieringa, 308–35. New York: Columbia University Press.

———. 2000. *Un amor que se atrevió a decir su nombre: La lucha de las lesbianas y su relación con los movimientos homosexual y feminist en américa latina*. Mexico City: Centro de Documentación y Archivo Histórico Lésbico (CDAHL), Plaza y Valdés.

Molina, Natalia. 2006. *Fit to be citizens? Public health and race in Los Angeles, 1879–1939*. Berkeley: University of California Press.

Mouffe, Chantal. 1992. Feminism, citizenship, and radical democratic politics. In *Feminists theorize the political*, edited by Judith Butler and Joan W. Scott, 369–84. New York: Routledge.

Mujeres Unidas y Activas (MUA). n.d. *Caring Hands / Manos Cariñosas Manual*. San Francisco, Calif.: Mujeres Unidas y Activas/Caring Hands.

Neilson, Victoria. 2005. Homosexual or female? Applying gender-based asylum juris-prudence to lesbian asylum claims. *Stanford Law and Policy Review* 16: 417–44.

Neuman, Gerald L. 1993. The lost century of American immigration law (1776–1875). *Columbia Law Review* 93: 1833–1901.

———. 1995. Aliens as outlaws: Government services, Proposition 187, and the struc-ture of equal protection doctrine. *UCLA Law Review* 42: 1425–52.

Newsom, Gavin. 2008. Sanctuary city. *San Francisco Chronicle*, August 8, B11.

Ngai, Mae M. 2004. *Impossible subjects: Illegal aliens and the making of modern Amer-ica*. Princeton, N.J.: Princeton University Press.

Office of the Mayor, City and County of San Francisco. 2008. Press release, April 2, http://www.sfgov.org/site/mayor_index.asp?id=78378.

Ong, Aihwa. 1995. Making the biopolitical subject: Cambodian immigrants, refugee medicine and cultural citizenship in California. *Social Science and Medicine* 40(9): 1243–57.

———. 1996. Cultural citizenship as subject-making: Immigrants negotiate racial and cultural boundaries in the United States [and Comments and Reply]. *Current An-thropology* 37(5): 737–62.

———. 2003. *Buddha is hiding: Refugees, citizenship, the new America*. Berkeley: Uni-versity of California Press.

Orloff, Ann Shola. 1993. Gender and the social rights of citizenship: The comparative analysis of gender relations and welfare states. *American Sociological Review* 58(3): 303–28.

———. 1996. Gender in the welfare state. *Annual Review of Sociology* 22: 51–78.

Osanloo, Arzoo. 2006. Islamico-civil "rights talk": Women, subjectivity, and law in Iranian family court. *American Ethnologist* 33(2): 191–209.

———. 2009. *The politics of women's rights in Iran*. Princeton, N.J.: Princeton Univer-sity Press.

Ovrebo, Beverly, Martha Ryan, Kelle Jackson, and Kimberly Hutchinson. 1994. The homeless prenatal program: A model for empowering homeless pregnant women. *Health Education Quarterly* 21(2): 187–98.

Pamuk, Ayse. 2003. *Children under five years of age in poverty in San Francisco, 2000*. San Francisco: Public Research Institute at San Francisco State University.

Pardo, Mary. 1990. Mexican American women grassroots community activists: "Mothers of East Los Angeles." *Frontiers* 11(1): 1–7.

———. 1991. Creating community: Mexican American women in East Los Angeles. *Aztlán* 20(1): 39–71.

———. 1995. Doing it for the kids: Mexican American community activist, border femi-nists? In *Feminist organizations: Harvest of the new women's movement*, edited by Myra Marx Ferree and Patricia Yancy Martin. Philadelphia: Temple University Press.

Park, Jin S. 1995. Pink asylum: Political asylum eligibility of gay men and lesbians under U.S. immigration policy. *UCLA Law Review* 42: 1115–56.

Parreñas, Rhacel Salazar. 2001. Transgressing the nation-state: The partial citizenship and "imagined (global) community" of migrant Filipina domestic workers. *Signs: Journal of Women in Culture and Society* 26(4): 1129–54.

———. 2005. *Children of global migration.* Stanford: Stanford University Press.

Pateman, Carol. 1988. *The sexual contract.* Stanford, Calif.: Stanford University Press.

———. 1989. *The disorder of women, democracy, feminism and political theory.* Stanford, Calif.: Stanford University Press.

Pendleton, Gail. 1997. Applications for immigration status under the Violence Against Women Act (VAWA). In *Domestic violence in immigrant and refugee communities: Asserting the rights of battered women,* by Deeana Jang, Leni Marín, and Gail Pendleton. San Francisco: Family Violence Prevention Fund.

Pérez, Gina. 2002. The real "real world": Gentrification and the politics of space in Chicago. *Urban Anthropology* 3(1): 37–88.

———. 2003. "Puertorriqueñas rencorosas y mejicanas sufridas": Gendered ethnic identity formation in Chicago's Latino community. *Journal of Latin American Anthropology* 8(2): 96–125.

———. 2004. *The near northwest side story: Migration, displacement and Puerto Rican families.* Berkeley: University of California Press.

Plummer, Kenneth. 1995. Intimate citizenship: The politics of sexual story-telling. In *Telling sexuality stories: Power, change and social worlds,* 144–66. London: Routledge.

Portes, Alejandro, and Rubén G. Rumbaut. 1996. *Immigrant America: A portrait.* Los Angeles and Oxford: University of California Press.

Pratt, Mary Louise. 1993. Criticism in the contact zone: Decentering community and nation. In *Critical theory, cultural politics and Latin American narrative,* edited by Steven M. Bell and Albert H. LeMay, 83–103. Notre Dame, Ind.: University of Notre Dame Press.

Putnam, Robert. 2000. *Bowling alone: The collapse and revival of American community.* New York: Simon and Schuster.

Quayson, Valentina Napolitano. 2005. Social suffering and embodied states of male transnational migrancy in San Francisco, California. *Identities: Global Studies in Culture and Power* 12: 335–62.

Quiñones, Sam. 2000. PRI's nearly naked ambition: Mexico's ruling party woos women. *San Francisco Examiner,* June 30, A1.

Ramos, Juanita. 1987. *Compañeras/Latina lesbians: An anthology.* New York: Latina Lesbian History Project.

Ramos-Zayas, Ana Y. 2003. *National performances: The politics of class, race, and space in Puerto Rican Chicago.* Chicago: University of Chicago Press.

———. 2004. Delinquent citizenship, national performances: Racialization, surveillance, and the politics of "worthiness" in Puerto Rican Chicago. *Latino Studies* 2: 26–44.

Razack, Sherene. 1995. Domestic violence as gender persecution: Policing the borders of nation, race, and gender. *Canadian Journal of Women and the Law/Revue Femmes et Droit* 8(1): 45–88.

———. 1998. *Looking white people in the eye: Gender, race, and culture in courtrooms and classrooms.* Toronto: University of Toronto Press.

Reed, Diane F., and Kathy Krebs-Dean. 1996. SB 697 community needs assessment: Executive summary indicator data report, Anthology of local studies of community perceptions on health related issues. Northern California Council for the Community.

Reiter, Rayna R. 1975. Men and women in the south of France: Public and private domains. In *Toward an anthropology of women*, edited by Rayna R. Reiter, 252–82. New York: Monthly Review Press.

Rich, Adrienne. 1995 (1977). *Of women born: Motherhood as experience and institution.* New York: Norton.

Ricourt, Milagros, and Ruby Danta. 2003. *Hispanas de Queens: Latino panethnicity in a New York City neighborhood.* Ithaca, N.Y.: Cornell University Press.

Romero, Mary. 2002 (1992). *Maid in the U.S.A.* New York: Routledge.

Rosaldo, Michelle Z. 1980. The use and abuse of anthropology: Reflections of feminist and cross-cultural understandings. *Signs* 5(3): 389–417.

Rosaldo, Renato. 1989. *Culture and truth: The remaking of social analysis.* Boston: Beacon.

———. 1994. Cultural citizenship in San José, California. *PoLAR: Political and Legal Anthropology Review* 17(2): 57–63.

———. 1996. Foreword. *Stanford Law Review* 48(5): 1037–46.

Rosaldo, Renato, William V. Flores, and Blanca Silvestrini. 1993. *Identity, conflict, and evolving Latino communities: Cultural citizenship in San Jose, California.* Stanford, Calif.: Stanford Center for Chicano Research.

Ruíz, Vicki L. 2000. Claiming public space at work, church, and neighborhood In *Las obreras: Chicana politics of work and family*, edited by Vicki L. Ruíz. Los Angeles: UCLA Chicano Studies Research Center.

Sandino-Glasser, Gloria. 1998. Los confundidos: De-conflating Latino/as' race and ethnicity. *Chicano-Latino Law Review* 19(Spring): 69–162.

Sarkar, Pia. 2000. Mexico not too far for ardent voters: Expatriates in U.S. trekking thousands of miles for elections. *San Francisco Examiner*, July 2, A1.

Scott, Joan W. 1992. Experience. In *Feminists theorize the political*, edited by Judith Butler and Joan W. Scott, 22–40. New York: Routledge.

Sharma, Aradhana. 2006. Crossbreeding institutions, breeding struggle: Women's empowerment, neoliberal governmentality, and state (re)formation in India. *Cultural Anthropology* 21(1): 60–95.

———. 2008. *Logics of empowerment: Development, gender and governance in neoliberal India*. Minneapolis: University of Minnesota Press.

Shepard, Paul. 2000. Race splits schools in U.S., officials say. *Boston Globe*, May 19.

Sheridan, Mary Beth. 2000. From homemaker to kingmaker, Mexico: Women have gained unprecedented attention amid changes in political participation. *Los Angeles Times*, June 30, A1, http://articles.latimes.com/2000/jun/30/news/mn-46340.

Shklar, Judith. 1991. *American citizenship: The quest for inclusion*. Cambridge, Mass.: Harvard University Press.

Silliman, Jael, Marlene Gerber Fried, Loretta Ross, and Elena R. Gutierrez, 2004. *Undivided rights: Women of color organize for reproductive justice*. Cambridge, Mass.: South End Press.

Siu, Lok C. D. 2005. *Memories of a future home: Diasporic citizenship of Chinese in Panama*. Stanford, Calif.: Stanford University Press.

Somers, Margaret R. 1993. Citizenship and the place of the public sphere: Law, community, and political culture in the transition to democracy. *American Sociological Review* 58(October): 587–620.

Soysal, Yasemin Nuhoglu. 1994. *The limits of citizenship: Migrants and postnational membership in Europe*. Chicago: University of Chicago Press.

Stanford, Leland. Jan. 10, 1862. Inaugural address as governor of California. http://www.californiagovernors.ca.gov/h/documents/inaugural_8.html.

Steinberg, Stephen. 1989. *The ethnic myth*. Boston: Beacon Press.

Stephen, Lynn. 1995. Women's rights are human rights: The merging of feminine and feminist interests among El Salvador's Mothers of the Disappeared (CO-MADRES). *American Ethnologist* 22(4): 807–27.

———. 1997. *Women and social movements in Latin America: Power from below*. Austin: University of Texas Press.

———. 1998. Gender and grassroots organizing: Lessons from Chiapas. In *Women's participation in Mexican political life*, edited by V. E. Rodríguez, 146–63. Boulder, Colo.: Westview Press.

———. 2001. Gender, citizenship, and the politics of identity. *Latin American Perspectives* 28 (6): 54–69.

Strazdes, Diana, 2001. The millionaire's palace: Leland Stanford's Commission for Pottier and Stymus in San Francisco. *Winterthur Portfolio* 36(4): 213–43.

Suárez-Orozco, Marcelo, and Mariela Páez. 2009. *Latinos: Remaking America*. Berkeley: University of California Press and the David Rockefeller Center for Latin American Studies at Harvard University.

Takaki, Ronald. 1990. *Strangers from a different shore: A history of Asian Americans.* New York: Penguin Books.

Tamayo, William R. 1995. When the "coloreds" are neither black nor citizens: The United States civil rights movement and global migration. *Asian Law Journal* 2(1): 1–32

Taylor, David. 1994. Citizenship and social power. In *Citizenship: Critical concepts,* vol. 1, edited by Bryan S. Turner and Peter Hamilton, 136–147. London: Routledge.

Thompson, Ginger. 2000. Women become the darlings of the candidates in Mexico. *New York Times,* June 30, A1.

———. 2008. After losing freedom, some immigrants face loss of custody of their children. *New York Times,* April 23.

———. 2009. After losing freedom, some immigrants face loss of their children. *New York Times,* April 23, http://www.nytimes.com/2009/04/23/us/23children.html.

Tjaden, Patricia, and Nancy Thoennes. 1998. *Prevalence, incidence and consequences of violence against women: Findings from the National Violence Against Women Survey.* Washington, D.C., and Atlanta, Ga.: National Institute of Justice and the Centers for Disease Control and Prevention.

Torruellas, Rosa, Rina Benmayor, Anneris Coris, and Anna Juarbe. 1989. Testimonio, identity, and empowerment. *Centro: Centro de Estudios Puertorriqueños* 2(6): 76–86.

———. 1991. *Affirming cultural citizenship in the Puerto Rican community: Critical literacy and the El Barrio popular education program.* New York: Centro de Estudios Puertorriqueños, Hunter College.

Tsing, Anna Lowenhaupt. 1990. Monster stories: Women charged with perinatal endangerment. In *Uncertain terms: Negotiating gender in American culture,* edited by Faye D. Ginsburg and Anna Lowenhaupt Tsing, 282–99. Boston: Beacon Press.

Turner, Bryan S. 1990. Outline of a theory of citizenship. *Sociology* 24(2): 189–217.

———. 1993. Contemporary problems in the theory of citizenship. In *Citizenship and social theory,* edited by Bryan S. Turner, 1–18. London: Sage Publications.

U.S. Bureau of the Census. 2000. Summary file 3 (SF 3) for San Francisco City, DP-2, profile of selected social characteristics. http://factfinder.census.gov/servlet/QTTable?_bm=y&-qr_name=DEC_2000_SF3_U_DP2&-ds_name=DEC_2000_SF3_U&-_lang=en&-_sse=on&-geo_id=16000US0667000.

———. 2003a. American Community Survey (ACS) Data Profile for San Francisco County, Table 3, Economic Characteristics. http://www.census.gov/acs/www/Products/Profiles/Single/2003/ACS/Tabular/001/A4000US0033.htm

———. 2003b. Foreign-born population: 2000. *Census 2000 Brief.* Washington, D.C.: U.S. Department of Commerce.

———. 2006. Estimates. http://quickfacts.census.gov/qfd/states/06/06075.html.

U.S. Congress. House. Committee on the Judiciary. Subcommittee on Immigration and Claims and Subcommittee on the Constitution. 1996. *Societal and legal issues surrounding children born in the United States to illegal alien parents.* 104th Congress. Washington, D.C.: GPO.

Van Derbeken, Jaxon. 2008a. S.F. fund aids teen felons who are illegals. *San Francisco Chronicle*, August 3, A1, http://sfgate.info/cgi-bin/article.cgi?f=/c/a/2008/08/02/MNJH120OUN.DTL.

———. 2008b. "S.F. gives teen drug suspect to Immigration." *San Francisco Chronicle*, August 28, A1, http://www.sfgate.com/cgi-bin/article.cgi?f=/c/a/2008/08/28/MNB412JFHB.DTL&hw=mayor+juvenile+court+ruling&sn=001&sc=1000.

Vigdor, Jacob L. 2008. Measuring immigrant assimilation in the United States. In *Civic report* No. 53. Center for Civic Innovation and the Manhattan Institute.

Voss, Barbara L. 2008. *The archaeology of ethnogenesis: Race and sexuality in colonial San Francisco.* Berkeley: University of California Press.

Walby, Sylvia. 1994. Is citizenship gendered? *Sociology* 28(2): 379–95.

West, Cornel. 1994. *Race matters.* New York: Vintage.

Weston, Kath. 1991. *Families we choose: Lesbians, gays, kinship.* New York: Columbia University Press.

White, J., et al. 1995. *Newcomer children in San Francisco: Their health and well-being,* edited by Child Health Initiative for Immigrant/Refugee Newcomers Project. San Francisco: San Francisco Department of Public Health.

Williams, Patricia J. 1988. On being the object of property. *Signs: Journal of Women in Culture and Society* 14(1): 5–24.

Wong, Edward. 2005. Swift road for U.S. citizen soldiers already fighting in Iraq. *New York Times*, August 9, http://www.nytimes.com/2005/08/09/international/middleeast/09soldiers.html.

Woodrow, Karen A., and Jeffrey S. Passel. 1990. Post-IRCA unauthorized immigration to the United States: An assessment based on the June 1988 CPS. In *Unauthorized migration to California: IRCA and the experience of the 1980s,* edited by B. E. Frank, D. Bean, and Jeffrey S. Passel, 33–75. Washington, D.C.: Urban Institute Press.

Yanagisako, Sylvia, and Carol Delaney. 1995. Naturalizing power. In *Naturalizing power: Essays in feminist cultural analysis,* edited by Sylvia Yanagisako and Carol Delaney, 1–22. New York: Routledge.

Young, Iris Marion. 1989. Polity and group difference: A critique of universal citizenship. *Ethics* 99: 250–74.

———. 1990. *Justice and the politics of difference.* Princeton, N.J.: Princeton University Press.

———. 1995. Polity and group difference: A critique of the ideal of universal citizenship. In *Theorizing citizenship,* edited by R. Beiner, 175–208. Albany: State University of New York Press.

Yuval-Davis, Nira. 1999. The "multi-layered citizen": Citizenship in the age of global-ization. *International Feminist Journal of Politics* 1(1): 119–36.

Yuval-Davis, Nira, and Floya Anthias. 1994. Introduction to *Woman-nation-state*, edited by Floya Anthias and Nira Yuval-Davis. In *Nationalism*, edited by John Hutchinson and Anthony D. Smith, 312–16. Oxford, U.K.: Oxford University Press.

Yuval-Davis, Nira, and Pnina Werbner. 1999. *Women, citizenship and difference*. London: Zed Books.

Zapor, Patricia. 2000. Immigration laws give families unsavory choices, say speakers. *San Francisco Catholic*, April 21, 6.

Zavella, Patricia, 1987. *Women's work and Chicano families: Cannery workers of the Santa Clara Valley*. Ithaca, N.Y.: Cornell University Press.

———. 1991. Reflections on diversity among Chicanas. *Frontiers: A Journal of Women's Studies* 12(2): 73–85.

———. 1996. Living on the edge: Everyday lives of poor Chicano/Mexicano families. In *Mapping multiculturalism*, edited by Aver F. Gordon and Christopher Newfield, 363–86. Minneapolis: University of Minnesota Press.

———. 2003. Talkin' sex: Chicanas and Mexicanas theorize about silences and sexual pleasures. In *Chicana feminisms*, edited by Gabriela F. Arredondo, Aída Hurtado, Norma Klahn, Olga Nájera-Ramirez, and Patricia Zavella, 228–53. Durham, N.C.: Duke University Press.

Zlolniski, Christian. 2006. *Janitors, street vendors, and activists: The lives of Mexican immigrants in Silicon Valley*. Berkeley: University of California Press.

Index

Abu-Lughod, Lila, 186
Act Relative to the Naturalization and Citizenship of Married Women, 54
affirmative action, ballot initiative to end, Prop. 209, 15, 63
African Americans, 15, 19, 142, 149–150, 194n14
agricultural workers, 58, 66
Aguirre, Adela (pseud.), 117–122, 124, 130, 144–148, 150
Aid to Families with Dependent Children (AFDC), 52, 196n2
amnistía, la (amnesty provisions) (IRCA), 33–34, 55, 56, 57, 58
amnesty, NACARA avenue for, 170
anti-Chinese laws, 205n3
anti-immigrant movements, 15–16, 51–55, 62–66, 171, 198n25, 205n3. See also Proposition 187, public benefits and services to the undocumented; Proposition 209 on affirmative action
Anzaldúa, Gloria, 11
apoyo (peer support), 32, 39–40, 47–48, 88–90, 101–103, 147, 176, 187
aprendiendo a hablar (learning to speak), 32; against violence, 125–129; desahogarse as step to, 116–117; in ethnography, 129–132
Arizona Border Rights Project, 91
armed forces, immigrants as active members or veterans of, 193n5, 205n6

Asians: demographics, 15, 194n14; historic prejudices against, 65, 148, 198n25, 205n3; Latina prejudices against, 147–148
asylee, defined, 196n7
asylum applicants, 66–68, 162, 193n5, 199n26
autoestima (self-esteem), 32, 112–115; concept of, 104–105; cultural citizenship and, 103–104, 113–115; developing in MUA meetings, 101–103; public claims for rights and recognition, 112–114; stories of forces undermining, 101–102, 105–109, 111–112
ayudando a los demás (community organizing), 32, 43–47

Balliger, Robin, 195n2
Baumann, Gerd, 139
Bayview–Hunter's Point neighborhood, 18, 52
belonging: to community, 96–98, 121–122; discursively constructing, 158; political, 115. See also membership, claiming a rightful place in society
Blackstone, William, 196n4
Bloemraad, Irene, 29–30
Blum, Richard, 174
Bracero Program, 66
Brown, Willie, 15
buena informacion (good information), 39–43, 48, 175
Bush, George W., 171, 205n6, 206n11
Butler, Judith, 189